FIX IT, CLEAN IT, AND MAKE IT LAST

The Ultimate Guide to Making Your Household Items Last Forever

By the editors of FC&A

Publisher's Note

The editors of FC&A have taken careful measures to ensure the accuracy and usefulness of the information in this book. While every attempt has been made to assure accuracy, errors may occur. We advise readers to carefully review and understand the ideas and tips presented and to seek the advice of a qualified professional before attempting to use them. The publisher and editors disclaim all liability (including any injuries, damages or losses) resulting from the use of the information in this book.

The health information in this book is for information only and is not intended to be a medical guide for self-treatment. It does not constitute medical advice and should not be construed as such or used in place of your doctor's medical advice.

"Now glory be to God who by 'tis mighty power at work within us is able to do far more than we would ever dare to ask or even dream of – infinitely beyond our highest prayers, desires, thoughts, or hopes."

– Ephesians 3:20 (TLB)

FC&A
103 Clover Green
Peachtree City, GA 30269

Produced by the staff of FC&A
Cover Images: ©1997 PhotoDisc, Inc.

Third printing January 2002

ISBN 1-890957-27-5

CONTENTS

INTRODUCTION

Do you ever wish you could go back to simpler times? The days when grandmothers baked cookies, gave warm hugs, and taught you the special way to care for everything in the house? When grandfathers puttered around the garden, built furniture in their workshops, and advised you on the best way to keep your car running? Most of us don't get the benefit of that good, old-fashioned know-how anymore. So where does a person turn for household advice?

Right here. In *Fix It, Clean It, and Make It Last: The Ultimate Guide to Making Your Household Items Last Forever,* you'll find quick, useful tips on how to repair, clean, or do most anything better, cheaper, faster, and simpler. It's like having your grandmother right next to you, patiently explaining how to clean burnt-on food from a saucepan, or the best way to ripen tomatoes. Your grandfather would surely give you the same good advice on storing your handsaw or caulking your windows. We provide simple, tried-and-true tips you can use to keep your home, and maybe even your life, running more smoothly.

But we haven't forgotten the complications of modern technology. You'll get help to clean your computer, store your videotapes, and make your state-of-the-art camera last longer. And you'll learn the newest tips on caring for your pets, traveling economically, and keeping yourself healthy. There's lots of helpful information here that even Grandma and Grandpa wouldn't know.

Fix It, Clean It, and Make It Last is divided into 16 easy-to-read chapters focusing on the most important areas in and around your home. Each chapter has sections that guide you to the kinds of tips you're looking for. If you have trouble finding a topic, check the index. Along with the page number, the index will list all the uses for that particular item. You may be surprised to learn how many ways you can use that baking soda in your cupboard!

Throughout the book, you'll find special boxes filled with helpful hints and fascinating trivia. Keep your eyes open for some top-notch advice from our household experts. They'll give you the scoop on everything from cleaning your carpet to getting your lawnmower in shape. Just for fun, we've also included a few "golden oldie" tips that provide a delightful peek into the households of yesteryear. We know you'll enjoy these charming glimpses into the history of homemaking.

Fix It, Clean It, and Make It Last is the reference book you've been waiting for to help you save time, money, and energy. Read on for a bounty of information, tips, and clever tricks to make life simpler – and simply better.

The Editors of FC&A

KITCHEN

Organization and meal planning

Get a grip on the grocery list

Take a sheet of paper, and make a list of items you buy from the grocery store on a regular basis. Leave space for additional items you might want to add later. Make photocopies of the list and the store where you can easily find them. Hang a copy on the refrigerator to remind yourself to check off the items you need. When shopping time rolls around, your list is practically done. The items not marked are also good reminders of essentials you may not have realized you need.

Cost-cutting strategy

Keep a list of the foods and other items you buy regularly. Make a note of the price you pay and the price you see in ads. You'll get a better handle on what an item should cost and recognize a good buy when you see one.

Recipe for order

Store only recipes you have used and liked in your "working" recipe box. Keep those you think you'd like but haven't tried in a file cabinet. You'll save time when hunting for an "old faithful." When you're feeling creative, go to your reserve and select a recipe that looks appealing.

Meal planning magic

Save money, time, and electricity by keeping an inventory on the door of your refrigerator. When you return from the grocery store, make a list of all the food items you store inside. Also note the date. As you use things up, cross them off the list. With this method, you can plan meals at a glance without having to dig around in the fridge with the door open, and you're less likely to waste food simply because it's out of sight. For even more savings, make a similar list for the freezer door.

Spices A to Z

If you take a few minutes to alphabetize your spice rack, finding spices when you are in the middle of preparing a meal is easy. Also, when you are preparing your shopping list or using a new recipe, you can quickly check to see if you have the necessary ingredient without looking at all your spice bottles to make sure. This is a real time saver.

Bag it on Sunday

Enjoy the leisurely pace of a Sunday afternoon to prepare bag lunch items for the week ahead. Make all the sandwiches that can be frozen. Wrap them in plastic wrap, and store them in a large zip-lock bag. Then into the freezer they go. Just grab one each morning as you rush out the door. It will thaw out by the time you're ready to eat it. You can put pretzels and carrots into individual baggies ahead, too. This is cheaper than buying prepackaged one-serving-size bags.

HALT for smart shopping

To save money when shopping for groceries, remember the word HALT – hungry, angry, lonely, and tired. Don't shop when you are feeling any of these. You'll make wiser choices when your appetite has been satisfied, you feel rested, and all is well in your world. Otherwise, you are likely to buy more of those "comfort foods" you think will make you feel better.

Shop alone whenever possible. With other family members along, you are likely to make more impulse purchases. Take their preferences into consideration when making your list, not in the grocery aisle.

Golden oldie

Picnic sandwiches will stay fresh twice as long if, after wrapping them, you seal the edges of the wax paper with a hot iron.

1003 Household Hints and Work Savers, 1947

Save $$ in the supermarket

Weigh prebagged items like a five-pound bag of potatoes. It's impossible to find the exact number of potatoes to match that exact weight, so some will weigh a little more than others. When you regularly choose a heavier one, the savings will add up.

_____

 If you buy juice made from concentrate, you might as well buy the frozen concentrate and add your own water. It's a little more trouble, but don't dwell on the inconvenience. Just concentrate on your savings — up to 75 percent over the ready-to-use juice.

_____

If your recipe calls for just a few broccoli or cauliflower florets, buy them in the supermarket salad bar. You won't have leftover parts that might go to waste, and you'll save preparation time as well.

Eggs and dairy foods

Freeze the 'egg'stras

Eggs are on sale so you buy that extra carton. Are you kidding? You can't use that many eggs! Don't panic. Just get out a spare ice cube tray, and crack each egg into the individual molds. Freeze until hard and then transfer the egg cubes to a plastic freezer bag. Use when needed. Warning: Wash your used ice cube trays and plastic containers carefully in hot water and soap. Raw eggs harbor bacteria that can make you ill.

_____

If you have egg whites left over from a recipe, pour them into an airtight plastic container. They'll stay fresh in the refrigerator for up to four days. Store them for six months to a year in the freezer. When you are ready to use them, thaw them out overnight in the refrigerator. They will work well for meringues. Or use them as a low-fat replacement for whole eggs in recipes.

Leftover egg yolks will last for a couple of days in the refrigerator. Slip unbroken yolks into a container of cold water and seal airtight until you are ready to use them. Or put them in a small bowl with two table-spoons of salad oil.

A shell of a scoop

If a piece of eggshell falls into the mixing bowl, scoop it out with half a shell. The larger piece will attract the smaller bit of shell.

Humpty Dumpty should have tried this

If your egg cracks during boiling, add a splash of vinegar to the water to seal the crack and save the egg.

When only the hen knows for sure

You can figure out how fresh an egg is by placing it in the bottom of a bowl of cold water. If it lies on its side, it's fresh. If it stands at an angle, it's at least three days old. If it stands on end, it's at least 10 days old.

Perfect peels and super slices

You can peel hard-boiled eggs perfectly. As soon as they are cooked, put them in ice water for one minute. The cold water will cause each egg to shrink away from its shell. Then put them back into boiling

7

water for 10 seconds. The hot water will make the shell expand away from the egg. Remove the eggs and crack the shells all over, then start peeling them at the large end. The combination of heat and cold will make peeling a snap.

To slice a hard-boiled egg cleanly, dip the knife into water before each slice. The egg won't crumble.

What eggs-actly is that green stuff?

You sometimes see a greenish-gray color around the yolk of a hard-boiled egg. What is it, and is it safe to eat? Before you crack your brain with worry, relax. It's a harmless combination of iron and sulfur that forms when you heat the egg.

Golden oldie

Here's a "butter stretcher": One pound butter plus two cups evaporated milk equal two pounds of butter, believe it or not. Bring the butter to room temperature and beat to cream – your egg-beater will do fine! Add two cups of evaporated milk, a little at a time. Keep on beating until all the milk is absorbed. Chill to a solid, and you're twice as butter rich.

1003 Household Hints and Work Savers, 1947

'Udderly' fresh

To double the shelf life of milk, add a pinch of salt when you first open it. And you can freeze it too! So when your grocery store has a big sale, go ahead and buy a few extra gallons and store them in your chest freezer. It doesn't affect the nutritional value, but it may make the milk separate. Just shake well before using.

Cottage cheese will stay fresh longer in your refrigerator if you store it upside down.

Say cheese!

You can turn plain yogurt into yogurt "cheese," a good substitute for sour cream. Line a strainer or funnel with cheesecloth or a paper coffee filter. Add the yogurt, and let it drain into a bowl overnight in the refrigerator. Simply discard the liquid, and you're ready to use the yogurt in your favorite recipe.

Put bad milk to good use

If your recipe calls for buttermilk, but you have only fresh milk on hand, here's how to sour your milk and save yourself a trip to the store. Add one tablespoon of vinegar or lemon juice to a cup of fresh milk. Stir it and wait five minutes. Then just add it to your recipe. You can also substitute equal amounts of plain yogurt for buttermilk or buttermilk for plain yogurt.

Easy, cheesy melt

When making dishes that contain cheese, remember high heat and long cooking can make it tough and stringy. So use a low temperature, and add the cheese as late as possible. By shredding or grating the cheese, it will melt faster.

Gratefully fast

In a hurry for melted butter for a recipe or favorite dish? Simply grate it with your cheese grater or vegetable peeler, and it will melt in seconds.

Fruits and nuts

Ripe and ready

Most fresh fruit you buy at the grocery store is gathered before it is fully ripe. But it will taste better if you allow it to ripen fully before eating. Some fruits, like peaches, pears, and tomatoes, will ripen faster if you place them in a brown paper bag. Just punch a few holes in the bag, and place pieces of fruit inside in a single layer, not stacked on top of each other. Fold over the top of the bag, and leave it on the counter. Check every day to see if it's ready to eat. When it's ripe, eat what you wish and store the rest in the refrigerator.

Some fruits, like blueberries, cranberries, and strawberries, do not ripen anymore after they are picked and should be refrigerated immediately. Bananas, on the other hand, are always picked green, but they ripen quickly. When they have brown speckles, called "honey spots," they are very sweet and ready to eat. You can store them in the refrigerator. The skins will turn black, but the banana inside will stay fresh for several days.

Do you have trouble figuring out whether a pineapple is ripe? Try plucking a leaf from the crown. If it comes out easily, it's ripe.

Fresh and fruity

Prolong the freshness of strawberries. Store them in a colander in the refrigerator, and don't wash them until you are ready to eat or use them in a recipe.

You don't have to wait until you are ready to eat fresh fruit before you can peel and slice it. It won't turn brown if you spray it lightly with lemon juice.

When you're craving banana bread

Your bunch of bananas has ripened, but you don't have time to eat them. Here's an easy alternative to the old idea of freezing them in their skins. Peel and slice the bananas, puree them in the blender, and add a little lemon juice to keep them from browning. Store them in a bag in the freezer for up to six months. Then when you're ready to make banana bread or a refreshing fruit smoothie, just thaw overnight in the refrigerator.

And in case you need to know, three or four medium-size bananas will make a pound. A pound will yield about one and three quarters of a cup of mashed bananas.

Make apple peeling appealing

Fresh apples make delicious pies. But if you are in a hurry you may feel there just isn't time to do all that peeling. Here's a tip to speed things up. Use the cutting board to quickly cut it into quarters. Remove the core and seeds. Then peel it. It really does go faster this way rather than peeling it whole.

Hit the juice

 Don't throw away the liquid from canned fruit. Store it in a jar or sealed plastic container in the fridge. The next time you prepare a congealed salad or dessert, make it tastier by substituting the fruit juice for the water in the recipe.

Pleasingly plump

If raisins dry out, soak them in hot water for a few minutes to soften them before putting them in your recipes.

A sticky solution

To cut sticky foods like dates or figs more easily, dip the knife in cold water frequently. Or use a pair of clean scissors. Just rub butter on the blades before cutting marshmallows or fruit, and the food won't stick.

Savor the tart taste

If your recipe calls for only the juice of the lemon, don't waste the peel. Cut it up and freeze it to use later when you need freshly grated lemon peel.

All it's cracked up to be

To make coconut cracking easier, cool it or heat it. First punch holes in two of the eyes, and drain the milk. Then either place it in the freezer for an hour or in a 350 degree oven for 20 to 30 minutes. While it's still cold or after it's cooled down from the oven, wrap it in a clean dish towel, and tap it all over with a hammer. When it breaks open, remove the meat and shred or grate it in a blender or food processor.

A kinder, gentler nutcracker

For an easy way to crack nuts that leaves the nut meat intact, soak walnuts or pecans in salty water overnight and then gently crack them the next day.

Vegetables and herbs

Get fresh with a cute tomato

Make your fresh tomatoes last longer by storing them with the stem-side down.

___

To peel a tomato quickly and smoothly, place it in boiling water for 20 to 60 seconds. The skin will come off easily.

Contain flying veggies

When tossing a salad, place the bowl in the sink. Vegetables that fly over the edge of the bowl won't

Delay the toss

Leftover tossed salad won't last very long. One way to extend its crispiness is to place several sheets of folded paper towel in the bottom of the plastic bag or container you're using for storage. It soaks up excess moisture and keeps the vegetables from getting soggy.

land on the counter top or floor. The cleanup will be a lot quicker.

Sack the celery

Celery may come in plastic bags from the grocery, but that isn't the best way to preserve it in the refrigerator. Place celery in a paper bag, and leave the outside stalks and leaves on it for best storage.

Keep the crunch to munch

Sagging veggies take the bite-appeal out of a green salad. Resuscitate limp lettuce by adding lemon juice to a container of cold water. Place the lettuce in the container and soak for an hour in the refrigerator.

Revitalize those rubbery celery stalks by cutting them into pieces or strips, and store them in a plastic container with enough water to cover the bottom.

Watch for waste with pricey veggies

When you buy expensive fresh vegetables, be sure you use every part you can. Broccoli stems can be peeled and cut into small strips, then cooked with the broccoli florets. Eat as is or puree in a blender to add to soup stock.

Pricey asparagus yields more than you think, too. Prepare each spear by cutting off and discarding the dried, light-colored end, which is too tough to eat. Bend the stalk in several places down the stem until the tender part snaps off. Peel the tough green piece below the break with a sharp paring knife and cook with the rest of the asparagus for a tender treat.

Keep your peppers in shape

Looking for something to keep your stuffed peppers in shape while baking? Try lightly greased muffin tins. Just choose small peppers that will fit into the muffin cups.

Does it make it boiling mad?

Adding a small amount of salt to water will make it boil faster. But add salt at the end when cooking dried beans, or you'll prolong the cooking time.

Smooth as silk

Fresh corn is tasty, but the silks aren't any fun if you get them in your teeth. Remove them with a wet paper towel or napkin. Wipe the ear down from one end to the other. The silks will stick to the paper towel and come right off.

Nail that potato

Shorten the cooking time of baked potatoes by 15 minutes by inserting a clean nail into the potato's flesh (for conventional oven, not microwave). The nail directs heat to the center of the potato.

What's that green stuff in my coffee?

Let your old percolator do double duty as an asparagus cooker. Just take out the basket mechanism, and stand the asparagus on end. Then add water, plug in, and steam the asparagus briefly to keep in flavor and nutrients.

Cut the clinginess

Herbs like parsley, cilantro, sage, and rosemary can cling to a cutting board. Use kitchen scissors to cut them, letting them fall directly into a dish or glass measuring cup. It will be easier, and you'll have less waste.

Foil the sprouts

Onions will last longer and not sprout if you wrap them in aluminum foil. If you cut an onion and use only half, rub the remaining onion half with butter on the cut edge. The butter will keep it fresh longer.

Slip sliding away

A clove of garlic, on the other hand, tends to slip around on the cutting board when you are trying to mince it. To keep it still, sprinkle the board with salt, crush the garlic by pressing down on it with the flat side of the knife blade, then chop it.

Storing ginger is a snap

Store ginger root dry in the refrigerator. Or you can freeze it for up to three months. Another way to preserve it is to peel it, cover it with sherry wine, and store it in the refrigerator.

Fresh herbal teas, no teasing

Store teas in airtight containers so they won't lose flavor, go stale, or pick up flavors from other foods.

Don't store them in the refrigerator, freezer, or any other place with high humidity. They should be used within a year of purchase.

Meats, chicken, and fish

Mess-free meat loaf

Make meat loaf and you make a mess, right? Not necessarily. Put all the ingredients in a large zip-top bag, push out most of the air, and seal the top. Then knead and blend the ingredients from the outside of the bag, form into a loaf shape, remove from the bag, and put into the pan to bake.

Be fast on the thaw

There's an easy way to store ground beef so that it will thaw faster when you're ready to cook it. Put about a pound of ground beef in a large zip-lock freezer bag, and then flatten it like a pancake. It stores more easily and thaws in half the time.

Fork over the spoons

That roast will stay juicy if, during cooking, you turn it with two wooden spoons. They won't pierce the meat and let the juices run out like a fork will.

A brush with the sauce

For basting meats or brushing on sauces, use a natural bristle paint brush. It will be flexible and easy to clean. And when grilling, dip the brush in olive oil and spread it on the grate to keep the meat from sticking.

'Tea'nderize it

Scientists continue to discover new benefits from one of society's favorite beverages – tea. Here's one for your kitchen: Try cooking tougher cuts of meat in tea. The tannin in it works as a tenderizer for melt-in-your-mouth goodness.

Bits about bacon

Keep bacon from sticking together in the package by rolling the package into a tube and holding it for a minute. The slices will loosen up and come out of the package one at a time.

Bacon won't curl up while cooking if you put it in ice-cold water before frying it. Just dip it for about five seconds, pat it dry with a paper towel, and pop it in the pan. You'll get nice flat bacon.

Any time is turkey time

It isn't always necessary to thaw a turkey before cooking it. You can cook whole turkeys without giblets or poultry parts from the frozen state. But it will take one and a half times as long to cook. Commercially frozen stuffed turkeys must not be thawed because of the possibility of bacterial contamination. Just follow the directions on the wrapper.

Soups, stews, and casseroles

Save your blood pressure

So you made a little mistake and put too much salt in the casserole? Don't throw it out. Add an apple sliced into thin strips to the dish for a while. Then take out the apple and the salt goes with it! Also, try this to remove the bad taste when foods and sauces burn. If it's salty soup you're having trouble with, add a peeled potato. It will absorb the extra salt. Just toss it out when the soup's done.

Shape up your soup

Freeze soup and other liquids in a plastic bag inside a coffee can. This makes a shape that's easier to store. Once the food is frozen, you can remove the can and use it again.

Fixings in the freezer

Keep two containers in your freezer for soup fixings. Use one for meat scraps and bones. Put vegetable leftovers like celery leaves and carrot tops in the other. Use for meat broth and vegetable stock.

'Soup'er degreasers

To remove grease from the top of soup or chili while it's cooking, put a cube of ice in a piece of cheese cloth. Run this across the surface of the soup, and the unwanted grease will stick to it.

Another quick way to get rid of the grease floating on top of your soup – drop in a leaf of lettuce. It will attract the grease. When you're done, just toss the lettuce and serve the soup!

Breads, grains, and staples

A soft touch

Do you like your bread slices soft? Keep a rib of celery inside a plastic bag with the bread. It helps it stay soft because it provides a slight amount of moisture.

Bag the bread crumbs

Save the end pieces and cut-off crusts from your loaves of bread in a plastic bag in the freezer. Next time you need bread crumbs for a recipe, get out the bag, and run the bread through a food processor or blender to make crumbs.

If bread gets stale, you can use it to make delicious croutons. Choose your favorite herbs and seasonings and mix with olive oil. Brush both sides of the bread with this mixture. Cut into cubes, and arrange in a single layer on a cookie sheet. Bake at 300 degrees until they are dry and crisp.

Squeeze to make it fluffy

When boiling rice, add a teaspoon of lemon juice to the water, and you'll get fluffier, whiter rice.

Ye olde yeast maker

Baking bread today may mean simply opening a box of mix and following the directions that come with your electric breadmaker. But in the past, breadmaking was an all day affair – mixing and kneading and waiting for the bread to rise, then punching it down and waiting for it to rise again.

Some housewives even made their own yeast. How would you like to follow this lengthy process? On Monday morning, mix two ounces of hops in four quarts of water and boil for one-half hour. Strain and let cool until lukewarm. Stir in a small handful of salt and one-half pound of brown sugar. Mix enough of this liquid with one-half pound of white flour to make a smooth paste. Then blend in the rest of the liquid. Let stand until Wednesday. Grate three pounds of raw potatoes and add to the mixture. Mix well and keep in a warm place until Thursday. Stir frequently.

This may have taken a long time, but housewives of the past could make their bread using half as much of this yeast as compared to regular yeast. That made it worth the time and trouble!

Ah, the fresh smell of frozen coffee

If you store your ground coffee in the refrigerator or freezer for freshness, that's fine. But for the best flavor, bring it to room temperature before brewing it.

Take a stab at it

How do you get ketchup out when it's stuck in the bottle? Take a chopstick, skewer, or plastic drinking straw and insert it in the bottle. Push it to the bottom, and then take it out. This lets in air so the ketchup can flow freely.

High or low grade oil?

Olive oil comes in several grades, with extra-virgin being the tastiest but most expensive. Save money by reserving that for salads and other cold uses. In cooking, you lose some of the flavor anyway, so you might as well start with a cheaper variety. You can also save money by making your own nonstick cooking spray. Just put your olive oil into a spray bottle.

Desserts and sweets

The bottom line on cake baking

To apply a fast and even coat of oil to a cake pan or a muffin tin, use a small paint brush.

———————————

To keep chocolate cake brown on the bottom, dust the cake pan with cocoa rather than flour.

———————————

Cake won't stick to the bottom of the pan if you cover it with wax paper. Use scissors to cut it to the shape of the pan. Spray the paper with cooking spray, then pour in the batter. When it's done, you can easily remove the cake from the pan and peel off the wax paper.

———————————

Out of wax paper? Prevent sticking by placing the pan on wet paper towels when you first take it out of the oven.

Pick a proper cake pan

You'll get a more tender crust, and one lighter in color too, if you use shiny metal cake pans. Glass and dark nonstick pans absorb more heat. With these, it's best to follow the manufacturer's directions. Usually, you have to reduce heat by about 25 degrees.

Tips for the top

Wait until the cake is completely cool before you frost it. Otherwise the frosting will melt and run down the sides.

___

Need a pastry bag with a decorating tip? Make one from a zip-lock plastic bag. Spoon frosting into the bag, press out the air, then snip off a bottom corner. Give a squeeze, and decorate your cake with no fuss or muss.

Cutting the cake without the crumbs

Try cutting a hot cake with thread, or even dental floss, instead of a knife. Hold the thread taut on both ends and run through the hot cake quickly. It's much easier and won't cause a crumbly mess. Thread works well to cut angel food and chiffon cakes when they are cold as well.

Beat the mixer mess

There's a neat way to use a hand-held mixer to whip cream or cake frosting. Tear a piece of wax paper big enough to cover the bowl. Cut a hole in the center. Push the mixer blade stems through the hole, and insert them into the mixer. Place the beaters in the bowl, and the wax paper will be in place to catch any splatters.

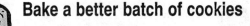

Bake a better batch of cookies

For best results, bake cookies on a shiny, flat cookie sheet that has no edge on one to three sides. It should be at least two inches narrower and shorter than the oven rack. And you don't need an insulated cookie sheet to keep cookies from burning. Just turn an old cookie sheet upside down and place the one you are using on top. It works just as well.

Make all cookies on a sheet the same size and thickness so they'll get done at the same time. Bake one sheet at a time, and place it in the center of the rack.

For chewy cookies, bake just until the edges are lightly brown. Centers may look underbaked. Let cool on the baking sheet for a minute or two before moving to the cooling rack. Leave bar cookies in the pan until completely cooled before cutting them. You'll have fewer crumbs this way.

'Chews' the best container

To keep cookies soft, put them in an airtight container. For crisper cookies, store them with a loose-fitting lid. Leave bar cookies in the pan you baked them in, and cover it tightly with foil or plastic wrap.

Sweet treats

If the people in your house like popsicles, you can have your own custom-made frozen treats at a fraction of the cost of commercial ones. Invest in a plastic

A 'swingin' snack

You may remember eating animal crackers as a child or buying them as a fun snack for your own children. But have you ever wondered why the famous circus-cage box has a string attached?

Of course, it makes it easier to carry. And after eating the cookies, a child can use the box as a play purse or to carry little treasures. But when the National Biscuit Company (Nabisco) introduced these edible "toys" during the 1902 Christmas season, it had another idea in mind.

The company hoped the handy string would encourage parents to hang the cookies as a gift on the Christmas tree!

popsicle set, sold in discount and drug stores. Fill the plastic forms with any kind of fruit juice, including the juice you strain from canned fruit. Make them interesting with bits of fruit or fruit-flavored gelatin. Or use flavored milk or yogurt.

A taste, not a temptation

If you like freshly baked cookies, but don't like your tendency to eat too many, this tip is for you: Store the cookie dough in the refrigerator. When you want cookies, take out just enough for two or three, and bake them in the toaster over.

The cookie crumbles

Do you have leftover broken cookies that nobody seems to want to eat? Crumble them even more and use as a topping for pudding or ice cream. Or make a tasty crust for pie or cheesecake. For one cup of fine crumbs you'll need 14 graham cracker squares, 14 Oreos (keep the middle), 22 vanilla wafers, or 15 gingersnaps. Just combine the crumbs with a bit of butter and press into a pie plate.

With sugar on top

Creamy pudding can be yummy. Keep it smooth by sprinkling a bit of sugar on top while it cools. This will keep it from forming a skin.

Pasta in the pie

When baking a pie, to prevent juice from running over and to let steam escape, cut holes in the top crust. Then stand short lengths of macaroni in the slits. They will act as vents while the pie cooks.

Slide home on the plate

If you sprinkle a few drops of water on the serving plate when you unmold a congealed dessert or salad, it will be easier to move around and center on the dish.

For your honey

To avoid a sticky mess when measuring honey, spray or wipe the measuring spoon or cup with cooking oil. The honey will flow right out into your recipe.

You can keep honey from crystallizing. Just pour it into small freezer containers and keep it in the freezer. Thawing takes no time at all.

If you have honey that has already "sugared," don't throw it away. Just put the jar in a pan of boiling water and watch the sugar disappear. If it's in a covered plastic container, hold it with tongs under very hot tap water.

Sweet substitute

Need brown sugar for a recipe but have none on hand? Don't rush to the store — make your own. Stir one to two tablespoons of dark molasses into one cup of white sugar, and you won't be able to tell the difference.

A sneaky treat

If your children or grandchildren are begging for sweets, try this healthier substitute. Older kids can help or even do it all by themselves.

Stir one tablespoon of honey and one tablespoon of raisins into a cup of peanut butter. Mix well, then drop by small spoonfuls (about one-half teaspoon) into a bowl of powdered sugar. Roll each blob of peanut butter mixture in the sugar to form a bite-size candy. Serve with a glass of milk, and you've sneaked in a little extra nutrition!

When it just won't cooperate

Has your opened box of brown sugar become so hard that you can't even scoop it out? Put a soft piece of bread in a plastic bag with the hardened brown sugar to soften it. Wait a few hours, and you'll be able to measure it again.

Need a faster way to soften it? Put the brown sugar and a heat-proof cup of water in a baking pan and cover. Place it in a warm oven on low heat and let the steam soften it quickly. Or use the microwave for even quicker results.

Super snacks

Turn tortillas into tantalizing treats

Make delicious corn chips out of stale left-over corn tortillas. Spray them lightly with nonstick cooking spray. Cut into wedges with a pizza cutter. Bake in a single layer in a 400 degree oven for 10 to 12 minutes until crisp.

Crisp up the crackers

Don't throw out slightly stale crackers or cereal. Spread them one layer deep on a baking sheet, and pop them in the oven to heat for a few minutes. The crispy texture will return.

Make mine a pepperoni

Reheat leftover pizza in your toaster oven. It will heat and crisp quicker and use less energy than the regular oven. Make sure the rack has the bumpy grid wires facing up for an easier slide in and out.

Cold corn for hot popping

Store microwave popcorn in the freezer to keep it from getting stale. This will also reduce the number of those irritating unpopped kernels when you pop it.

Spread a no-sog sandwich

Keep your peanut butter and jelly sandwich from getting soggy with this quick trick. Spread both slices of bread with a thin layer of peanut butter, then spread a layer of jelly in between. The jelly won't soak through and moisten the bread.

General cleaning

Down with dangerous disinfectants

It's best to go slow with those expensive new anti-bacterial disinfectants and antiseptics you now find on the grocery shelves. They were developed for use in hospitals, and you may sometimes need to use them in the sick room. But for regular cleaning, these powerful, long-lasting antibacterial cleansers may kill "good" bacteria. And they may lead to more resistant forms of bacteria as well.

A dangerous mix

When doing household chores, never mix vinegar, or anything else, with chlorine bleach! This could produce toxic fumes and make you extremely sick.

29

A regular soap or detergent is all you'll need for most household cleaning. If you need something a little stronger – for cleaning utensils and countertops after contact with raw meat, for example – use a fast-evaporating chemical like chlorine bleach, alcohol, hydrogen peroxide, or ammonia. They remove potentially dangerous bacteria but do not stick around doing damage after they have done their job.

Do-it-yourself formulas save money

What are you really paying for when you buy those expensive cleaners advertised on TV? Mostly water! Save money and clean without harsh chemicals by mixing your own. Here are two tried-and-true formulas that outshine the commercial brands.

All-Purpose Cleaner

1/4 cup baking soda

1 cup ammonia

1/2 cup white vinegar

2 pints warm water

Fill a spray bottle or use with a mop or rag.

Drain Opener

1 cup baking soda

1 cup salt

1/2 cup white vinegar

Mix and pour down the drain. Wait for 15 to 20 minutes, and then pour a big pot of boiling water down the drain. Bonus: this drain opener doesn't damage the pipes. Do not use this method, however, if commercial drain cleaner has been used and is still present in the standing water.

Don't splurge on detergents

Don't fall for those expensive, name-brand concentrated dish detergents. Use the cheapest brand you can find, but add a few tablespoons of vinegar to the wash water. The amazing power of vinegar cuts the grease and leaves the dishes squeaky clean.

Zero in on germs

A kitchen sponge can pick up a lot of bacteria. Clean it regularly by putting it in the automatic dishwasher

---

The little scrubber that could

Door-to-door salesman Edward W. Cox needed a gimmick. The year was 1917, and the housewives of San Francisco weren't interested in looking at his aluminum cookware. If he could just come up with an appealing free gift, maybe that would get him in the door.

Cox knew that one of his customers' biggest complaints was how hard it was to clean dried-on food from their pots and pans. So he went to work. He mixed up a soapy solution and hand-dipped squares of steel wool into it. When they were dry, he dipped them again. He repeated this dipping and drying process until the pads were saturated with dried soap.

By combining the abrasive quality of steel wool with the cleansing power of soap, Cox had invented a handy scrubber. The soap pads were such a big hit with housewives, he soon began to devote all his time to producing and marketing them.

It was his own housewife who came up with the name for the original steel wool soap pad – S.O.S., which stands for "Save Our Saucepans."

---

each time you run it. Or after using the sponge, rinse it, wring it out, and microwave it for 30 to 60 seconds.

A cool end to rust frustration

A wet, soapy steel wool pad makes quick work of cleaning baked-on food from a metal pan. But have you ever reached for one only to have it disintegrate in your hand, leaving you with a palm full of powdered rust? What a mess! But keep your cool. Your used soap pad doesn't have to get rusty. Just drop it in a zip-lock plastic bag, and stash it in the freezer until you need it again.

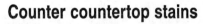

Counter countertop stains

White laminate countertops are easily stained, but they are also the easiest to clean since you can bleach them without having to worry about removing color from the countertop material. If a stain won't come out of your white countertop, soak a paper towel in household chlorine bleach, and lay it over the stain. Cover this with another paper towel soaked in water. Leave the paper towels in place overnight, and the stain should be gone in the morning.

If little Jimmy's morning juice has left bright red blotches, you don't want to have bleach on the countertop all day. Blot up any liquid, then pour rubbing alcohol on the spots and spread it around. After about one minute, pour a little full-strength household bleach on the stains, and let it stand for another minute. Rinse thoroughly with clean water, and the stain should disappear.

What if you have an ugly purple stain from a grocery pricing label that stuck to your wet countertop? Spray on a generous amount of your regular household or kitchen cleaner, and allow it to liquefy the stain. Blot with a paper towel, and rinse with clean water. Repeat this process until the stain is gone.

A super scrubber for a greasy grill

Looking for a good way to get that cooked-on grease off your barbecue grill? Fold a six-inch square of aluminum window screen until it's about an inch square. As soon as the grill is cool enough, start scrubbing. You'll be surprised how quickly it will do the trick.

Cleaning for klutzes

If you're like one young homemaker who admits she's hopeless with a dustpan, Donna Harp has the answer for you.

"You don't really need a dustpan to do a good job of sweeping your floors," says this professional cleaner who, with four children, knows just how dirty the kitchen floor can get. Her advice? "Sweep all the dirt to a pile in the middle of the floor. Then dampen a paper towel and, starting from the outer edge of the dirt pile, wipe up the dirt in a circular motion until you gather up the dirt in the middle of the pile and wipe the floor clean."

This method will keep dust from flying around and effectively catch those wayward particles that tend to miss the dustpan anyway. So if you feel like a klutz every time you sweep the floor, just turn in your dustpan for a roll of paper towels, and you'll have that floor sparkling in no time!

'Egg'stra quick cleanup is no 'yolk'

 Drop a raw egg, and it will definitely break. Now you've got a mess on your kitchen floor. But you can make short work of the cleanup by sprinkling salt over the egg. It changes the consistency, allowing you to wipe it up easily with a paper towel.

Put a holey lid on hot splatters

A boiling sauce can pop out and make a mess. Place an inverted metal colander on top like a lid, and it will allow the steam to escape but catch the hot spatters. This will also protect you from burns if you get too close.

Get yourself out of a tight spot

It's easy to clean under your refrigerator when you've learned this trick: place an old sock over the end of a fly swatter. It will be flat enough to run it deep under the refrigerator for a clean sweep.

For those hard to reach spots between cabinets and under appliances, clean with a small foam paint brush.

Ah, but here's the scrub

Burnt-on food in the bottom of a saucepan can take you all night to clean. Here's the easy way. Pour baking soda in the pan, covering the burned area well. Add enough water to make the consistency like paste. Let the pan sit for several hours, then scrub, rinse, and see how fast the cleanup is!

To remove cooked-on food from glass cookware, scour with a non-abrasive scrubber and ammonia. Or soak it in water to which you have added baking soda (three tablespoons per quart of water). Scrape as needed with a wooden spoon or plastic scouring pad.

But does it soften the dishes?

To clean a difficult casserole dish, save your used laundry softener sheets. Just put one or two used sheets in the pan, fill it with hot water, and let it sit for 20 minutes. It should wipe clean.

Help for dirty dinnerware

Pretreat baked-on foods on cookware you wash in the dishwasher (stainless steel, glass, ceramic, or porcelain). Put liquid automatic dishwashing detergent directly on the cooked-on food before putting it in the dishwasher.

Teflon trickery

For stubborn stains in nonstick cookware, boil one-half cup vinegar, one cup water, and two teaspoons of baking powder in the stained pan for 10 minutes. Rinse and dry. Before using it again, season the non-stick surface with a coat of cooking oil.

Germ warfare

You can sanitize wood or plastic cutting boards by first spraying a mist of vinegar over the surface. Follow that with a mist of hydrogen peroxide. This combination can even kill bacteria on meat or produce without harming the food. Bacteria require moisture to survive more than a few hours. So keep cutting boards and other food surfaces dry when not in use.

Another way to kill germs on and below the surface of a wooden cutting board is to put it in an 800-watt microwave oven for 10 minutes on high heat. But don't try it on plastic. Microwaves don't get plastic boards hot enough to kill the germs. You should clean plastic cutting boards with a mild bleach solution. Even full strength, bleach won't sanitize wooden boards. The organic composition of wood neutralizes the disinfectant.

Don't bother with these boards

What about anti-bacterial cutting boards? Save your money. The EPA has ordered at least two companies to stop selling them and other anti-bacterial kitchen products. These were treated with a pesticide that eliminates odor-causing bacteria. But it has not been proven effective at killing disease-causing organisms.

Rub out stubborn stains

To get rid of unsightly stains on a wooden board, first sprinkle it with ordinary table salt. Then take a lemon wedge and rub the salt in. If the stain is particularly stubborn, this might not complete the job. In that case, pour liquid laundry bleach over the stains. Leave it for about 10 minutes, then rinse it off. Sometimes you must do this a second time to remove the worst stains.

A+ aluminum cleaner

It's easy to keep your aluminum cookware clean inside and out. Keep smooth aluminum surfaces shiny by rubbing with the outside of a lemon. And to remove stains from the inside of aluminum pots and pans, mix three tablespoons of vinegar in two pints of water. Boil until stains disappear. (If your stained pot is larger than two pints, you can increase the ingredients proportionally.)

———

To clean and remove lime deposits from your aluminum coffeepot, boil equal parts of white vinegar and water.

Clean your little teapot

Remove lime deposits from your tea kettle with this recipe:

1 cup apple cider vinegar

2 tablespoons salt

1 cup water

Boil this mixture in your tea kettle for 15 minutes. Let stand overnight, then rinse it out with cold water.

How to make metals shine

To clean copper, bronze, brass, or pewter, dissolve a teaspoon of salt in a cup of white vinegar. Mix in enough flour to make a paste. Coat the item with the paste, and let it sit for 15 minutes to an hour. Rinse with warm water and polish dry with a clean cloth.

Buff up the brass

Try these easy brass polishers for a no-fuss shine:

▶ Clean tarnished brass by coating it with a paste of lemon juice and cream of tartar or baking soda. Let it stay on for five minutes. Wash in warm water, rinse, and polish dry.

▶ Sprinkle baking soda directly on a slice of lemon, and rub the brass with it.

▶ Pour vinegar over tarnished brass items, and sprinkle with salt. Rub, rinse, and polish.

▶ After cleaning, rub brass with a little olive oil. It will brighten the brass and retard tarnishing, so you won't have to polish it as often.

Polish stainless steel cutlery with undiluted white or apple vinegar and a clean cloth.

Mama mia — now that's a solution!

Plastic bowls with tops that seal good and tight are ideal for storing leftovers. But when dinner was your favorite Italian or Mexican dish, you may be left with unsightly grease and tomato sauce stains. Remove them by rubbing on a little dry baking soda with a damp paper towel or sponge, then washing in warm sudsy water. You may have to do this several times to remove the stain.

Shake, rattle, and rinse

Trying to clean a vase or bottle with a tiny opening can be frustrating. But here's a trick to save time and energy.

Grind up some eggshells and mix with water and vinegar. Pour the solution into the container, cover, and shake until it's clean. Rinse and you're done.

The kitchen sink

Chase dirt and stains down the drain

You can clean your stained porcelain sink overnight as if by magic. Just wet down some paper towels with household bleach. (Wear dishwashing gloves to protect your skin.) Lay them in the sink, particularly over any stained areas. In the morning the sink will be clean and sanitized too.

If you have a stainless steel sink, you can brighten it in only a few minutes as well. Polish it with a cloth dipped in a little vinegar or ammonia. Or use a bit of baking powder on a damp sponge. To remove streaks, rub with olive oil or club soda. But never scrub stainless steel with abrasive powders or scouring pads.

A salty kiss

Having to explain a bright pink smear on your cheek or collar might make you a little uncomfortable. But no need to be embarrassed by lipstick stains on cups and glasses. Just give them a quick rub with salt before washing, and the stains will come right off.

The cold truth about disposals

To keep your kitchen garbage disposal running smoothly, don't pack material into the drain before you start it. Let the unit self-feed. Run cold water with maximum force just before, during, and for several seconds after operating the disposal. The water helps process the disposed material and flushes the pipes clean. And cold water congeals grease so the machine can deal with it.

Lick the leak in your kitchen sink

If your sink stopper is worn and no longer tight-fitting, put some plastic wrap into the drain before putting in the stopper. You'll have an airtight seal.

A spray mildew remover will clean drains or garbage disposals if it contains chlorine bleach. Or you can pour a little undiluted bleach down the drains and let it sit for a while before running the water. Turn on the disposal as you run water through it. This will clean, disinfect, and remove most odors.

Blindingly clean faucets

To clean stains from chrome faucets and the chrome trim on kitchen appliances, polish with a little baby oil on a soft cloth. They'll shine so bright you might need sunglasses to see your way around the kitchen.

Cleaning appliances

Hot tips for a clean oven

To keep an oven clean, sprinkle salt or baking soda on spills while they are warm. When the oven is cool enough, wipe them up.

To clean an oven with baked-on grease, heat the oven on warm for about two minutes and turn it off.

Put half a cup of full strength ammonia in a small glass bowl on the top rack. Place a large pan of boiling water on the bottom rack. Close the door, and let stand overnight. The next day, wipe off the loosened grime with paper towels or newspapers. If there are stubborn spots remaining, scrub with baking soda. For particularly resistant spots, use steel wool or a soap pad. Wipe the suds away with a paper towel. Wash with warm soapy water, and rinse thoroughly.

Don't exhaust your options

To clean those stubborn exhaust fan filters that get coated with kitchen grease, soak them in a strong solution of grease-cutting dishwashing detergent and water. After soaking for an hour or so, clean with a scrub brush or old toothbrush.

Golden oldie

Keeping the kitchen stove clean is one of a housekeeper's hardest tasks. After blacking the metal, try slipping brown paper bags over each hand for the polishing.

Ladies Home Journal circa 1920

A steamy affair

The microwave oven is one of the most popular kitchen appliances these days. Lots of use means lots of baked on food spills inside. Take the work out of cleaning up your microwave by boiling a cup of water in it for a few minutes. The steam from the water softens the debris and makes wiping it clean a breeze. Never use abrasive powders or soap pads to clean the microwave oven.

A bath for the dishwasher

Sometimes even your dishwasher needs to be cleaned. The first sign of buildup is a film left on the glasses and plates. An easy way to clean your machine is to fill a bowl with one cup liquid bleach and put it on the bottom rack of the dishwasher. Run the dishwasher on a setting that excludes the "dry" cycle. Open the machine and fill the bowl with one cup of white vinegar. Run the dishwasher through a full cycle. Repeat if necessary.

Banish dirty blender blues

Blender cleanup can be easy if you do it as soon as you finish mixing that milkshake or chocolate pudding. Just squirt a little dish detergent inside, add a cup of warm water, replace the cover, and give it a spin.

Throw in the paper towel

Clean your electric can opener by feeding a paper towel through it. It will remove grime and leave the blade clean and ready to use.

Cleaning magic for your coffee maker

About every four weeks, clean your coffee maker system with a half-and-half mixture of white vinegar and water. (Do it more often if you have hard water.) Pour a pot of the mixture into the coffee maker and turn it on. Let about half of it drip into the carafe. Turn off the coffee maker, and let it cool for about 30 minutes. Pour that solution back into the coffee maker, turn it back on, and finish the cycle. Do a second cycle with clear water to rinse.

Care for kitchenware

Like a new penny

Try this home formula to make copper pots or pots with copper bottoms look beautiful. It's cheaper and faster than commercial copper cleaners. Mix three tablespoons of salt with four cups of vinegar. Spray it on the copper. Let stand for a few minutes and then rub clean. If you don't have any vinegar on hand, you can use liquids that have salt and vinegar in them – like Worcestershire sauce, ketchup, or sauerkraut juice. You can use these cleaners on tarnished brass as well.

Black is beautiful

Protect your iron skillets and pots from rusting by rubbing wax paper inside and outside the pan. Why does this work? The wax paper leaves a thin coat of wax on the pan and prevents air from interacting with the metal and any moisture. If you store smaller pieces of iron cookware stacked inside larger ones, leave pieces of wax paper between them. If light rust spots do appear on cast-iron cookware, remove them by rubbing with half a lemon dipped in salt.

Glassware is gonna clear up, put on a happy face

If your glass bakeware gets a cloudy appearance from mineral deposits, make it clear again by soaking it in a solution of hot water and vinegar.

Say no to a hot dish

Want to know if a glass container can be used in the microwave oven? Do a quick test by putting the empty dish in the microwave on high for one minute. If it's still cool, you can safely use it for cooking. If it's lukewarm, it's OK for short periods of reheating. If it's warm, don't use it in the microwave oven.

No chip off the butcher block

There are fancy and expensive products for protecting your butcher block or cutting board. But there's an everyday product that can measure up to the best store-bought mixture. Try rubbing mineral oil (it has no taste) on your butcher block surface, and let it stay on for 15 minutes. Then blot up the excess oil, and you're ready to start chopping again.

'Wooden' a light wax be 'lov-er-ly'?

Dry your wooden salad bowl thoroughly as soon as you wash it. Then rub it inside and out with wax paper. This light coat of wax will reseal the surface of the bowl.

Special-care items

No stained history here

If your prized family heirloom china has dark stains from years of use, return it to like-new condition. Mix equal parts of white distilled vinegar and salt, apply, and let the solution dissolve the discoloration.

For tea or coffee stains in the bottom of your china cups, add one and a half teaspoons of chlorine bleach to a cup of water, and pour into the cup. Let stand for about two minutes, then pour it out and rinse the cup immediately. To gently scrub stains from fine china, use dry baking soda. And if china gets dull, bring back the shine with petroleum jelly (Vaseline). Just rub it on, let it sit for about an hour, and polish.

Keep your silver and gold bold

Keep china or glassware with a silver or gold edge or decoration far away from ammonia, heavy duty detergents, and washing soda. And don't even think of scrubbing them with any abrasive cleaners.

Get a handle on ivory

Has the ivory on the handles of your knives and forks turned yellow? Clean them by dipping a piece of lemon in salt and rubbing it over them.

Ousting kitchen odors

Put a stop to unsavory smells

To keep onion and cabbage odors from spreading through the house, simply boil a cup of vinegar in a saucepan at the same time they are cooking. Remove the onion smell from a pot with a tablespoon of vinegar in hot water.

Say good-bye to stinky boards

For odor-free fingers

Have onions to chop? Rub your hands before you start, and again afterwards, with white vinegar. Rubbing them with the end of a stalk of celery also works. To get the scent of fish off your hands or kitchen utensils, rub them with vinegar and lemon. And if all else fails, just get out your toothpaste and use it to wash your hands. The ingredients in toothpaste that clean and freshen your mouth will do the same for your skin.

Clean odors from your cutting board by sprinkling it with salt and rubbing with a damp cloth. Then wash in warm, soapy water.

Spice up the air

Did you know that commercial air fresheners don't really freshen the air? What they do is cover up the odor with a stronger, more pleasant scent. Or they deaden the nerve endings in your nose so you just don't smell the bad smells. You can make a safe and fragrant alternative to a commercial air freshener from two popular kitchen spices — cinnamon and cloves. Tie them in a piece of cheesecloth for an easy cleanup. Then boil them together, and fill the air with a pleasant scent.

Bid adieu to disposal 'pewh'

Remove food debris, and leave a fresh scent in the garbage disposal. Put in about a half-dozen ice cubes, run the system, and flush it well with cold water. Then put in half of a lemon and grind it up. Or, for a warmer deodorizing, pour in one-half cup of salt, then add hot water and run the disposal.

Trash those yukky smells

To prevent odors in garbage cans, empty them frequently. And add a sprinkle of borax in the bottom of the can to prevent growth of odor-producing molds and bacteria.

Good 'scents' for your refrigerator

If odors don't come out with a regular sudsy washing, spread one of these in a container, and place it in your smelly refrigerator or freezer. Let the appliance run empty for a few days:

► activated charcoal

► cat box litter

► imitation vanilla extract (not pure extract)

► ground coffee

Waves of odor

Clean offensive odors from your microwave oven with a solution of one cup warm water and one tablespoon baking soda. Rinse and dry. Or mix one part lemon juice to three parts water in a glass dish. Place in microwave and boil for three to five minutes. Cool, remove water, and wipe dry.

Are those fajitas I smell?

Plastic storage containers really come in handy for storing leftovers. But chili, pesto sauce, and other strong-smelling foods can leave them with a permanent aroma. Crumple black and white newsprint, and place it inside the offending container. Cover and leave for a day. The smell should be gone when you remove the paper.

Stuff it

If you're having an extra difficult time with refrigerator odors, stuff the shelves with wads of newspaper. Put a bowl of water on the top shelf. Also sprinkle newspaper with water. Allow refrigerator to run five or six days. This usually works well with strong odors.

Appliance savers

Fill 'er up!

Your freezer can be a wonderful time and money saver, but to really work efficiently it needs to be at least two-thirds full. If you don't have enough food to keep it this full, fill plastic milk jugs or plastic food storage containers with water, and place them in the freezer. Once the water turns to ice, you can count on a peak performance from your freezer.

Running hot and cold

If your refrigerator is located right next to your stove or dishwasher, figure out a way to move it. This arrangement of a "hot" appliance next to a "cold" one makes both these machines function less efficiently. By separating your refrigerator, it will last years longer.

Stove-top savings

For the most efficient cooking, either on top of the stove or in your microwave, use a container just slightly larger than the food. When you're cooking something in a pot on the stove, be sure to cover it. By leaving the lid off, you may be losing up to one-third of the heat produced.

On an electric stove, you can usually turn the heat off about five minutes before the cooking time is over, and the residual heat will finish cooking your food. This is also true for foods you cook in your oven.

Don't toast your toaster

Be careful about overloading your home's electrical circuits. Don't plug in your toaster and your electric skillet, or any two heat-producing appliances, in the same regular circuit at the same time. You might find yourself with a burned out appliance or circuit. If, however, your circuit is designed for heavy-duty appliance use, go ahead and plug them both in. It shouldn't do any damage.

Short-circuit safety

Do not leave toasters, blenders, can openers, or any small countertop appliance plugged in after you use them. If an electrical component malfunctions, the appliance could catch on fire.

Cord care

To get the longest life from your appliances, take care of the cords. If a cord gets knots or crimps in it, it can break and cause a short. And heat can do a lot of damage, so don't let the cord touch any hot surface — like a hot iron or toaster oven. Also, don't wrap the cord tightly around an appliance, especially if it's hot. It's better to store it with the cord coiled loosely beside it.

Pay attention to those arrows

Your toaster is probably marked to indicate which slot to use when toasting just one piece of bread. But does it really matter which side you use? Yes. The temperature gauge is usually located on one side of the toaster. To accurately judge when the toast is done, there should be a piece on that side whether or not the other side is being used.

Go small for big savings

Your toaster oven preheats in less than half the time it takes to heat the range oven. And it uses a lot less energy. It's great for browning foods, crisping casserole toppings, toasting nuts, warming a slice of pizza, even baking a potato.

If you have an electric skillet, use it. Stovetop cooking burns up about three and a half times as much energy as an electric frying pan. And don't forget about your reliable old pressure cooker. It may not be glamorous, but it cooks faster than conventional methods while using 50 to 75 percent less energy.

Don't wash away dollars

Be kind to your dishes, and save water and electricity, by routinely using the "china and crystal" setting on your dishwasher if you have one. If you have dirty pots and pans, wash them separately by hand instead of running them in a load. And always wait until your dishwasher is full before running it.

Pest proofing the home

Stop those ant-ics

To keep ants away, wipe down your countertops, cabinets, and floors with a solution of one part vinegar to one part water.

You can also squeeze lemon juice in the hole or crack where ants are getting in. Slice up the lemon peeling and scatter it around the entrance to make sure they get the hint!

Keep fleas at bay with basil

To repel fleas, grow a pot of basil in your kitchen window. Water it regularly from the bottom for a stronger smell. Or it works just as well to put crushed dried basil leaves in small bowls or hang some in muslin bags.

Ants usually will not cross a line of bone meal, powdered charcoal, cream of tartar, red chili pepper, paprika, or dried peppermint. So find out where they are entering, and create your own homemade barrier.

The ants crawl in but don't crawl out

Make your own ant traps. Use one cup of clear corn syrup and a half cup of warm water. Microwave for 40 seconds and stir to blend. Add two teaspoons of boric acid powder to the mixture and stir. Find some shallow containers (like bottle caps or small pieces of aluminum foil, bent up at the edges) and pour some of this mixture in them. Set these "traps" where you see ants but out of the reach of children or pets. Your ant problem will be short-lived.

Make frequent fliers flee

Flies are repelled by citrus, so scratch the peel of an orange and leave it out. Or hang a bundle of cloves, or keep a pot of fresh mint in the kitchen window.

Sprinkle borax or dry soap in the bottom of the garbage can after it's washed and dried to keep flies away.

Make your own fly paper by boiling sugar, corn syrup, and water. Spread the sticky mixture on brown paper, and lay it out or hang it where it will attract flies.

Rid your digs of roaches

Control roaches by scattering a mixture of equal parts baking soda and powdered sugar in the infested area. (The sugar attracts them; the soda kills them.) Or repel these creepy critters by cutting hedge apples (Osage orange) in half and placing them in the cabinets, in the basement, or under the house.

Combine half a cup of borax with one-fourth cup of flour. Put it in a jar. Punch holes in the lid and sprinkle it along baseboards and door sills. Or try a combination of oatmeal, flour, and Plaster of Paris. Put it in dishes in areas where roaches are likely to hide. Take care that no pets or children will get into either of these mixtures. Borax is toxic if eaten.

Put saucers of red wine under the cabinets. (Use the cheapest you can find. No need to waste the good stuff on pests.) Roaches crawl in, drink it, get tipsy, and drown.

Resourceful recycling

Easy coupon carrier

After opening your mail, save your envelopes and use the outside for your next shopping list. Place coupons you plan to use inside the envelope, and you're set for the next trip to the grocery store.

Milk that jug for all it's worth

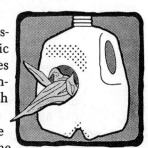

Make a handy dispenser for your plastic grocery bags from a clean plastic milk jug. Cut a hole, about four inches in diameter, in the side. When you finish putting away groceries, just push the empty bags through the hole one at a time. When you are ready to use one, it will pull out neatly while the others stay put.

Knot just for clean clothes

Recycle the plastic bag that comes from the dry cleaners. Just tie a knot in the end with the hole for the hanger and use it to line a trash can.

Get 'board' with your groceries

Using canvas grocery bags may be a better choice for the environment than the plastic or paper ones. But they also can fall over, letting bottles and cans roll to the deepest part of the trunk where it's hard to reach. To solve that problem, cut a piece of plywood to fit snugly into the bottom of the canvas bag. Items will sit firmly on the bottom, making it easier to retrieve them when you get your groceries home.

Kitchen safety

Sure-fire prevention

Always keep a multipurpose fire extinguisher handy. But if you use one for a grease fire, be careful not to spray burning grease out of the pan.

If a grease flame is small, it may be quicker to slide a tight-fitting lid carefully over the flame and turn off the heat. Wait until it's cool to uncover it. Never lift the flaming pan to take it outside. You can also smother a grease fire with baking soda, but never use flour or water.

If a fire starts in the oven, you can use a similar procedure to smother it. Keep the door closed, and turn the heat off. The fire should die out on its own.

Avoid hot splashes

Remember, oil and water don't mix. So when cooking a dish that contains hot oil, never add water. It can spatter hot grease and burn you.

HOUSEHOLD

Home accessories

Hang in there

Hanging artwork in your home will be easy and fast if you use this terrific tip. For each painting or photo you want to hang, use newspaper or a brown paper bag to make a paper cutout. To do this, lay the item face down on the paper and draw around it, then cut out the shape. Use masking tape or transparent tape to stick the cutouts to the wall to see how the paintings will look. Change the arrangement as many times as you like until it's just the way you want it. Then nail your picture hangers in place right through the paper. The paper tears off easily, and you haven't put any unnecessary holes in your wall.

The straight and narrow

You may have hung that painting straight on the wall, but the vibrations of people walking by have knocked it crooked. For a more permanent position, loop a rubber band around the hanging wire of the painting to mark the correct spot for hanging the picture straight. Wind some masking tape several times around the wire on each side of the rubber band. Remove the rubber band, and hang the painting. The little rolls of masking tape will keep it from jiggling out of position again.

Doily delights

You just couldn't throw away those crocheted doilies you inherited from Aunt Dorothy. So now what do you do with them? Put them to good use.

▶ A doily framed on a background that coordinates with your room becomes a piece of art.

▶ For a small, special gift, make a unique wrapper. Thread narrow ribbon through the edge of a large doily, and pull it up to form a decorative pouch for your gift.

Craft some pretty candles

Tired of plain candles? You can dress them up with spring finery by adding pressed flowers to their surfaces. Purchase pressed flowers, or make your own by gathering small, fresh blooms and leaves and placing them between layers of wax paper. Lay several heavy books on top, and in a week or so the flowers will be ready to use. Purchase wax as "paraffin" in the canning section of your local supermarket, or recycle used white candles. In a tin can placed in a saucepan full of water, melt some wax until it is transparent. (If the wax begins to smoke, it's too hot.) Brush a small amount of wax on the candle, then place a pressed flower over the wax, and press it in place with a toothpick.

Paint hot wax over the pressed flower and candle with an artist's brush while continuing to press the flower in place. One or two thin layers of wax should be enough.

Smoke out

Fewer and fewer people smoke these days, but if you have friends or family who do, ashtrays are still a part of your life. Wash ashtrays with a paste of baking soda and water to remove the smoky odor. Or sprinkle some baking soda in the ashtray before it's used to prevent cigarettes from smoldering and to keep down the smell.

Give dust the brush-off

A clean, dry paintbrush can be a wonderful tool for dusting. Use a fairly small brush with soft bristles to dust china, resin, and wooden knickknacks as well as computers and sewing machines. A soft brush works well on lampshades, too. A larger brush with stiffer bristles does a good job on carved furniture, windowsills, baskets, and wicker furniture.

All washed up

If you have lots of small knickknacks made of glass, china, or pottery, try washing them instead of dusting them. You'll save time and effort in the long run, and the pieces will stay much cleaner. Use a serving tray to carry them back and forth from the kitchen, and simply dip them in soapy water, rinse, and put them on a towel to dry. To wash a larger, fragile object, place it on a thick, folded towel in your kitchen sink. Spray it with glass cleaner or spray chandelier cleaner, and rinse it off with a water spray after a few minutes. Place it on another thick towel to dry.

Chipped cup camouflage

A chipped china cup or coffee mug may no longer be nice enough to drink from, but it makes a pretty flowerpot for a small plant on your windowsill or table. Just turn the chipped area away from you, and no one will see the flaw.

Tread softly with that sculpture

Decorative accessories of pottery, metal, and stone can be a lovely addition to your home decor. They can also scratch the living daylights out of your furniture if you aren't careful. Use inexpensive stick-on felt or cork pads on the bottom of each pot, bowl, or sculpture, and save the finish of your furniture.

In the dining room

The wax will wane

Scrape off melted candle wax from candlesticks, candle holders, or furniture with a plastic spoon. It will remove the wax without scratching.

Don't be a drip

To keep dripping wax from running all over your candlesticks, refrigerate your candles for several hours before lighting them.

Dining room downsizing

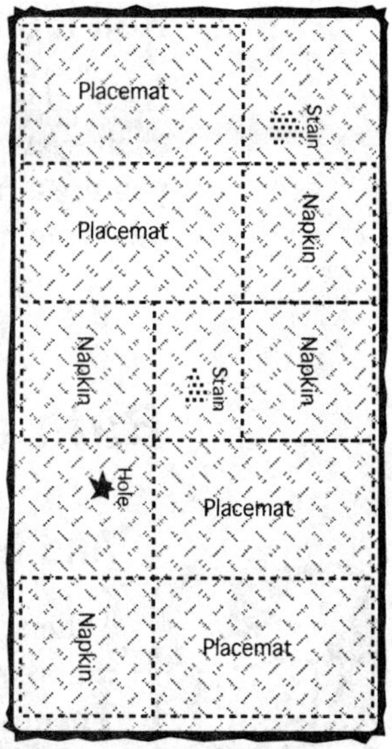

If your favorite tablecloth has acquired some large holes you can no longer cover up with your dinner plates, consider recycling it. Cut it up into large squares or rectangles, and hem the edges by hand or machine to make napkins or place mats. You can also bind the edges with bias-cut fabric or bias binding in a matching color.

The diagram on the right shows a tablecloth with labels: Placemat, Stain, Napkin, Placemat, Napkin, Napkin, Stain, Napkin, Hole, Placemat, Napkin, Placemat.

Nifty, thrifty napkins

Avoid the daily expense and waste of using paper napkins by using cloth ones for your family instead. Buy either good quality all-cotton napkins, or use dishcloths in pretty colors. Washcloths that are nicely finished on all sides serve well as napkins, too. Identify the napkins so that each person in your family has his own. You can embroider a monogram in the corner of each one, or simply buy a different color for each person. When you buy your napkins, pick colors that are not too far from the colors of your normal clothing and other laundry (no bright purple ones if your family dresses mostly in shades of beige). This way, it will be easy to throw your napkins in with your other laundry instead of having to wash them in a separate load.

Golden oldie

The ravelings cut from new table cloths before hemming is the best material that can be used in darning holes or thin places in the worn ones.

Household Hand Book, 1860

Roll it on

A smudge of dust or dry dirt on your upholstered chair seats or tablecloth will be picked up cleanly if you use a rolling lint remover. If you don't have one, use some masking tape rolled around your fingers.

Bath and shower

And two shall become one

When you're down to that last sliver of bar soap and ready to start a new one, moisten them both. Then work up a bit of lather on the new one and stick the sliver on it. It will soon become one with the new bar of soap, and there's no waste.

For a super shower, hide the soap!

Here's another way to use up those last little bits of soap – slip them into a bath sponge. To make your own, take a new household sponge and use a sharp knife to slit a little pocket into the side of the sponge. Insert small slivers of soap, and use the sponge instead of a washcloth for showers or baths.

A lemon-fresh view

Keeping your glass shower doors clean may seem like a full-time job. After cleaning the glass, wipe it with a little lemon oil to help keep it from getting cloudy.

Give your tub a good shampoo

Is your tub greasy from bath oil or other dirt? There's a product in your bathroom that will clean it in a flash. Pour some shampoo on a rag, and wipe off the greasy ring with ease.

This will do for mildew

No need for expensive mildew and mold cleaning solutions for your bathroom tile or shower. Add liquid bleach to a spray bottle, label the bottle "bleach," and spray away the fungus. Be careful, though; bleach fumes can be irritating, and you don't want to inadvertently spray bleach in your eyes or on fabrics.

It's 'curtains' for mildew

If you have a shower/tub enclosure with a shower curtain, shake out the curtain at the end of every

A mildew-free zone

Keeping mold and mildew out of the bathroom is a tough problem for many people. As a professional house cleaner, Donna Harp knows how much work it takes to maintain this particular room. She suggests you give your tile and grout a good scrubbing, then get in the habit of maintaining it.

"Spray the problem areas with a mildew-removing spray or an all-purpose cleaner a couple of times a week before you step into the shower," she advises. "Then take a minute to scrub down the walls and rinse them. Just be sure you have plenty of ventilation when you're using strong chemicals."

shower and drape it on the outside of the tub. This will help prevent mildew on the curtain and in the shower. If the curtain gets mildew on it, you can put it in the washer with detergent and a little bleach.

Mop it up

In order to make shower cleaning quicker and easier, try cleaning with a mop. Not only does this prevent you from having to get in the shower to sponge everything down, it's also easier on your back and knees. Simply spray on the shower cleaner of your choice, and give your shower the once-over with the mop. Rinse the mop, then go over the shower walls again. If it needs it, you can mop the bathroom floor at the same time without having to switch cleaning tools.

Steam cleaning

When it's time to tackle cleaning the shower, help yourself by turning on the shower at the hottest water temperature for about a minute. The steam from the shower will speed the process by loosening grime.

Hairspray haven

Step into the shower stall when you spray your hair. This way the floor and other stuff in the bathroom doesn't get sticky, and the shower gets rinsed every day anyway. If your bathroom is carpeted, this is especially useful for preventing a damaging buildup of dust and dirt on the carpet.

Curtain call

If your plastic shower curtain is still good except for a tear, mend it with some heavy-duty tape. Masking tape and transparent tape won't hold up to the moisture. Try some strapping tape (the kind with fibers embedded in it) or packing tape, which is thin, wide, and a light brown color. Be sure the curtain is completely clean and dry before you apply the tape, and smooth the tape carefully so no moisture can get under it. Your curtain should last for a while longer.

Caulk it over

When you need to re-caulk your tub, first remove the old caulk completely. Then wash the area thoroughly, and finally, clean the surfaces with rubbing alcohol. This will remove any remaining grease or soap, as well as disinfect the area of mold or mildew. Your new caulk will stick like a dream.

Clever cleaning with simple stuff

You can make a good, general cleaner by mixing one-half cup of borax in one gallon of hot water. This solution disinfects your bathroom, too.

A sprinkle a day

Recycle a small spice jar with a sprinkler top to keep by your bathroom sink. Fill it with baking soda and use it with a sponge daily to keep your basin and faucets sparkling clean. If you have stains on your porcelain, a gentle scrubbing with cream of tartar sprinkled on a damp cloth should remove them.

Take a shine to it

If you need to shine your bathroom quickly, get out the bottle of rubbing alcohol and a soft cloth. Isopropyl (rubbing) alcohol shines chrome faucets and fixtures and cleans hairspray film from mirrors.

Be nice to your enamel

If you have a porcelain enamel sink or bathtub, you need to treat it more carefully than you might realize. Avoid using scouring powder. If you must use it, go with the very finest grit you can find. Harsh abrasives shouldn't be necessary unless the surface has already been scratched. Then it may be necessary to use abrasive cleanser to get the dirt out, but be as gentle as you can.

Here are some other tips for keeping your porcelain enamel fixtures in tip-top shape:

▶ You may have heard that muriatic acid will remove stubborn stains from porcelain enamel. Don't buy it. You may get out the stains, but you'll also remove part of the enamel. Even acetic acid, found in vinegar, is too harsh.

▶ If you use chlorine bleach or hydrogen peroxide to remove stains from your bathtub or sink, don't use it full strength. Don't leave it on the surface for more than a few seconds, and wash it off thoroughly.

▶ To clean your porcelain fixtures safely, you can use a solution of warm water and ammonia. Or you can clean with one tablespoon of trisodium phosphate (TSP) diluted in one gallon of hot water.

Cure for cloudy chrome

You can soften and remove the hard water deposits around the handles of your chrome faucets by soaking paper towels in white vinegar and draping them over the deposits. After an hour, remove the paper towel and wipe the faucets clean. If your sink is porcelain enamel, be sure to keep the vinegar-soaked towels on the chrome and not on the porcelain, which could be damaged by the acid in the vinegar.

Soap stretchers

Liquid hand soap is wonderfully convenient, but more expensive than bar soap. Make your liquid hand soap last as long as possible. Here's how:

▶ As soon as the dispenser is half empty, fill it with water and agitate it gently to mix it. It will still do a good job of washing your hands for half the cost.

▶ Once you have bought the first soap dispenser, keep refilling it with replacement soap thinned with water. If the dispenser gets a little grubby looking, scrub it with a recycled toothbrush.

▶ Instead of buying liquid soap refills, try the least expensive brands of shampoo. They can also be watered down, come in various scents, and in the large containers are less expensive than soap refills.

▶ Make your own liquid soap and finally get some use out of those soap slivers. Break the slivers into small pieces and throw them into a blender with some warm water. Blend and then pour the soap mixture into dispensers.

Toilet care

Give your bowl a smile

You have guests coming tomorrow, and you'd like to clean and freshen the powder room toilet, but you just don't have the time. Do it effortlessly, overnight. Drop a couple of denture cleansing tablets into the bowl before you go to bed, and in the morning give it a swish with the bowl brush.

Commode cleaning

Forget expensive toilet cleaners! Flush your toilet to wet it down and sprinkle a little scouring powder over stained areas. After this has worked for a while, come back to it and swish it with a toilet brush. Use a liquid or spray all-purpose cleaner on the toilet seat. Scouring powder will leave it gritty and will eventually wear away a painted finish.

Tidy your toilet bowl

For space-age cleaning that adds a citrus freshness to your bathroom, sprinkle about half cup of Tang drink mix into your toilet. Leave it in for a couple of hours, then flush.

Top tips for toilets

Your toilet should last 50 years if you care for it correctly (and don't get tired of that avocado green color you selected). Here are some do's and don'ts:

▶ Do replace your toilet bowl cleaning brush when the bristles are bent or worn. Any metal on the brush that comes in contact with your toilet bowl may permanently scratch the porcelain.

▶ Don't hit the toilet bowl with anything hard, not even to break loose a fitting. A cracked toilet can't be repaired.

▶ Do use household oil or some other kind of lubricant to break loose a fitting.

▶ Don't sit or stand on the toilet lid. It isn't designed for that kind of use.

▶ Don't store heavy items or small loose items on top of the tank. You're risking a crack or getting an object stuck inside the toilet. Both can mean costly repairs or replacement.

General cleaning

Versatile vinegar

Vinegar is the mainstay of your non-toxic cleaning arsenal. Try these concoctions to clean everyday problems:

Copper pots – scrub with a pinch of salt and vinegar.

Bathtub film – remove with vinegar alone if it's not a porcelain enamel surface.

Windows – spray with equal parts of water and distilled vinegar, dry with soft cloth.

Grout stains and mildew – apply a straight solution of vinegar and wipe clean.

That old devil, dust

Are you constantly battling for control over the dust in your house? One way to win the battle is to capture dust as it's moving through the air. Housecleaning veteran Donna Harp has some good advice. "Be sure to replace furnace and air conditioner filters regularly. They're the first line of defense against dust and dirt. You also need to clean your floor and ceiling vents often; that's where dust gathers. You can remove most of the dust with a vacuum attachment. But every once in a while, you should remove the vents and give them a good scrubbing with soap and water."

Another hiding place for dust is your ceiling fan. Donna's advice? "When you clean your ceiling fans, don't just dust them — the dust will fly all over your room. Use a cloth and some warm, soapy water in a bucket to wash down the blades and get them really clean."

Getting unhooked

To remove stick-on hooks from painted walls, use plain white vinegar warmed in your microwave oven. Soak a sponge or cloth with the warm vinegar, and saturate the adhesive. After a few minutes, you should be able to remove it easily. This also works for getting sticky labels off glass, china, or wood.

Sock it to dust

A simple, more effective alternative to a dust cloth — an old athletic sock! Wear it over your hand and wipe around, behind, and over every nook and cranny.

Here's the wrap-up

To clean louvered doors, use a sock or a piece of cotton fabric wrapped tightly around a plastic ruler, spatula, or stiff paint brush. Secure the sock or fabric in place with a rubber band, if you like. Spray with a dust-attracting spray or saturate it with rubbing alcohol and wipe across each slat for thorough cleaning. This method works well for plastic mini-blinds, too.

O-mitt the dust

Another easy way to dust your furniture is with a clean car-washing mitt. Spray it lightly with dust-attracting spray or furniture polish, and you can quickly swipe your way to clean furniture. When it's dirty, just wash it in the washing machine, and let it air dry.

Golden oldie

Take that old broom you were just about to throw out, cut the bristles away, then tie an old felt hat (or scrap of flannel or carpet) around the "business end" – and, presto! You've got a perfectly good floor polisher.

1003 Household Hints and Work Savers, 1947

Try a little litter

Even though cat litter is associated with odor, unused litter is actually a great deodorant. Sprinkle some in the bottom of the garbage can to keep it smelling fresh. Change the litter after a week or so or when it becomes damp. Litter also works to prevent musty odors in a house that will be closed up for a while. Simply place a shallow box filled with cat litter in each room.

Stains take a powder

For a grease stain on your upholstered furniture, apply talcum powder generously and rub into the stain. Leave for a while until the grease is absorbed, then brush off with a stiff, dry brush such as an old, clean toothbrush.

Clutter control

Hold it right there

Use the plastic cases from rolls of 35-millimeter film to store small objects like paper clips, buttons, or thumbtacks. Recycle metal coffee cans to hold nails and screws.

Ace your storage problems

Save empty tennis ball canisters to store loose objects like sewing bobbins, drill bits, or tie wraps. Attach Velcro fasteners to the canisters and the other adhesive strip to a pegboard or wall to hang the containers.

Baby your stuff

Reuse small jars with lids, such as baby food jars, by nailing the lids to the underside of a shelf and screwing the jars to the lids. This is a handy way to keep small items like keys and earrings organized.

Perfect placement

Experts in household management live by the axiom, "a place for everything and everything in its place."

Follow their lead by creating specific places for the everyday necessities. For instance, hang car keys on a hook next to the back door, put mail that hasn't been read in the wicker basket on the desk, stack the newspaper on the television. Make sure you also create permanent "homes" for frequently used items like light bulbs, batteries, or cleaning supplies.

Address your concerns

It's a constant battle to keep an address book updated and legible. When your old one is ready to be retired, transferring the information to a new book is a tiresome task. Try keeping address and phone information on index cards and filing them in a recipe box instead. Larger index cards allow for additional information like business addresses, anniversaries and birthdays, or directions to a friend's house. When addresses become out-of-date, throw out the old cards and save the rest.

A better home for your 'Better Homes'

If you absolutely can't bear to part with those magazines you spent so much money on, cut out the articles that interest you most and keep them. Get several file folders, and label them with the names of your specific areas of interest. Go through each magazine and rip out the pages that contain articles in these areas, then staple them together and put them in the file folders. Start working on the magazines you already have, and any time you buy a new one, go through the same procedure. You'll be amazed how little space the articles take up compared to entire magazines. Soon you should be free of magazine clutter!

The second time around

If you have a computer and printer at your house, consider recycling your own printer paper. When you print off a letter or report that isn't quite perfect, don't throw the paper in the trash; put it in a special "recycle" pile. Turn the used paper over, and run it through your printer again when you know you're writing something that is a "first draft." You'll get the maximum use of your paper, save money, and help the environment at the same time.

Atten-hut!

Messy stacks of magazines every place you look? Tired of the clutter? Make magazine holders for free by diagonally cutting off the top part of empty cereal boxes and neatly storing your magazines upright on a bookshelf. To add a decorative touch, cover the boxes with pretty contact paper or wallpaper.

What is that plastic thing anyway?

Keep a small laundry basket or plastic box for odd items that are either missing something, like an unmatched sock, or are separated from the original, such as a game piece or an unusual screw found on the floor. Label the container with a question mark. Then periodically go through the basket when you have time to figure out where the pieces go.

For serious supplies

Minimize clutter and keep dangerous cleaning solutions from spilling by standing cleaning supplies upright in a plastic crate under your sink. If there are some supplies you need to use throughout the house, store them in a plastic tool carrier so you can easily use them on cleaning day.

Flatten it and forget it

You've just bought a computer, and you think you might be moving in a year or two, so it makes sense to save the box it came in. But there is nowhere to store that bulky box. Simply slit the tape holding the box together, and flatten it out. Now you can store it under a bed or flattened against the back wall of a closet. If you don't have any place to keep the Styrofoam packing, try to recycle it or discard it if you need to. When the time comes for moving, wadded newspaper or household linens can substitute for the packing, and your computer can move safely to its next home.

A tisket, a tasket

If you don't have any cabinet space in your bathroom to store towels, use a small basket on the counter for hand towels and a larger basket on the floor to hold bath towels. You can fit more towels in the baskets if you roll each towel up and stand it on its end.

Electrical problems

Where were you when the lights went out?

Every adult in your household should know where your fuse box is located, what it's for, and how to change a fuse. If not, take a few minutes for a family training session. This will save you lots of time and trouble next time the lights go out.

The map that lets you see the light

While you're at it, take a few pieces of masking tape and label each fuse or circuit breaker in the box. On each piece of tape, write the main room or area that is served by a particular fuse. That way, in an emergency, you'll be able to tell at a glance which fuse needs fixing. Many fuse boxes come with a pre-drawn map on the inside of the door, sort of like a family tree. If yours doesn't have one, you can simply draw it out on a piece of paper, or use the masking tape labels.

When time stands still

If your electric clock stops running, turn it upside down for several days. This redistributes the oil in the clock's mechanism so it will start running again.

You can sing happy birthday, too

A storm is coming, and you're trying to prepare for strong winds and probable power outages. Of course, a good flashlight with lots of backup batteries would be great. How about a few emergency candles that will burn a long time? If these are not available, don't panic. Grab a jar of petroleum jelly and search for the leftover birthday candles in the kitchen. Stick a birthday candle into the middle of the jar, and light it when needed. This homemade candle should burn for several hours.

Potato power

When a light bulb breaks off as you're trying to unscrew it, you're in a bit of a pickle. Vegetable to the rescue! First, make sure the light is turned off. With a hammer, knock away the remaining broken glass into a trash can. Then cut the top third off a baking potato and stick the cut side into the socket. Holding on to the potato, you can safely unscrew and remove the rest of the bulb and replace it with a new one.

How enlightening

Did you know that an incandescent bulb covered with dust provides up to 50 percent less light than a clean one? Make it a habit to dust your light bulbs when you dust everything else.

Golden oldie

Brilliant light – A pinch of salt put into the lamps when they are filled with oil will cause them to burn with more brilliance.

Household Hand Book, 1860

A little ambience for the closet

When the top two wattages of your three-way bulbs burn out, try using the low-wattage bulbs in a hall or a closet. You'll be recycling and saving yourself money at the same time.

Cool bulbs for a cool house

Compact fluorescent light bulbs cost more than incandescent ones, but in the long run they are less expensive. They last up to 10 times as long as regular bulbs, and they use much less electricity. And since they produce less heat than incandescent bulbs, there is not as much heat for your air conditioner to overcome during the summer months.

A bright idea

You'll save energy, and therefore money, if you use one larger bulb with higher wattage instead of several smaller bulbs with lower wattage. For example, you can get just as much light from one 100-watt light bulb as you can get from six 25-watt bulbs. And it's cheaper to buy the one larger bulb.

Battery power

To prolong the life of a battery, lightly file both ends of the battery with an emery board or some fine-grit sandpaper.

Gifts and giftwrap

Goodies for a gardener

To create an inexpensive gift for a gardener, look in your garden for a clay pot that is in good condition. Scrub it thoroughly with soap and water, and let it dry completely. Use leftover house paint or craft paint to paint the exterior of it in pretty colors, either abstract shapes, lines, and squiggles, or a garden-theme design. Cut a square of fabric to tuck inside the pot and extend over the top edges. Add an inexpensive pair of gardening gloves and a packet of seeds. A small trowel with a handle in a matching color or an old spoon with the handle painted would make the gift extra-special and practical.

A gift of romance

If you have a person on your gift list who is really hard to buy for, or a gift to buy for an upcoming wedding, consider an "evening in a basket." Start with an inexpensive basket purchased at a garage sale and one of your favorite main-dish recipes. Line the basket with pretty paper or leftover fabric and add all the non-perishable ingredients in your recipe. Finish with something to drink, such as exotic tea, fruit juice, or a bottle of wine, and a small box of chocolates for dessert.

Um, thank you for the lovely gift

Everyone gets "white elephant" gifts from time to time – nice things that you have absolutely no use for. Save them in their original packages, and attach notes saying who gave them to you. Then when one of your white elephants turns out to be just the right gift for someone else, it's still fresh and new and ready to go.

A bonus gift

Get creative when it comes to wrapping gifts. Things like fingertip towels, cloth napkins, bandannas, and scarves dress up a gift in a unique and reusable wrapper that the recipient will appreciate twice as much!

Card party

Make your own gift tags, greeting cards, and postcards. Carefully cut the fronts off cards you receive, and reuse them as they are, or paste them onto folded heavy paper or index cards.

It's a wrap

Get more creative with wrapping paper, and save money to boot. Use the pages of fancy gardening magazines for small gifts, or the cartoon section of the newspaper for a wrap with a different look. Old posters are another good substitute for more expensive wrapping paper.

Cards for a cause

Here is a great way to recycle old Christmas cards. A home for abandoned, abused, and troubled children recycles as many as 500,000 old cards each year. The children cut the front off the cards and paste new backs on them.

To donate your old cards, mail them to:

St. Jude's Ranch for Children
100 St. Jude's Street
Boulder City, Nevada 89005

To order a package of 10 recycled cards and envelopes, send $6.50. Price includes postage and handling charges. For more information, call 702-293-3131.

A tasty tin

When you'd like to recycle pretty, decorative tins for gift giving, you often have a label to remove first. Spread it lightly with creamy peanut butter and leave it overnight. In the morning, the label should come off easily.

Vase the facts

Here's a great way to recycle and save money, too. Buy inexpensive vases from garage sales; you can often get them for about 25 cents. Then provide your own vase the next time you go to the florist to buy flowers as a gift. You'll save as much as $3, depending on the size of the arrangement.

Holiday decorations

Bow beauty

If you recycle bows for your holiday gifts, you may find them a little squashed when you take them out of the storage box. A hand-held hair dryer set on high heat can perk them up and make them usable again.

Christmas all year round

Consider buying a live tree in a planter instead of an expensive, cut Christmas tree. You may need to start with a smaller tree, but it can be used for several years as it grows. When it gets too big for your house, plant it outside. One word of advice: trees can be heavy and hard to move, so you may need to set your planter on wheels.

Light the way

To keep Christmas lights from getting tangled up, wrap them around an empty wrapping paper tube or a rolled-up newspaper when you store them. This also makes it easier to put them on the tree the next year. Just unroll them gradually around the tree.

Treats for your tree

Make your cut Christmas tree last longer with a simple recipe. Add four tablespoons of iron powder from your plant nursery, four teaspoons of liquid bleach, and two cups of clear corn syrup. Mix it thoroughly and add approximately one gallon of hot water. Insert your tree into the plant stand and pour the liquid into the stand. You should be able to keep your tree looking fresh longer with this recipe but, of course, you have to check the water daily and never let the level get low. A six-foot tree can absorb as much as a quart of water every day.

To help keep the needles from falling off your Christmas tree, try an antidessicant spray. This product coats the needles so they don't dry out as fast. It will work on live trees or cut trees. You should be able to find antidessicant spray at your local garden center.

Bug off

To keep bugs from bugging you and your Christmas tree, treat it before you bring it inside. Fill a spray bottle with a mixture of one quart of water and one and one half teaspoons of liquid dishwashing detergent. Spray all over the needles, the branches (especially underneath), and the trunk. Wait until the spray has dried before bringing the tree inside.

Houseplants

A clean plant is a happy plant

To keep your houseplants healthy, you need to give them an occasional bath to get rid of dust and spider webs. You can stand them in a shower and let the water douse the leaves, put them in the kitchen sink and use the sprayer, or take them outside and rinse them off with a hose. Just don't do this in bright sunlight, or the leaves may burn. After a good bath, houseplants should be dusted regularly, about as often as you dust your furniture. A soft, dry cloth or a feather duster will do the trick. Then about once a month, wipe leaves clean with a damp cloth or sponge.

A drip in time

If you don't have a helpful neighbor with a watering can when you go on vacation, try suspending a baby bottle full of water above your plants. The water drips out slowly, so your plant will be quenched long-term. If your plant is large, you can use a soft drink bottle with a tiny hole punched near

It must be the lovely smell

Mothballs repel not only moths but lots of other bugs you don't want indoors with you. So put a mothball in your houseplants that you put outside in spring, and you won't have to bring the bugs with them when they come back inside in the fall.

the bottom. Fill it with water and place it in the pot with the plant. Your greenery will be watered slowly over a long period of time.

Off, off, darn bugs!

To get rid of insects on your indoor plants, fill a quart-size spray bottle with water. Add two tablespoons of liquid soap and stir well to dissolve. Spray the leaves and stems of your plants and any bugs that you see hanging around.

Give your plants a squeeze

You can recycle a squeeze bottle from liquid detergent into a watering can just the right size for small plants. Or you can use it to mix and distribute your plant food.

Keep soil in its place

Houseplants need good drainage through the bottoms of their pots. It's common to use broken pieces of clay pots or rocks to block drain holes, but both can still let soil run through and out of the pot. Instead, try a piece of window screen over the drain holes. It's fine enough to keep in soil but let out water. Another idea is to reuse the plastic tops from milk or juice jugs. Cut small notches around the edge of the cap and put it over the drain holes. Or use the old-fashioned metal bottle caps (from beer or soft drinks) with ruffled edges. For hanging baskets, recycled pieces of Styrofoam will plug the drain hole and provide good drainage without any extra weight.

Poinsettia pointers

Although poinsettias usually last only one season, you can keep them going longer with some special loving care. To bloom at Christmas, they need total darkness for 10 hours a day for the entire fall. Trim the stems back after the flowers die in winter, and give them only a little water for several months. Once you start back to regular watering, the plant will begin to grow again.

Cap it off

To prevent dripping from hanging plants after you water them, cover the bottoms of the planters with old shower caps. Remove the caps after several hours, and your floors should stay dry.

Don't knock it 'til you've tried it

If you can't tell whether your plant needs water, just knock. A thump on the side of the flowerpot should tell you if the pot sounds hollow. If it does, the plant is dry. When your knocking yields a solid thud, there's probably enough moisture in the plant.

Cold comfort

Here's another great way to water hanging plants without having a drippy mess on your hands. Put a few ice cubes around the edge of the pot, not touching the plant. As the cubes melt, they will provide a slow watering that the soil can absorb – with no messy dripping on the floor.

Having a dry spell?

Houseplants can get so dry sometimes that when you water, it runs right through and doesn't soak the soil thoroughly. Try this technique to make sure they get a complete soaking. Set the plant in a medium-sized trash can or five-gallon bucket. Gradually add water until it flows over the lip of the pot, and the soil is immersed. Let the plant sit in the water for about a half hour. Then carefully lift the pot, let the excess water drain out the bottom, and put it in a plant saucer or tray.

It's in the bag

Save those bags that cover your dry-cleaned clothes to cover houseplants when you go on vacation. They make a great mini-greenhouse that keep houseplants moist while you're gone. First you'll need to put plastic or terra cotta saucers under your plants. Water as usual, letting some water overflow into the saucer. Then bend a wire coat hanger to make an arch, straighten the hook end, and stick it straight down into the soil near the pot's edge. Put the dry-cleaning bag over the hanger, trim off any excess, and tuck the ends under the saucer.

The root of the problem

You don't want a plant to be too crowded in a pot, but be careful not to replant it in a pot that is much too large. Instead of putting its energy into growing foliage, the plant will grow more roots to fill the pot. Aim for a good balance.

Gloss over it

To give your houseplants a healthy shine, wipe their leaves down with some glycerin on a soft cloth. It won't attract dust the way some "leaf glossing" products will.

Pamper your plants

▶ Regularly remove dead leaves and spent flowers. Not only do they look bad, but they can also promote disease.

▶ Give your plants fertilizer during the same seasons you would your outdoor plants, and give them winters off.

▶ If the tips of the leaves turn brown, cut off most of the brown part, leaving a narrow brown edge. Cutting into the green may promote disease.

Step by step

When you're looking for a good way to display several potted plants together, consider a ladder. A small wooden step ladder from your local hardware or discount store makes an attractive, movable shelf for plants. You can paint it to match your decor, stain it with wood stain, or leave it natural. Or you might find an old wooden or metal step ladder at a garage sale or in your basement. A ladder works especially well in the kitchen or on a patio or screened porch.

Floral arrangements

Spruce up your silk flowers

An easy way to clean silk flowers is to blow the dust off with your hand-held hair dryer. Be sure to use only the "cool" setting so any plastic parts won't melt. If you do this on your deck or patio, even better. You'll be removing the dust from your house.

Dry but durable

Dried flowers can be so brittle and flaky that they are a mess to work with. Try giving them a light spritz of hairspray before you start, and leaves and petals should stay in place instead of ending up on your floor.

Your plants need a treat, too

Everyday foods from your kitchen can give a real boost to your houseplants. Try these tips for healthier plants:

▶ A little bit of diced banana skin or ground-up eggshell is like a vitamin for your plants.

▶ A package of unflavored gelatin dissolved in a quart of water makes a plant food that is full of nitrogen, an important nutrient for plants.

▶ Ferns like a cup of tea as much as the rest of us do. Or mix wet tea leaves into their soil.

A breath of fresh air

When your silk flowers begin to look a little tired, spruce them up by adding a few stems of dried flowers. They will blend in well and look realistic. Or you can add a touch of life with some fresh flowers. Check your local florist or craft store for floral "picks." These are small, pointed containers that hold a flower stem in place while surrounding it with water. Fill each pick with water, insert the stem of a blossom, and push the pick into the foam base of your silk flower arrangement. Blossoms will last a day or two on the water in the pick, or you can replace the water to keep them going longer.

Show your support for cut flowers

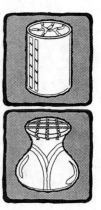

To arrange flowers in a vase with a wide mouth, you can cut strong twigs the diameter of the opening and wedge them horizontally in the vase, just down from the top edge. Or you can use masking tape or green florist's tape to construct a grid across the opening of the vase. Either method supports the flower stems so the flowers can be arranged easily and will look pretty longer.

Don't be daffy with your daffodils

Cut flowers from your garden are a beautiful addition to your home. If you're lucky enough to have tulips and daffodils, here's a tip: don't bring them in from the garden and put them together in the same vase. The slime from daffodil stems can ruin cut tulips. So put the daffodils in a separate vase for about a day, then rinse off their stems, and you can safely add them to the tulips.

The last straw

If your cut flower needs a longer stem to go in the vase you've chosen, give it a little lift. Put the short stem into a plastic drinking straw cut to the length you want.

Perk up your posies

When you bring cut flowers into your home, there are certain things you can do to keep them fresh as long as possible. Before you put them into the vase, cut about an inch off the end of each flower stem at an angle. This will let the flower soak up as much water as it needs. When you fill the vase with water, add a dollop of 7-Up (regular, not diet) to the water. The soft drink acts as "plant food" for the flowers. Every day, pour out the old water in the vase and fill it with fresh water. Add a little fresh 7-Up, as well. Finally, keep your vase of flowers out of direct sunlight if you can. These steps will prolong your enjoyment of the beautiful blossoms.

A penny for this thought

Put a penny in the bottom of your vase of cut tulips. It will help keep the tulips from opening up too fast.

Make it clear

If you're arranging cut flowers in a clear vase, they'll look much better if the water doesn't turn cloudy. Add a teaspoon of household bleach to a quart of water to keep the water clear. Add bleach each time you change the water.

Party plans

See it in the right light

Planning a party and don't have time for a thorough house cleaning? Replace your regular light bulbs with low wattage bulbs, and use candles for "atmosphere."

Bargain bandannas

To brighten your table and give it a Southwestern flair, use inexpensive bandannas as napkins. You'll find them in a rainbow of colors in craft stores or the scarf department of discount stores. If you choose the polyester/cotton kind rather than all cotton, you'll never need to iron. You can also sew bandannas together to make an easy, inexpensive tablecloth.

Pretty natural placecards

For unusual place cards, use magnolia leaves or medium to large ivy leaves. Wash and dry the leaves, then write the guests' names with a marker containing opaque white, gold, or silver ink.

Glass glowing

Need pretty holders for votive candles? Look again at your own glassware. A small sherbet bowl (the kind that stands on a low pedestal) makes a perfect votive candle holder. So does a sturdy wine or champagne glass. Put a teaspoon of water in the bottom of the bowl to keep the candle from sticking. To remove any remaining wax after the party, scrape the glass gently, and wash it with hot soapy water.

Here comes the bride

To save money on a wedding cake, have one layer of real cake and the rest decorated Styrofoam. After cutting the cake for the traditional photographs, ask the servers to roll it back into the kitchen. Have sheet cakes waiting to be cut and served. Sheet cakes are much less expensive than tiered cakes and will serve a crowd neatly and easily.

Remember the times of your life

If you are hosting a special party for someone and want to give a gift that is inexpensive but effective, consider a "memory canvas." At a craft store, buy an inexpensive piece of canvas board. Using craft paints, paint the canvas board a pale color, and add a scene or designs around the border. Paint the words "Happy Birthday" or whatever is appropriate. Then, during the party, let each guest use a fine-tipped permanent marker to sign or write a special message on the canvas for the guest of honor. After the party, the honoree has a wonderful memento of the occasion.

Here's the scoop

For ease in serving ice cream at your child's birthday party, prepare ice cream servings ahead of time. Simply scoop the ice cream into paper muffin cups, place them on a cookie sheet, and return them to the freezer. When it's time to serve the cake, take out the ice cream all ready to serve. No mess, no delay!

Photo realism

For every special event in your life, there are usually photos to be developed. When you pick up your photos, remember these money-saving tips:

▶ Look through the photographs on the spot. Most developers will not charge you for the ones that didn't turn out, such as a photo of the ceiling or someone's feet. You can reject those photos and simply be charged for the ones you keep.

▶ If the color processing is bad (for example, your friends have green faces), ask the photo lab to redo the photos. It will probably reprint them for free.

▶ Avoid "one-hour" processing. It's the most expensive way to go.

Urn your keep

If you have a large coffee urn for serving big groups, always store it with the spigots open to prevent the handles from sticking. Wash it thoroughly before storing it.

Shoo fly

Don't let a party on your deck or patio be ruined by pesky flies, gnats, or mosquitoes. Borrow or invest in a portable electric fan. Aimed at the center of the party action, a fan will cool the area while it discourages flying insects. A second fan aimed at the same area from another direction will help even more.

Tea-riffic

Always wash out any container you use to serve coffee or tea with a solution of baking soda and hot water. Your serving pieces will be clean and stain free, and the beverages will taste fresher.

Don't be a target

If you want to discourage mosquitoes from biting you at your next outdoor party or picnic, avoid wearing shiny jewelry, bright colors, or flower prints. And don't wear cologne or perfume.

Purchasing power

Give yourself some credit

The next time you're tempted to pull out your credit card to pay for a purchase, stop just a moment. Mentally calculate how many hours you will have to work to pay for that purchase, including credit card interest. Is it really worth the time? This trick may help you decide what you really want to buy.

A sample in time saves nine

Each time you paint a room in your house, take a minute to brush a wide band of paint onto a plain index card. When the card is dry, label it with the room and the date and keep it in an envelope in your car's glove compartment. When you are shopping for furniture, linens, or accessories for your home, you have an easy, instant way to make sure they will coordinate with the walls. To be even more accurate in your purchases, add a small swatch of the major fabrics you've used in the room. On ready-made or upholstered pieces, you can usually cut a little sliver of fabric from the inside of a seam allowance. Tape these to the card with the paint, and you'll save time

The bottom line

This is the best money-saving tip you can follow. Before you purchase any item of significance, ask yourself these questions:

▶ Do you really have to have it?

▶ Is it the best buy for the money?

▶ What do you have to give up to have it?

▶ Will it enrich your life?

▶ What would happen if you didn't buy it?

▶ By buying it, are you trying to meet some other unrelated need in your life? (For example, a fancy car will give you "status.")

▶ How much will it cost to maintain it?

▶ Will it lose its value quickly?

If you answer this checklist honestly and thoughtfully, it can save you from making many costly, unnecessary purchases.

and money by never having to return an accessory that doesn't match your room.

Be p-repaired

Sometimes it pays dividends later to invest in something now. That's how it is with many home repairs. A fresh tube of super glue may fix that special china platter you were going to throw away. An inexpensive eyeglass repair kit may keep you from a trip to the eye care center at a really inconvenient time. And the $50 you spend on the repair manual for your car will seem small when you save $350 on your next repair job. Look around your house, and see what types of repairs could save your possessions if you spent a little on repair equipment. Maybe you could even rent it or borrow it from a friend.

Off the wall

If you are lucky enough to find a sample book of discontinued wallpaper, buy it. That also goes for rolls of discontinued wallpaper in a pattern you like, especially if the sale price is good. Wallpaper makes attractive wrapping paper for small gifts, and it can also cover an old lampshade to make it new. It can be used to line drawers, make a mat for a photo or painting, or cover a notebook or photo album. Along with some clear contact paper, wallpaper can be used to make place mats or coasters to protect your furniture. You'll invent your own uses for this wonderful paper if you have some at hand.

HOME INTERIOR

Carpet care

Get 'mower' dirt from your carpet

Your carpet's worst enemy is dirt. To be sure you get it really clean, vacuum like you would mow your lawn – in orderly rows. This way you are less likely to miss a spot. Be sure to make several passes with the vacuum over every strip of carpet because it takes more than a "once over" to do it right.

Stand up right

When you go to the store to buy a vacuum, you'll find a dizzying array of machines to choose from. If you can, go for an upright vacuum cleaner over the canister type. They generally do a better job.

It's in the bag

You'll get the best results from your vacuum cleaner if you make sure the bag isn't too full of dirt and dust. Once the bag is filled to a height of about eight inches, you need to replace it. What if you haven't finished vacuuming and you don't have any more bags? You can remove the bag, put on a rubber glove, and

Golden oldie

Do not use cornmeal or tea leaves in sweeping carpets. The cornmeal has been known to attract water
bugs if not carefully swept up, while tea leaves, unless
well washed, are liable to make a stain. If anything is
used let it be small pieces of newspaper, well dampened and sprinkled about the floor.

Household Hand Book, 1860

take some of the dirt out by hand. Then reattach the
bag and continue.

How many hoses?

When your vacuum cleaner hose is clogged, use a
piece of old water hose to unclog it. The piece of
water hose should be a little longer than the vacuum
hose. Unplug the vacuum cleaner and remove its
hose. Push the water hose through the vacuum hose.
The water hose is small enough to fit, but sturdy
enough to quickly dislodge any clog.

Flea free

If you have a pet, you may sometimes find it necessary to vacuum up fleas from your carpet. Put two or
three mothballs in your vacuum bag before you
begin, and the fleas should be dead before you turn
off the machine. Immediately remove the used vacuum bag. Put it in a plastic trash bag, close it up tight,
and take it outside to the garbage can.

Don't push on plush

Always lift heavy furniture to move it across nylon carpet. If you push it, the weight and the friction can actually cause the carpet fibers to melt. This may leave permanent streaks.

Where there's smoke

A burning cigarette, if dropped, will usually melt a hole in synthetic carpet. But some carpets can catch on fire. If this happens, grab a box of baking soda and put out the fire. It will cause less mess than a bucket of water and can simply be vacuumed up.

To repair a cigarette burn in carpet, cut out the blackened fibers using small scissors. Fill this indentation

No bare feet allowed

Taking off your shoes and walking on plush carpet may make you feel like a kid again, running barefoot in the grass. But it may not be as good for the carpet as it seems. Professional carpet cleaner Robert Clay recommends that you adopt the Japanese custom of removing your shoes at the front door. But don't go completely barefoot.

"It may be pleasant to walk around your house this way, but the oil from your feet rubs off and attracts more soil to your carpet," Robert notes. "Slip on a pair of clean white socks instead." Tennis-style socks, which only come to your ankle, might be a comfortable compromise between sock feet and bare feet.

with some liquid glue and carpet fibers cut from a remnant of your carpet.

Pre-treat your carpet

When your carpet looks like it needs cleaning, try brushing it well with a clean broom. Then vacuum thoroughly. This should bring up the nap and make it look much better. Maybe you can hold off a little longer before shampooing it. On the other hand, if it is definitely time for a good cleaning, you'll have it all ready.

Spot cleaning

Don't let stain remain

When you get a spot or stain on your carpet, deal with it immediately. The longer you wait, the less likely you are to get it out. Begin by removing as much of the stain-causing substance as possible. For thick, "gloppy" stuff, use a paper cup, a spatula, or a credit card to lift the substance up and away. For liquids, blot it with paper towels or a clean white cloth. If it's a dry mess, vacuum it up.

Do the closet test

Always test your cleaner first in an inconspicuous area, such as the back corner of a carpeted closet or behind a heavy piece of furniture that you aren't likely to move. Some carpet spot cleaners contain bleach to help remove spots, but they could ruin your carpet instead.

Spot the best spot cleaner

Whenever possible, use club soda to remove spots from your carpet.

Its carbonation works to loosen the soil so you can blot it up. Unlike soap, it doesn't leave any sticky residue to attract even more dirt to the area. Here are some other spot cleaners you might want to try:

▶ Commercial window cleaner or a half-and-half mixture of water and white vinegar works well on most carpet.

▶ Try equal parts of water and liquid dishwashing detergent. (Not the kind used in automatic dishwashers.) Just be sure the detergent doesn't contain bleach.

▶ For acid stains, apply a solution of one tablespoon baking soda mixed in one cup of cold water.

Just a spoonful of solution

To avoid mildew and other problems, don't soak your carpet. Begin with small amounts – maybe one teaspoon – of the cleaning solution. Spoon it directly onto the spot and use the spoon to gently rub it in, working from the outside of the stain inward toward the center. Then apply a little clear water with a white cloth. (With a colored towel, there is a risk that its color might cause an additional stain.) Blot. If the stain remains, repeat the process. When you finish, spread a clean white cloth over the entire treated area and apply pressure with your foot to absorb as much of the moisture as possible.

Don't play chicken with your carpet

You trip on the way to the dining table, spilling greasy fried chicken on the floor. Never fear. Your kitchen cupboard has the carpet cleaning remedy you need. Remove the chicken and scoop up all the grease you can. Pour baking soda over the remaining stained area and rub it in. Wait for about an hour so the oil can be absorbed. Then run your vacuum cleaner over the soda. You'll squawk with delight at the results!

Carpet odors

If you delay, your nose will pay

Nothing smells worse than an old pet stain in carpet, so you need to act quickly if your pet has an accident. Blot up all of the urine and rinse the area with warm water. Then apply a solution of one teaspoon of white vinegar, one teaspoon of liquid detergent and two cups of warm water. Work this into the carpet and let it stand for 15 minutes. Rinse and dry the area. (Caution: vinegar may affect dark colors, so be sure to test this formula in an area that is hidden.)

Sprinkle a subtle scent

Make your own carpet freshener and add a gentle fragrance to any room. Combine one-fourth cup of talcum powder with your favorite scent, three-fourths cup of baking soda and two tablespoons of corn starch. Mix it all together. Then sprinkle this over your carpet and let it stand for at least 15 minutes. Vacuum and enjoy the fresh scent.

Shake out odors

Knock out odors in your carpeting by applying a mixture of one cup of Borax and two cups of cornmeal. Shake the mixture over your carpet and let it stand for at least an hour before vacuuming.

If your carpet is completely dry, another good odor-removing substance is baking soda. Sprinkle it on your carpet and leave on for 15 minutes or more. For really stubborn odors, leave it overnight, then vacuum thoroughly in the morning.

Hardwood floors

Squelch that squeak

Can't sneak up on anyone in your home because the "creak" of your floors gives you away? You can fix a squeaky floor like a professional by following these steps:

▶ Locate the floor joists near the squeak. Joists are usually 16 inches apart, laid in the direction of the front to the back of your house.

▶ Drill a number eight wood screw, one-and-one-fourth inches long, through the carpeting and into the floor joists where the squeak occurs.

This should fix your squeak, since most are caused by the sub-flooring boards rubbing on dried-out joists that have shrunk.

Put a damper on flying dust

Vacuuming just seems to make the dust fly around on hardwood floors. So use a dust mop instead. You can spray it with a little commercial dusting spray if you'd like to help attract the dust.

The big chill for a grease spill

If you spill some grease on your hardwood floor, immediately put a couple of ice cubes on the spot. This will harden the grease so you can scrape it up with the side of a credit card and throw it away. Then wipe the floor with a clean, dry cloth to remove any remaining grease.

A clean sweep

If you cut your child's hair at home or you have pets that shed, this tip will be a time saver. Tie a soft, cotton cloth around the bristles of your broom and sweep up the loose hair. The cloth attracts the fine hair and keeps it from scattering.

Don't seep it under the rug

Be sure you protect the hardwood floor underneath when cleaning stains off rugs. Some cleaners designed to remove stains will also remove the finish from your floor. You may think your carpet is too thick for any of the solution to seep through, but don't risk it. Place a thick, white, terry towel under the section of the rug you're cleaning, just to be safe.

Sock out scratches

Put thick socks over the legs of furniture before moving it. This will prevent scratches on your hardwood floors.

Nix the Nicks

Clear nail polish can fill in small nicks and scratches on varnished wood floors and glass or plexiglas surfaces – and no one will ever know.

Vinyl, linoleum, and tile floors

Soft on shine

Your floor needs mopping but you hate to lose that high wax shine. Can you clean it and keep the sparkle? You bet you can. Just use a mixture of one cup of fabric softener in half a pail of water.

Scrub with the club

Remove wax buildup from your vinyl or asbestos floor tiles with club soda. Pour it on a small section at a time. Scrub it in, let it soak a few minutes, then wipe it clean.

Erase heel marks

Black heel marks really stand out on your clean, light-colored floor. But they are easier to get rid of than you might think. Just rub them away with an art gum eraser.

Shine the light on linoleum

Is your kitchen's linoleum or no-wax floor getting dull? To make it bright again, wash it with one-half cup of white vinegar to one gallon of water.

Dump, don't deal with dirty water

When you have a lot of dirty, soapy water remaining after scrubbing a floor, don't waste time mopping it up. It's quicker to use a squeegee to push it into a puddle. Quickly scoop it up in a dust pan and dump it down the drain. Then just damp mop lightly and your floor is done.

Windows

End window washing worries

If your windows are really dirty with soil and grease, you'll usually do better to clean them with an alkali like ammonia, baking soda, or washing soda. But to remove hard water deposits and some soils, a mild acid like vinegar is best. Avoid harsh acids that can etch the glass.

For cleaning and de-fogging your windows, mix either two tablespoons of vinegar to one quart of water or two tablespoons of sudsy ammonia per quart of water.

For a mixture that should keep your windows clear in cold weather, mix one-half cup of sudsy ammonia, two cups of rubbing alcohol, one teaspoon of liquid dishwashing detergent, and one gallon of water.

Steer clear of the heat

Avoid washing windows on days when the temperature soars. The heat will cause your windows to streak.

Bring back sparkle and shine

To make your windows sparkle, after washing and drying them, rub them with a clean blackboard eraser. Or dry your windows with coffee filters and you won't leave any lint behind – just shine.

Don't damage your window sills

A spray bottle can be handy, but not when window cleaning solutions drip. They can damage the finish on varnished or painted surfaces, especially if they are alkaline or contain alcohol. It's best to spray cleaning solution directly onto the cloth, sponge, or chamois. Wring it out until it's almost dry before wiping the glass.

A trick when windows stick

Never strain to open a window again! Your windows won't stick if you apply a thin coat of petroleum jelly to the window tracks. Just brush it on with a small paint brush. Try this method with sticking drawers and cabinet doors, too.

Polish off this shade problem

Got a torn window shade? Try clear nail polish to mend the tear. Lay the shade flat on a table, hold the tear closed, and apply the nail polish in thin coats.

An eye on the world

When early Norwegian carpenters built houses, they needed a hole or "eye" to let the smoke from their fires escape. Since the cold wind frequently blew through this opening in the roof, it became known as "the wind's eye." The British borrowed the Norse name, eventually changing it to "window." Today's windows with glass panes give us an eye to the out-of-doors. But when closed, they keep the wind out.

Windows and warmth

If you count on your windows for solar heat in winter, be sure to keep them clean. Clear glass lets more sunlight through to help warm your home.

Shades and blinds can help keep out the winter's cold. To get the best insulation, mount them outside rather than inside the window frames. There they'll do a better job of keeping the cold air from leaking into the room.

Walls, doors, and ceilings

Mix-it-yourself cleaner

Use this formula to clean painted walls:

1/2 cup white vinegar   1/4 cup baking soda

1 cup ammonia   1 gallon warm water

Don't let this crack you up

Cracks in plaster are an eyesore. Mix plain white school glue and baking soda into a paste and rub into the cracks. Cracks disappear!

Arm yourself against dripping water

You reach up to wash your walls, and soapy water goes running down your forearms. What can you do to keep sleeves and arms dry? Wear a terry cloth athletic wristband to stop and soak up drips.

Picture-perfect plaster

Here are two tips to keep your plaster walls from splitting when you hang a picture:

▶ Make an "X" with scotch tape on the spot where you intend to place the nail.

▶ Heat the nail with a match or lighter before hammering it in.

Sock it to debris on rough walls

A sponge or cotton cloth is likely to leave little pieces behind when you clean rough plaster walls. Try using old nylon or Ban-Lon socks instead. They won't fall apart so easily.

Soak up a solution to wallpaper removal

Don't break your back trying to remove old stuck-on wallpaper! Do it the easy way with a solution of white vinegar and hot water. Using a roller brush, soak the paper several times with this solution. The paper will peel off without a struggle.

Doughy cleaner for wallpaper

Use a few slices of crustless, fresh bread to clean non-washable wallpaper and other delicate surfaces. The softer and doughier the bread, the less abrasive it will be on your delicate surfaces.

North, south, east, west, put this stud finder to the test

Need to find wall studs but don't have a stud finder? You can easily improvise if you have a compass on hand. Simply hold the compass level at a right angle

Hold the lettuce

Mayonnaise isn't just for sandwiches and salads. You can use it to clean white water marks from wood paneled walls and cabinets. Just rub it on, leave it for 12 hours, then wipe it off.

to the wall. Pass it slowly across the wall until the presence of a nail makes the compass needle move. When you are trying to locate studs, it helps to know that 16 inches is the usual distance between stud centers. Electrical outlets are usually mounted on one side of a stud, and the nails in ceiling moldings or baseboards should also indicate the approximate position of studs.

Spray on resistance

Hallways and stairway walls attract plenty of fingerprints and grime, especially if you have young children around. Try spraying these areas with a light coating of spray starch. The sprayed areas will resist marks longer and will be easier to wash off when the dirt begins to build up.

Color it clean

Remove crayon marks from a painted wall by rubbing first with a dry cloth just on the marks. Then use a little toothpaste on a soft cloth to scrub off the remaining stain.

For crayon marks on vinyl wall coverings, use silver polish or concentrated dishwashing detergent.

Brush on grease relief

You can't scrub grease spots on non-washable wallpaper. So what can you do? Try dusting on talcum powder with a powder puff or soft brush. Leave it on for about an hour, then brush it off. It may require a second treatment to make the grease disappear completely.

Handy tips for hanging wallpaper

To make sure your wallpaper will stick, cover old grease spots on the walls with shellac. Let it dry before you begin papering.

Paint a one-inch strip at the top of the wall to match the ceiling. You won't have a dark line showing if there's a small gap or an uneven line where wallpaper and ceiling meet.

If you use wallpaper paste, stir in a few drops of food coloring. You will be able to tell if you miss any spots when you apply the paste.

To make things easier when soaking prepasted wallpaper, use a large cooler that is wide enough for the paper. Since the cooler is insulated, the water will stay warm longer and do a more effective job.

Creative solution to a rough problem

Is your wall rough from the buildup of old paint or from where wallpaper was pulled off? You can conceal it and give your room an unusual, rustic appearance at the same time. Just mix some common hay or dried grass into wall board compound, available at the hardware store. Spread it all over your wall, as thick or as thin as you like, with a wide putty knife.

111

Warm your walls

For greater energy efficiency, cover your walls with fabric (flame-retardant, of course) by sewing rod pockets in the top and bottom, gathering them on curtain rods, and attaching the rods to the wall.

Move a filled bookcase to a wall that needs additional insulation, such as a wall that doesn't get much exposure to sunlight.

Hang decorative rugs or wall-hangings on walls that stay cool to keep them from losing energy.

Squeaky hinge spray solutions

That squeaky door hinge is driving you crazy, but you don't have anything to oil it with. Check your cupboards before you drive to the hardware store. Cooking spray will eliminate that annoying squeak. Or try shaving cream – it should work just as well.

The fireplace

A 'mist' opportunity

You can make fireplace cleaning a little neater. Spread newspapers around the hearth before you start. Get out your plant mister, or any spray bottle, and fill it with water. First mist the newspapers. Then, as you sweep the ashes onto the newspaper, lightly mist them as well. You'll find that no ashes will blow onto your carpet. Put the whole mess into a garbage bag and throw it away.

Smoke and stains get the brush-off

To clean the surfaces of a brick or stone fireplace, mix together an ounce of powdered soap, an ounce of table salt, and enough water to make a paste. Rub it on with a cloth and let it dry for at least 10 minutes. Scrub it off with a stiff-bristled brush.

Make soot scoot

Toss a handful of salt into your fireplace occasionally. It helps prevent soot accumulation, and makes more colorful flames.

Give dust a hand

When it's time to clean the dust from your crystal chandelier, here's an easy way to bring back the sparkle. Wearing white gloves, dip your hands in a solution of water and ammonia. Squeeze your hands together to remove excess moisture. Take each individual prism in a gloved hand to clean it.

Indoor painting

Scent-sational tip

Don't like the smell of oil-based paint? Give your nose a break. You'll improve the scent and make your painting job more enjoyable if you stir a spoonful of vanilla extract into the can of paint.

Handle your woes with a garden hose

Don't throw away that old garden hose! It can make carrying a paint can easier on the hands. Cut a small section the width of your hand and split it lengthwise on one side. Place the section of hose around the wire handle of the paint can, and you have an instant "comfort grip."

Take the pain out of painting

Painting the wood near the glass panes on your windows is definitely a pain. This trick is so easy, you'll wonder why you didn't think of it before. Take a cotton swab or small applicator and rub petroleum jelly on the glass next to the wood. Any stray brush marks won't stick to the glass, so you can easily wipe away your mistakes. This works for painting around doorknobs and hinges, too.

Believe it or not

To prevent white paint from turning yellow, stir in a drop of black paint.

News you can use

Here's a cheap, nifty way to keep paint off glass when painting window frames. Dampen strips of newspaper and press them onto the glass right next to the wood. The strips stick to windows as well as masking tape, and you can remove them much more easily.

On a clear day you can see forever

No matter how carefully you paint, it seems some spatters will get on your windows. Newly dried ones will come off by wiping windows with a cloth soaked in hot vinegar.

No drips allowed

Prevent paint spills and catch paint drippings at the same time. Trace the bottom of a paint can on the side of an old cereal box. Make a hole to fit the can by cutting out the circle on the side of the box. Place the paint can inside it. Any drips will be on the cereal box and not your floor.

114

Rim shot

Before you begin painting, punch a few holes in the inside rim of the paint can. When you dip your brush and wipe off the excess paint on the edge of the can, the paint will flow back into the can instead of dripping down the outside. Not only will the cleanup be easier, but you'll save paint as well. And without paint in the rim, the lid isn't as likely to stick when you close the can.

Foil, don't fret

You're in the middle of painting a room and suddenly there's a more pressing need elsewhere. No need to clean your brush or roller if you'll be ready to use it again shortly. Simply wrap it in aluminum foil or put it in a plastic bag and stick it in the freezer. It will stay moist while you take care of your other chores.

Foiled again

If you're using a paint tray, let aluminum foil help with the cleanup. Just line the tray with foil before you begin. When you finish painting, you can pour any unused paint back into the can. Then toss the aluminum foil liner and your cleanup is done. When you are ready to start again, simply put in fresh foil.

Roll on

Here's a simple way to get more mileage from your paint roller sleeve. Just remove it from the frame from time to time and reverse the ends.

Under cover

Aluminum foil comes in handy for covering door knobs and thermostats while you paint the doors or walls. It's flexible and stays in place until you're ready to remove it.

Make a handy, disposable soaking bin for your paint roller cover. Just cut the top out of an empty milk carton, fill it with solution or water, and put your roller pad in to soak.

When you finish using a disposable paint roller sleeve, you can make quick and neat work of removing and discarding it. Just slip a plastic or paper bag over it. Pull it off while holding the outside of the bag, and it's all ready to drop in the trash.

Don't come unhinged

Painting around hinges doesn't have to be aggravating – just try this trick. Cover the hinges on your doors or cabinets with a layer of rubber cement, and let it dry before you paint. It's easily removed when the paint is dry. Just peel it off with your fingers or rub it off with a gum eraser.

A neat trim

When painting trim, use a wide wallboard finishing knife or wide putty knife to get neater, straighter lines. With one hand, hold the edge of the putty knife in the joint where the trim and the wall come together. With the wall area shielded by the putty knife, you can paint the trim without getting any stray strokes on the wall. Wipe the edge of the putty knife occasionally with a rag to prevent any seeping paint from going astray.

Undercover stains

You thought you could cover that stain with fresh paint. But there it is again, bleeding through. You should always wash off grease and hand prints with detergent and warm water before you paint a wall, but sometimes that isn't enough. Professional painters put a stop to this problem by painting over the stains with pigmented white shellac before painting. If you can't find this product, you can use any spray or liquid shellac to seal the stains so you can paint over them without the stains bleeding through.

A quick nick trick

It's simply too much trouble to get out the brush and paint can to touch up every little mar or chip on a painted surface. So when you finish painting walls, trim, or cabinets, save some paint and save yourself some work. Clean out an old fingernail polish bottle with polish remover. Fill it with paint, cap it tightly, and store it in a handy place. Or simply fill a small, capped bottle with paint and keep an inexpensive craft brush attached to the bottle with a rubber band. When your wall or woodwork gets a scratch, open the bottle, brush it on, and recap it. With touch-ups so convenient, you won't hesitate to fix that nick when you need to.

High plate dripper

Make a paint catcher from a paper plate or the plastic lid of a

Hit the ceiling

Holding your arm in the air to paint a ceiling is bad enough without having wet paint run down your arm in the process. To solve this problem, wear rubber gloves and turn the cuff back a few inches to catch paint drips.

117

coffee can. Just cut a slit in the middle and push the paintbrush handle through it. Now you can even paint overhead without getting drips in your eyes.

A fan-cy cover

When you are ready to paint around the ceiling fan, here's a quick way to do it neatly without having to remove the blades. Save your plastic wrappers from your daily newspaper. Slip one over each blade and continue painting.

Basic baseboard preparation

Check your baseboards before you paint them. If they picked up coats of wax when you waxed your floors, the new paint may not stick. To avoid this problem, scrub them with an ammonia solution, sand them lightly, and then proceed with your painting.

Back away from a tough move

Need to paint behind a piano or big chest of draw-ers? If it's not too close to the wall, you may be able to avoid the back-breaking work of moving it. Staple a thin plastic sponge to the end of a yardstick or other long, narrow strip of wood. The sponge will hold enough paint without dripping while you reach behind to give the wall a neat coat of paint.

Stair stepping

Don't let wet paint on the stairs prevent you from using both levels of your two-story house. If you paint every other step, you can still walk up and down on the unpainted steps. When the painted ones dry, you can stand on them while you paint the remaining steps. If skipping steps seems too risky, paint one half of each step, all on the right side, for example. When they are dry you can use them as you paint the left side.

Carpet care for paint spills

No matter how carefully you place that drop cloth, drops of paint will sometimes, somehow, manage to get on your carpet. Act quickly. If the paint is latex, dab it with a mixture of one part dish detergent to 20 parts water. Blot, rinse, and blot again. If the paint is dry, try a little lacquer thinner. But do a spot test first. This product can melt some kinds of carpet.

Go easy on yourself

Cooking oil, baby oil, shaving cream, or shampoo will soften and remove paint from your hands and face more pleasantly than harsh turpentine or mineral spirits.

Did you forget to wear a cap while painting the ceiling? Baby oil is a good choice for removing the paint that dripped onto your hair.

For fresh oil-based paint or varnish spills, use the specific thinner or solvent recommended on the label. If it has dried on, you can soften it by soaking paper towels with the solvent and placing them on the paint spots for several hours. Then brush the spot. You may need to repeat the solvent treatment. Then work in a solution of detergent and water. Blot up the excess. Rinse, using warm water, and blot the carpet dry.

Starch right up

To remove paint that has dried on a vinyl or linoleum floor, apply a paste of starch and hot water. Leave it for 30 minutes and then wipe it up.

If brushes make you bristle

Before you start painting, give your brush a good combing. Use a comb with plastic or metal teeth to remove loose bristles that might otherwise get stuck on your freshly painted wall.

If a bristle does stick to a freshly painted surface, remove it with a pair of tweezers while the paint is still wet. Then brush over the spot to smooth the surface.

Brush up on brush care

Before you use a new paintbrush for oil-based paints, soak it in linseed oil for a day. It will be easier to clean and will last longer, too.

To restore natural bristle brushes to their original softness after you use them, clean them as usual with solvent and wipe them dry. Then soak them briefly in hot water with a little fabric softener added.

To soften hardened paint on brushes, soak them in hot vinegar. Follow up by washing with warm, soapy water.

Mess-free brush cleaning

Cleaning up after painting with an oil-based paint can get pretty messy. Make cleaning your paintbrush easier with the "bag method." Pour cleaning solvent into a large, strong, plastic bag and insert the brush, handle end up. With one hand, hold the bag tightly closed and hold the brush by the handle. Use the other hand to swish and massage the bristles through the plastic bag. You'll clean your brush without getting your hands dirty.

Do-it-yourself hanger

When you have cleaned your brushes, hang them to dry with the bristles straight so they won't get bent and broken. Make a handy hanger for a couple of brushes from a coat hanger and two large paper clips. Bend the hanger corners down and push the bottom of the wire up in the center. Loop the paper clips over the corners, hook the brushes on the clips, and hang it all up to dry.

Storing leftover paint

When you finish painting a room, take an extra minute to label the side of the paint can. With a wide black permanent marker, write the room you painted and the date. If the color number is not on the top of the can, be sure to add it, too, in case you want to buy the same color again. Store paint cans with the labeled side showing. Next time you're cleaning out your paint supplies, you'll know at a glance whether the cans are keepers or not. And if your room needs a touch-up, you'll find the right paint quickly.

Use a permanent marker to draw a horizontal line indicating how much paint is left in the can. You won't have to open it to find out if there's enough for a project that comes up later.

A "skin" won't form on leftover paint if you store it upside down. Just be sure the lid is on tight!

Not just grease paint

Consider donating leftover cans of paint (still usable, of course) to a high school drama or art department for painting scenery and art projects.

Safe at the plate

Guessing how much paint you need for your rooms can lead to wasted paint or extra trips to the paint store. Now that you have painted and know how many gallons it takes to cover your room, don't write this important information on some little piece of paper you'll probably lose. Record it on the back of a light switch plate in the room. You'll have to take those off next time you paint anyway, and the vital statistics will be right there.

Take your lumps

Don't throw out lumpy paint! Pantyhose stretched over a paint bucket makes a perfect strainer. Pour the paint through slowly, and you'll catch the lumps that can be thrown away. Stir the strained paint a little and it's ready to use again.

FURNITURE

Looking for bargains

A quality that lasts

The best way to have furniture that lasts is to buy good quality pieces to begin with. When you're shopping for new furniture, take the time to test it out thoroughly for comfort and sturdiness. Sit on chairs and sofas; lie down on beds. Stay long enough to really get a feel for how comfortable it is. Here are some other key points to remember:

▶ Look for furniture made of good quality wood. By reading the label carefully, you should be able to tell about the materials used. A label that says "cherry finish" is probably referring to the color or a simulated wood grain, not to a piece made of cherry wood.

▶ Stay away from simulated wood such as particle-board unless you are looking for an inexpensive item to last for a short time. Keep such pieces away from dampness, or they can swell and warp.

▶ Inspect the finish carefully. Make sure it is smooth and evenly applied.

▶ Test doors and drawers to be sure they fit properly and glide easily, especially in a piece of furniture that will get a lot of use.

123

Unfinished business

To get the best quality for your dollar when buying new furniture, consider unfinished furniture. Today, you can purchase solid hardwood pieces, either assembled or ready to assemble (RTA) in an unfinished state, and finish them yourself. With a little bit of sanding, staining, and sealing, you'll have furniture you can be proud of at a much lower cost than you find in furniture showrooms. If you don't want to do the finishing yourself, you can have your furniture finished at the store and still come out ahead on the price. And you can pick exactly the color and finish you want.

Golden oldie

A few drops of oil of lavender scattered through a book case, in a closed room, will prevent mould in damp weather.

Household Hand Book, 1860

Table the issue

Garage sales are wonderful places to shop, but sometimes you have to "think outside the box" to get what you want. If you're looking for a large, sturdy coffee table for a living room, den, or family room, you may not find the quality or size you want. Look instead for a sturdy old dining room or kitchen table and cut off the legs to coffee-table height. You may even have an extra table in your attic that you had not thought of using this way. Try it; it works!

Easy repairs

Give rings the runaround

No matter how many times you ask your kids and friends to use drink coasters, accidents still happen, and an ugly white water ring appears on your favorite piece of wood furniture. To remove the ring, use extremely fine steel wool (4/0) with a dab of mineral oil. Be careful not to rub too hard, and rub with the wood grain. If you don't have any steel wool, you might try regular white toothpaste or automotive rubbing compound. Just be sure to remove these substances carefully when you're done with a clean, damp cloth. Then rub some mineral oil into the spot. To seal the oil in so the spot doesn't reappear, apply a thin coat of paste wax or beeswax over the surface of the furniture.

Please pass the jelly

Remove imperfections in your wood furniture, like water spots and heat marks, by coating them with petroleum jelly and letting it stand overnight. Wipe clean in the morning.

Originality counts

If you look at your antique furniture as an investment, the last thing you want to do is refinish it. Stripping off the original finish of an antique, no matter how scratched or cracked it is, can take away more than half of its value. To care for a piece of antique furniture that has scrapes, gouges, or other problems, use a thin coat of paste wax to even out the finish. You can always remove the wax later if you want to, and the original finish is not damaged or changed in any permanent way.

All that glitters

Don't throw out an old mirror just because of a few scratches in the silver backing. Get some metallic silver auto spray paint and give the scratches a couple of coats. Then seal with clear shellac spray.

Coffee cure

Hide small nicks in wood furniture with instant coffee! Make a thick paste with a little instant coffee and water and press into the blemishes with a clean soft cloth. For longer-lasting coverage, mix the powdered coffee into a bit of beeswax or paste wax, and apply to nicks and scratches. You can also buy an inexpensive wax crayon to match the color of the furniture and fill the scratch. Even a child's brown crayon may do the trick.

More than skin deep

You may have heard that iodine makes a good cover for scratches on your wood furniture. The problem is, if a permanent substance such as iodine penetrates into the wood, it won't come out simply by refinishing. You'll have to sand it out. Stick with less-permanent solutions for furniture scratches.

Just scratching the surface

If you use a "scratch cover" polish on your furniture, use it sparingly and wipe it off quickly. If you leave the polish on too long, it can make a dark stain on the finish.

Too bad it's only for chairs

The woven cane seat of a chair will sag after years of use, but don't throw it out. Give it its very own "seat lift." Carefully remove the caning from the chair and lay it in a bath of steaming hot water with a little lemon oil added. Once it is well soaked, remove it and let it dry in the sun. As the seat dries, it will return to its normal shape. Then rub on a thicker coat of lemon oil to help keep the caning supple. Reattach it to the frame and you're all set!

A leg to stand on

A spindle has come loose from the legs supporting one of your kitchen chairs. It looks like you might be able to fit it back in place, but you'd like to add a little glue for insurance. What kind should you use? If you want a quick setup, opt for one of the "tacky" glues. Yellow carpenter's glue is a type of tacky glue made just for wood, and will work very well. If you don't have any, go for tacky glue, fit the piece back in place, and hold for a few minutes. The repair should be done without any extra equipment. Be sure to wipe off excess glue with a damp cloth, and let the piece dry overnight or even 24 hours before using it again.

Polish it off

Does the knob on your dresser drawer keep coming off, even though the screw holding it on seems to fit tightly? Here's a quick solution to the problem. Remove the screw and give its threads a thick coat of clear fingernail polish. Put it back into the knob and screw into place. When the nail polish dries, the knob should be secure.

Don't toss those T-shirts

You don't have to buy new cloth or paper to clean or refinish your furniture – recycle. Clean, all-cotton T-shirts cut into sections make good rags for furniture polishing or refinishing.

This is 'oil' you need

To shine the surface of your furniture, one of the best products is plain old mineral oil, the kind you can find in the pharmacy section of discount or grocery stores. It's the main ingredient in lemon-oil furniture polishes.

Upholstery

Mattress maneuvers

How can you lengthen the life of your mattress? Use the seasons to remind you when to turn it. For the first time, turn it over in spring. Then in summer exchange the head and foot on the same side. When fall arrives, turn it over again. For winter, reverse the head and foot again. By the end of the year, you've slept on it every possible way, which helps prevent those uncomfortable body-size imprints that usually form on older mattresses.

Lather your leather

Sofas and chairs upholstered in leather are comfortable and durable but notoriously difficult and expensive to clean. Here's a simple method for cleaning your own leather furniture. Using warm water and a gentle bar soap such as Ivory, make a lather on a soft cloth, and clean a small area gently. Immediately rinse with another soft cloth dampened with clean water. With a third cloth, dry the cleaned area immediately.

Even the dog can't hurt it

When you buy a nice piece of furniture, invest a few more dollars in one or two cans of spray-on fabric protector. That way, you don't have to ban food, drink, shoes, and children from your nice furniture. The fabric will look nice for years in spite of accidental spills.

One good turn deserves another

Sofas and chairs with loose cushions will last longer and look better if you turn the cushions frequently. At the end of the day, turn the back cushions around to the other side, and turn the seat cushions over. This will ensure that the upholstery fabric doesn't get pulled too far out of shape in one direction and that the cushion inside will wear evenly.

Finishing and refinishing

Don't stick it to your furniture

Most home furniture refinishers will lay newspaper under the piece they're working on to protect the floor from paint or refinishing liquids. Then when it's time to move the repainted or refinished object, pieces of newspaper often stick to the bottom of the piece. Try using a folded square of wax paper or plastic wrap under each leg on top of the newspaper. Paint and sticky residue won't adhere, and your project stays neat.

Instant attraction

If you use steel wool for a final light sanding when refinishing furniture, tiny metal shavings will be left on the surface. To be sure you remove them all, run a magnet slowly over the surface of the wood to attract the metal particles. Then wipe the wood with a sticky "tack cloth" to remove the remaining dust.

Dancing with Mr. Sandman

Who doesn't love the smell of cedar? Unfortunately, old chests and closets can lose some of their fresh scent as the wood ages and dries out. Bring back a bit of that great smell by giving your cedar furniture a light once-over with very fine sandpaper.

That's pretty slick

Aerosol spray furniture polish is not a good choice to use on wood furniture if you think it might ever be refinished in the future. Such polish contains silicones, which give it a shiny, slick finish, but never really go away. When you try to refinish a piece that has several years' accumulation of silicones, the new finish may not stick.

Padding along

For refinishing your furniture, a less messy alternative to a steel wool pad is a plastic abrasive pad such as Scotch-Brite, available at your local hardware store. These pads are washable and reusable, won't fall apart like steel wool, and avoid the problem of metal shavings that can go through rubber gloves and into your skin. If you can't find these pads, you can use the abrasive side of scrubber sponges from your local grocery, the kind that are cellulose on one side and plastic scrubber on the other.

The fine art of stripping

The process of stripping furniture and applying new stain and finish is a slow one; there is not much you can do to speed it up. When working on such a project, do yourself a favor and allow plenty of time. The time required for a coat of stain or finish to dry is always listed on the can. However, these times apply to the very best of conditions. A good rule of thumb is to double the drying time listed on a product. That way, you should be safe in putting on the next coat, and you'll end up with a fine finish.

Don't play with fire

Be extremely careful when you use the highly toxic and flammable chemicals associated with furniture care and refinishing. Always wear heavy-duty rubber gloves when using these chemicals, and treat the rags you use properly. When rags are damp with mineral spirits, other solvents, or refinishing products, spread them out flat to dry somewhere away from your house. Do not wad them up; they can spontaneously burst into flame. Once the rags are completely dry, they are safe to throw in the garbage can.

If you want to take it off ... and put it back on

When you chemically strip the finish off furniture, be sure to neutralize the stripping chemical when you are done. Otherwise, it can interfere with the new finish you put on. If you work with a water-based stripper, use lots of water. If you use an oil-based stripper, neutralize with plenty of mineral spirits.

Care and maintenance

Say it, don't spray it

Be really careful when you use aerosol spray furniture polish. Overspray from this type of polish can create dangerously slick situations if it falls onto vinyl or hardwood floors where people walk. You can't really see it, but you can feel it when you slip and fall.

Not too hot, not too cold

After you've invested in quality furniture, take care of it by giving it a healthy environment. Wood expands and contracts with the changing humidity in the air, so it doesn't do well with extremes. If you are comfortable with the humidity in your home, your furniture probably will be, too. If possible, use an air conditioner in the summer and a humidifier in the winter. Don't place your furniture close to a fireplace or radiator or directly over a furnace vent. Try to protect your furniture from too much exposure to direct sunlight, which can bleach the finish and cause cracking. If a piece is in front of a window, remember to close the curtains to shield it from the brightest part of the day.

The care and feeding of furniture

Do you think your furniture needs expensive polish to "feed" the wood? If so, you're subscribing to an old myth that's just not true, says longtime woodworker and furniture maker Zach Etheridge.

"The idea that applying a polish to the surface of furniture is 'feeding the wood' is a myth. If the surface of a piece of furniture is sealed by lacquer, varnish, paint, or polyurethane, polish cannot penetrate into the wood. It is only treating the finished surface."

A furniture expert, Zach has taught classes on furniture making, refinishing, and repair. He recommends using a small amount of mineral spirits on a clean cotton cloth to clean the finish of your wood furniture.

"This will not damage any 'sound' finish, which is one without deep cracks, gouges, or areas where the finish is completely gone. Don't buy 'paint thinner,' but check the label for 100 percent mineral spirits. Wear rubber gloves when you use mineral spirits, and work in a well ventilated area."

Always use coasters or saucers to keep damp glasses, cups, and vases from making white rings on the furniture. Likewise, don't put hot bowls, plates, or pans on furniture without lots of pads for heat and moisture protection.

Cinnamon won't let 'em in

If silverfish are a problem, a pinch of cinnamon inside your drawers and cabinets will keep them away.

Not just for chalkboards

When you are lining dresser drawers with shelf liner or contact paper, a chalkboard eraser is a handy tool for smoothing out the wrinkles and getting the paper to lie flat.

Outdoor furniture

Gloss over it

When your wooden patio furniture soaks up moisture through its legs, the wood can weaken and split. Avoid the problem by coating the legs all over, especially on the bottom, with a couple of coats of paste wax. Or you can brush two coats of polyurethane on the bottom of the legs and a few inches up the sides. Be sure to match the finish of the wood, either satin or gloss, with the polyurethane so it won't show.

Wash and wear

The feet on metal patio furniture are usually covered with plastic or rubber tips to cushion them. However, with all the wear the furniture gets, especially scraping against concrete, the tips wear out and the sharp metal legs scrape against the floor, causing scratches and sometimes even rust stains. To eliminate the problem, remove one plastic tip and take it to the hardware store with you. Look for a thin metal washer that will fit inside the tip. Put washers inside the tips of all your patio furniture legs, and the tips (and the furniture) will last much longer.

PLUMBING, HEATING, AND COOLING

Water heaters

Cool it and save

To avoid scalding and save money on your electric or gas bill, turn your water heater down to 120 degrees or lower. About the only appliance that would need water hotter than this would be your dishwasher, but most dishwashers these days have their own internal heater to raise the water temperature to 140 degrees for washing.

Is your water heater in a sweat?

If you think your hot water heater is leaking, it should be replaced. However, don't mistake condensation for leakage. During cold months, the incoming cold water in the morning may cause condensation on the outside of the tank. When this water drips down to the floor, it may appear that the water heater is leaking. When the water has warmed up, the condensation will evaporate. If your water heater is too small for your household, it will be more likely to have a condensation problem. Make sure it is

Taking yourself to the cleaners

While taking a long bath can be luxurious and relaxing, the water you use may indeed be a luxury. A bath requires 50 to 60 gallons of water, while a quick four-minute shower will get you clean with about eight gallons.

big enough to keep up with your cleaning, laundry, and bathing demands.

Don't let a leak sneak up on you

To keep your hot water heater in top shape, drain two to three gallons of water from the valve at the bottom to remove any sediment that may have collected. If you do this about every six months, you may save yourself the trouble of repairing a leaky faucet valve. Removing sediment will also help the heater work more efficiently, saving you money each month on your power bill.

The right jacket for the job

If the outside of your water heater is warm to the touch, it's wasting energy. Cover the outside of the tank with a specially designed blanket of insulation. Home improvement stores carry water heater "jackets" that are either one and a half or three inches thick and fit any size water heater. Just wrap it around the heater, tape it, and trim off any excess.

Drain problems

The weekly steep

The simplest method to keep drains from becoming clogged requires no harsh chemicals or hard work.

Just heat about a gallon of water to boiling, pour half down the drain, wait a few minutes, and pour in the rest. Don't risk cracking a porcelain basin – pour directly into the drain. Repeat this procedure once a week.

String a leak

If you have a leak in the plumbing under the sink or any place you can easily reach, you can make a quick fix with a piece of string and a cup until you have time to deal with the repair. Just wrap and tie the string around the pipe at the leak, and let the string hang down into the cup. The drips will run down the string into the cup, keeping the area dry.

Sweeten 'drain breath'

Ever notice a slight stench wafting up from your tub or sink drain? You can prevent this by giving your drains a monthly dose of baking soda. Rinse it through with hot water and wash away that odor.

Before you ask the plumber, ask the plumber's friend

If you have a clog in your sink, try using a sink plunger first. Plug the sink overflow opening with a wet rag, and smear some petroleum jelly around the rubber rim of the plunger. Place the plunger over the drain and move the plunger handle up and down with enthusiasm. If that doesn't work, then you can try drain cleaner. Don't use a plunger on a clog if you have already used chemicals. It could blast dangerous drain-cleaning chemicals all over your room and all over you.

Blast from the past

When your bathroom sink is clogged or barely draining, here's the all-natural, old-fashioned way to get it flowing again. Pour in one cup of baking soda, one cup of salt, and three-fourths of a cup of vinegar. Let the ingredients stand in the drain for about 20 minutes. Then carefully pour in one gallon of boiling water. The drain should be in working order again.

Put a stopper in it

If you have to do any repair work on your bathroom faucet, no matter how simple it is, take a moment first to plug the drain with the stopper. If you don't have a built-in stopper, use a cloth. It's much easier to pick up a dropped part than to fish down the drain for it.

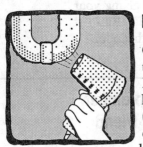

Hair dryer helper

Grease will clog drains faster than anything else. Here's a quick, simple solution. Hold a portable hair dryer, set on high heat, under the sink to heat up the trap. (The trap is the U-shaped portion of the drain right under the sink.) As the trap heats up, the grease will melt and the clog will loosen. Then run hot water to clear out the grease completely.

Toilet, or not toilet ...

What works for your clogged drain may not work for your toilet. Commercial drain openers are not usually effective on clogged toilets because the structure of the toilet prevents the drain solution from reaching the clog. Your best bet is to use a plunger.

Don't let your septic get dyspeptic

Keep your septic tank in the best condition – give it a weekly cup of baking soda by flushing it down the toilet. This should help keep its pH in balance so everything perks along as it should.

Smooth out the squeak

If your faucet handle squeaks when you turn the water on, it needs lubricating. Take the handle off and remove the stem, then apply petroleum jelly to both sets of threads. This will quiet the squeak and make your faucet easier to turn.

A good rule of thumb for the health of your septic system is to never use any product labeled "antiseptic." Bleach and other chlorine-containing products can also keep your system from working properly. These substances kill the bacteria that work to break down waste products in your septic system.

Be careful what you flush. Any type of plastic is a no-no. Cigarette butts, sanitary products, coffee grounds, dental floss, and bones will also accumulate and cause you to have your tank pumped out sooner than usual.

Don't flush petroleum-based paint or solvents, which can also cause septic tank problems and pollute your water.

Home water supply

Heaven's own sprinkler system

Want to bring down your water bill the all-natural way? Collect rainwater right off the roof by connecting the downspouts on your house to "rain barrels," the way people did generations ago. Any kind of wooden or plastic barrel or container will do the trick. You can use this free, natural resource to water your garden and flower beds all summer long.

A trick of the tap

Want to make it seem like you have lots more water pressure while you use half the water? Install a low-flow faucet aerator. One of these devices will reduce water flow by 50 percent, but your water pressure will seem stronger because air is mixed with water as it leaves the tap. A family of four typically saves 3,300 gallons of water a year. You can find low-flow faucet aerators at your local hardware store. Only one caution: Don't install a low-flow aerator on your kitchen faucet if you have a portable dishwasher that hooks up to it. The reduced flow would affect the dishwasher's performance.

Know your water

Is your water hard or soft? To find out, just add 10 drops of liquid detergent to a large glass about two-thirds full of tap water. Cover and shake. High, foamy suds mean relatively soft water. A low, flat cover of soap means relatively hard water. Hard water costs more than soft water: an estimated $40 a year in soap and detergent, $60 in plumbing repairs and replacements, $25 in extra fuel, and $30 in wear and tear on linens and clothes. If your water is very hard, you might want to consider adding a water softening system to your home.

Stop flushing your money away

If you don't already have a low-flush toilet, consider installing a displacement device in your toilet tank. This nifty gadget saves one to two gallons per flush by reducing the amount of water your tank will hold. With a small plastic bottle, such as a juice or a laundry soap bottle, you can make your own displacement device. Remove the bottle's label, place a few stones in the bottom for weight, and fill it with water. Place the bottle in your toilet tank, being careful that it doesn't interfere with the flushing mechanism. You may have to experiment a little to see what size bottle your tank will hold and still have enough water to flush effectively.

Dye, leaky toilet, dye!

A tiny faucet drip can waste 50 gallons of water a day, but a leaky toilet will waste 46,000 gallons of water in six months. To tell if you have a leak in your toilet, add some dye to the tank. If you don't flush and the dye shows up in the bowl anyway, you have a leak.

Flow free

If your shower head gets clogged, make it free-flowing again with this simple trick. Unscrew and remove your shower head, then put it into a pot filled with equal portions of vinegar and water brought to a boil. Simmer the fixture for five to seven minutes. The chemical action of the vinegar will dissolve the mineral buildup. If you can't get the shower head loose, or if it's made of plastic, try the cold vinegar method. Fill a sturdy plastic bag with vinegar and tape it closed around the fixture overnight. In the morning, your shower head should be flowing free again.

Heating and air conditioning

This audit will save you money

Contact your utilities about having an energy audit done to help you find out where your house is wasting energy. Many utility companies offer this service for free. If yours doesn't, it still might provide a guidebook to help you do your own audit.

Golden oldie

Keep the ash pit clean. Piled-up ashes interfere with your getting the maximum amount of draft. Keep the fire pot full. It is not economical to run a low fire bed.

1003 Household Hints and Work Savers, 1947

Cleaner air is cheaper air

Clean or replace your heating and air conditioning system filter every one to three months. A dirty filter makes the system work harder and use more energy than a clean one. Home improvement stores and discount stores carry inexpensive standard filters as well as special filters that are designed to last as long as several months. You can also buy permanent metal filters that can last years because they're washable. Whatever kind of filter you have, keep it clean.

Take care of the air that takes care of you

To keep your heating and air conditioning system running at top efficiency, you should have it inspected regularly. Gas and electric units should be looked at every two years, and heat pumps and oil burners should be checked yearly. Things you can check that may signal trouble include low refrigerant level, a stuck master cutoff switch, loose insulation on ductwork, and uneven heat distribution in your house.

A clean sweep for your system

Your regular heating and air conditioning inspection should include vacuuming the heater vents and return air grills. They gather dust over time, slowing down the flow of air and keeping dust loose in the system. Remove the vents and grills and vacuum the area every few months to promote efficient heating and cooling.

Dodge flying dander

If you keep a pet indoors, you should change your heating and air conditioning filter often, perhaps every month. Otherwise, your pet's hair and dander will keep circulating throughout your house, lessening

Quicker stripper-upper

To save time when you're installing weather stripping, staple it down instead of nailing it. Later you can go back and nail it down if you want to.

air quality and possibly worsening allergies in the human inhabitants.

Get with the program

You can reduce heating and cooling expenses by 20 to 30 percent just by changing your thermostat setting while no one is home and while you sleep at night. In winter, set it back 15 degrees (maybe from 70 to 55 degrees). In summer, raise it from 70 to 75 or 80 degrees. To make this cost savings easier, consider investing in a programmable automatic thermostat. It will take care of the desired temperature changes in the house before you get up in the morning and before you get home in the evening. With the money you'll save on utility bills, the thermostat should pay for itself in about six months.

Thermostat alert

To make sure that your heating and cooling system's thermostat is helping your system operate at peak efficiency, check inside the wall behind where it's mounted and make sure the wall is properly insulated. If it's not, hot air or cold air could creep in from outdoors and alter the thermostat reading, causing the system to work harder than necessary.

Don't do windows this summer

Do your window cleaning in late fall or winter. A clear window will let in more light and heat, which will lower your winter heating bill. In summer, a little film of dirt won't hurt, deflecting some sunlight and letting in less heat.

Who says insulation has to be pink and itchy?

During hot summer months, draw your shades to block out sunlight. Shade trees, awnings, and overhangs can prevent heat buildup as well. In winter, let shrubs help insulate your house from the cold. Evergreens planted a couple of feet from the house will help block the wind and keep it from creeping in through the cracks.

Made in the shade

If your air conditioning unit is exposed to direct sunlight, you can boost its performance by building a privacy or lattice work fence beside it to provide shade and ventilation, as well as protection from rain and snow. However, don't let leaves, shrubs, and grass grow too close to the unit. They will cut down on the air circulation around it and make the unit work harder.

Don't let your dryer vent its frustration on you

If your central air conditioner's outdoor unit is located near a dryer vent, it will have to work harder to cool your house. Find a way to move the dryer vent so that the hot, moist air is directed somewhere else.

Handling humidity

Don't let humidity get the upper hand in your home. Not only does it smell musty, it will damage clothes, books, papers, furniture, walls, and ceilings, and can even lead to rotten wood in walls, floors, and rafters. If you don't have central air conditioning, consider purchasing it. It's a big investment, but it may save your whole house from mildewing away. If the moisture problem is only in one part of your house, then buy a stand-alone dehumidifier. Portable units can be moved around as needed.

Clear the air

If your humidifier begins to smell musty, add a tablespoon of bleach to the water and let it run for a while. This should kill any germs the humidifier is harboring, and once the bleach smell is gone, the water vapor will be fresher.

Peak protection for window units

Window air conditioners need attention too, or they won't run at peak efficiency. At the start of the cooling season, get out your owner's manual and learn how to clean the fan blades and the evaporation coil. Check the caulking and weather stripping around the unit. Oil the motor and fan. Then clean the air filter each month throughout the summer.

Shun the sun

When installing a new window air conditioner, choose the window carefully. Try to put it in a window on the north wall of your house or on a wall that doesn't get much sunlight. Mount it up high in the window if possible. Since cool air falls, it will circulate the air in the room much better.

Winterize your window AC

If you leave your window unit in the window, be sure to close the vents. Cover it with a purchased air conditioner cover, or take the economical way and cover it completely with heavy plastic sealed all around with duct tape.

If you remove a window air conditioning unit from the window, don't put it directly on the floor of your garage for storage if you live in a part of the country where roads are salted in winter. The salt from your car tires could corrode the metal of the air conditioner.

Sure-fire energy waster

Don't turn your air conditioner's thermostat down lower than normal when you first turn it on, thinking it will cool the house faster. It won't, but it will waste energy.

Fans and vents

Keep a cool head

Poor or nonexistent attic ventilation costs you money year-round. In summer, it strains your air conditioning system, because the heat that builds up in the attic eventually radiates back down into the house. Your attic can get up to 150 degrees, which can actually cause the shingles to buckle. In winter, proper ventilation keeps moisture from accumulating on rafters and insulation, and helps prevent ice dams on top of the roof. Attic ventilators such as gable fans, passive and electric turbines, soffit vents, and ridge vents will help preserve your roof, prevent water damage, lower your cooling costs, and keep your house more comfortable.

Stir up the air

To help circulate the air in your house in both winter and summer, consider installing ceiling fans. Especially in rooms with cathedral ceilings and in stairwells, hot air can get trapped up high and cause both your heating and your air conditioning systems to work overtime.

Down in summer, up in winter

In summer, set your ceiling fans to blow down so that you'll feel cooler. In winter, reverse them to pull air up, which will keep blankets of cold air from forming near the floor. Both settings keep the air moving, which will keep you more comfortable. You'll find the switch that reverses the fan blade direction on the side of the fan motor housing.

Fan-handle your whole house

If you want to get tough on cooling costs, consider getting a whole-house fan that exhausts through your attic. The idea is to operate it in the evenings, when outside temperatures cool off but your house is still warm inside. By opening a few windows, you can pull in the cool night air and force the accumulated warm air out through the attic. In some areas, it can be used instead of air conditioning for a good cost savings. In really hot climates, it can be used in addition to air conditioning.

You need to vent

Make sure your house has adequate "natural ventilation." That means enough windows and doors, located on all sides of the house; crawl space vents; soffit vents; and attic vents. Install kitchen, laundry, and bathroom exhaust fans if you don't have them. They do an excellent job of removing heat, humidity, and odors from the house. Make sure they are properly vented to the outdoors, not just into the attic or crawl space.

LAUNDRY

Laundry room organization

Opt for order in the laundry room

Family members can sort their own dirty clothing if
you organize the laundry room to make it easy. Buy
three inexpensive laundry hampers or tall kitchen
trash containers. Use a permanent marker to label
them in large letters: "darks," "lights," and "colors."
Let your family members know that you expect
them to put their dirty clothes into the appropriate
container. You may have to do some additional sort-
ing, but a big part of the job will be done.

Although you stress the importance of emptying
pockets before putting articles in the dirty clothes
hamper, people will still forget sometimes. So keep
two containers handy, one for trash and one for valuables that get left in pockets. You'll know where to
look for extra change or that missing pocket knife
without having to sift through lint and wads of tissue.

Tag it for charity

Keep a bag in the laundry area for items that are
ready for a new home. If you noticed that the jeans

your son was wearing are two inches above his ankles, put them directly from the dryer into the bag. Things that no longer fit, are out of style, or are no longer needed for whatever reason will be ready to go to someone who can use them. And you can save that valuable closet and drawer space for the things you really use.

Preparing the wash

A mutual attraction

Load "linty" items together – things like fuzzy sweatshirts, flannels, terry cloth towels (especially new ones), and chenille bedspreads and bathrobes. Keep these away from permanent press and corduroy items, which are magnets for hard-to-remove lint.

Secrets of sorting

Remember when you went away to college and did your own wash for the first time? Everything turned that drab-looking gray color. But somewhere along the way you figured out that if you kept the light and dark clothes separate, your wardrobe could look as bright as your future. But separating the laundry by colors is just the beginning. It's also a good idea to wash articles together that need similar soap or detergent, wash cycles, and water temperatures.

To keep whites bright, always wash them separately. It's all right to wash pastels and medium colors together. But brights and darks need to be washed by themselves. Whites and lights can pick up dyes from more colorful items. And darks can dull them.

Separate the wash by how soiled the items are. Lightly soiled items can actually pick up soil from the wash water. Light items will get grayer or yellower, and colors will be duller if regularly put in with heavily soiled articles. Also sort by fabric type. Loosely knit fabrics and delicate items can go together in a gentle wash cycle.

Select a variety of sizes and weights to wash together, like king-size sheets with blouses or hand towels. Bigger items can move freely so you get a cleaner wash.

Neon know-how

It's fun to perk up a tired wardrobe with some of those really bright colors – hot pinks, neon oranges, and electric blues. But they may not be colorfast, so wash each color alone the first time, following the instructions on the label. They'll probably lose some of their brightness with each washing for a while. If you get a stain, you may need to treat the whole article so the color will be uniform.

Protect your duds in the suds

Be sure to empty the pockets of every article you put in the washing machine. And here are some more things you can do to protect your clothes from washday woes.

▶ Close zippers and any other closures, such as hooks and eyes and belt buckles, that might catch on fabric.

▶ If there are any small rips or tears in your clothes, sew them up before you wash them. They may turn into bigger holes during washing.

▶ Brush off loose dirt or dried mud from your clothes before putting them in the washer. Otherwise, the dirt may get deposited on the other clothes in the wash.

▶ Don't overload the washer. Clothes need room to circulate freely. If you didn't catch a small hole or tear or there was one that couldn't be mended, it is more likely to get bigger in an overloaded tub.

Laundry products

Know your soaps

Soap and detergent both help clean clothes by removing soil and suspending it in the wash water so it doesn't settle back into the fabric. Soaps are made from fat, lye, and a few other ingredients. Laundry soaps generally come in boxes of flakes or granules. They are used mainly for washing baby clothes, lingerie, or other gentle-wash items. Soap should only be used with soft water. In hard water it can form a scum that remains on clothing. It may build up and make them look gray, dingy, and greasy. It sometimes remains on surfaces of the washing machine as well.

Detergents are used for most of today's laundry chores, machine and hand washing alike. They have ingredients that quickly penetrate and loosen the soil and keep it suspended in the wash water until it's rinsed away. They are available in liquid or powder forms. The liquid is especially good for use in cold water since it dissolves more easily. And you can choose either heavy-duty or light-duty detergent.

The light-duty type is good for hand washing delicate fabrics.

The scoop on detergent

The detergent container gives a recommended amount. But that's based on an average load of five to seven pounds of fairly soiled clothes using moderately hard water. Use more detergent if the clothes are heavily soiled, your water is hard, or you are doing a bigger than average load in a large-capacity washer. If, on the other hand, your water is soft, your clothes are lightly soiled, or you are doing a smaller load, you can cut back on the amount of soap or detergent you use.

A hot tip for saving cold cash

Detergents dissolve best in warm or hot water. But some clothes are more likely to shrink or fade in hot water. And using cold water saves energy. One compromise is to put in the detergent and run enough hot water to dissolve it. Then switch the dial setting to cold water and begin adding the clothes as you finish filling the tub. Rinsing with cold water is almost always a good idea. Not only does it save energy, it keeps permanent press articles from wrinkling and makes others easier to iron.

Mind the 'mild' label

If the care label says "Use a mild detergent," be sure you really do use a light-duty one. Otherwise you may wind up with light spots on the garment. If this occurs, try soaking the entire article in a strong solution of regular detergent and water. This will lighten the garment, but the color should even out.

A little salt on that shirt, please

Colorsafe bleaches are designed to keep colors bright. But there's no need to spend money on those products unnecessarily. Try adding a couple of pinches of salt to the wash water. Your clothes should keep their vivid colors. And they'll wear longer, too. That's because bleach is harder on the fabric than salt is.

Stretch the soap

You have one more load of wash to do, and your laundry soap is almost gone. Make it stretch by adding a quarter cup of baking soda. As a bonus, your clothes will smell fresh and feel soft as well.

Ready, aim, paint

Pretreating heavily soiled parts of clothing with liquid laundry detergent is a good idea. But it can be messy and sometimes wasteful if your aim isn't exactly on target. Instead of pouring it on, use an old paintbrush (about one-and-a-half to two-inches wide). Just dip it into the liquid, and "paint" it onto the dirty spot without the mess and waste.

Reach for the right bleach

Bleach works with water and detergent to remove soil and stains and can help restore brightness and whiteness to some fabrics. It also deodorizes and disinfects. If used correctly, bleach will not break down fibers or cause fading. But read labels carefully. There are two kinds of bleach – chlorine and oxygen. The chlorine type comes in liquid and dry form. Don't use it on spandex, wool, silk, or fibers like mohair, angora, and cashmere. It is safe to use on other colorfast fabrics.

If you aren't sure about an article, test a hidden area like a seam allowance or facing. Mix one tablespoon of bleach with one-fourth cup of water. Put a drop on the spot you are testing. If there is no color change, the fabric should be safe with chlorine bleach added to the wash water. But if the label says not to bleach, then don't.

Bleach alert

When doing laundry or other household chores, never mix vinegar, ammonia, or anything else with chlorine bleach! This could produce toxic fumes and make you very sick.

Oxygen bleach is not as strong as chlorine bleach and works better when used on a regular basis as a preventative. It usually comes mixed with a water conditioner and brightener. Both the liquid and the powdered forms are generally safe for all fabrics. When using bleach, put it and the water in the washer tub before adding the clothes.

Unbeatable whitener

Keep a spray bottle of a bleach and water mixture (at least four parts water to one part bleach) handy in the laundry. Spray it directly on heavily soiled spots on white washables that can take bleach. Read the label if you aren't sure. Be careful to keep it away from colored and dark items, including any you might be wearing.

Soften without spotting

When using liquid fabric softener in the washer, dilute it before adding it to the rinse. Never pour it full strength onto clothes. It can leave spots that look greasy. If you do make that mistake, here's how to get rid of the spots. Moisten them if they have dried. Rub with bar soap, rinse, and wash as usual. If they still remain, sponge them with rubbing alcohol, rinse thoroughly, and wash again.

Save cents on softeners

Fabric softener sheets can pull double duty. Use them twice, once in the dryer and again in the rinse cycle of the next wash load.

You can also use liquid softener in the dryer. It's a bit more trouble, but it's cheaper than the softener sheets and works just as well. Just dampen an old washcloth or other clean rag and pour on a small amount of softener. Make sure it all soaks in, and toss it into the dryer.

Stocking stuffers

Do you have tiny items like baby socks or hair ribbons that are hard to keep up with in the wash? Just put a few of these items in a woman's knee high stocking. Loosely knot the top, and toss it in the washer. Be sure to wash only colorfast items together. And don't pack them in too tightly, especially if you plan to dry them the same way.

For a natural fabric softener and static cling remover, try adding about a cup of white vinegar to the final rinse cycle of your wash. It is mild enough not to harm your clothes. But it's strong enough to dissolve alkalis in soaps and detergents. Vinegar gets rid of extra suds and soap deposits and leaves your clothes soft and fresh.

Vinegar even breaks down uric acid, a plus if you're washing baby clothes. Add two cups of vinegar to a full tub of rinse water, and you'll have soft, fluffy blankets and sleepers for the little one.

The wash cycle

Overloaded with temptation

It can be so tempting to add just one more towel or a couple of shirts to an already full washing machine. But to get clothes really clean, don't overload the washer. You need to allow lots of room for items to move. And they need plenty of water to carry away the dirt, so choose the appropriate water level for the amount of clothing. When washing large articles like sheets, check from time to time to be sure they haven't wrapped around the agitator post.

A 'mitey' allergy aid

Do you or someone in your family suffer from asthma or allergies? If so, you know how miserable dust mite droppings in clothing and bedding can make you feel. You can get rid of both the droppings and the dust mites by adding eucalyptus oil to your wash. The *Journal of Allergy and Clinical Immunology* reported that this "recipe" can kill up to 95 percent of dust mites:

   1 part detergent

   3 to 5 parts eucalyptus oil

Make sure the detergent dissolves in the oil. If not, switch detergents. Add this mixture to the washer after it's filled with water. Put in the items to be washed and soak 30 minutes to an hour. Wash normally.

Refresh your wash (along with your memory)

Oh, no! You forgot about that load of clothes you washed a couple of days ago. Now they smell sour. Quick! Wash them again with a little ammonia added to the water. Your wash should be "sweet" again.

Golden oldie

As a short cut in washing clothes, first boil them with kerosene in an old boiler.

Ladies Home Journal circa 1920

Throw in the towel

Bath towels, especially new ones, shed a lot of lint that can cling to other clothes, so wash them by themselves. And they'll stay fresher later when they are damp from use if you add a quarter cup of baking soda with the detergent.

Presto — just like new!

If you're tired of replacing your shower curtain every time it gets a little dirty, just throw it in the wash with a couple of large towels and your regular detergent. Add a cup of vinegar to the rinse cycle, and it'll come out fresh as new. Then put it in the dryer on low for a few minutes and hang while still warm. The wrinkles will smooth right out.

Top-of-the-line care for your washer

Taking care of your washing machine will make it last longer and run more efficiently. Protect the top of your washer by wiping up spills of laundry products at once. Some surfaces and plastic parts can be damaged by ammonia, chlorine bleach, abrasives, and solvents. Use soil and stain-removers in the sink. Carefully follow the label instructions for clean up.

Be sure that water hoses connected to the washing machine are not bent or kinked. Hoses will last longer if you turn off the hot and cold water faucets leading to the washer between washdays. Water pressure puts strain on the hoses.

Vinegar can help keep the hoses clean. It also removes soap residue and reduces the build up of

An explosive situation

If hot water isn't used for a long time, hydrogen gas can build up in the water heater or hot water pipes. This gas can catch fire or explode. So when you are away from home for more than two weeks, take this safety precaution when you return. Let the hot water from all faucets run for several minutes before using the washer or other appliances that might be connected to hot water. Don't smoke or allow any flame nearby while the faucets are running.

mineral deposits in the machine. Add one to one-and-a-half cups of vinegar to a normal wash cycle (without any clothes) every couple of months. But be sure to continue through the rinse cycle. You don't want to leave vinegar on the surface of porcelain enamel tubs. It contains acid that can etch the surface if it remains in contact too long. This can cause rust and rough spots that could damage your clothes.

When you do a load of heavily soiled or linty wash it may leave a residue in the washer tub. Wipe it out with a damp cloth, and leave the washer open to air dry.

The dryer cycle

Save $$$ in your dryer

Whenever you use your dryer, try to run it more than once. By the second time, the dryer will already be heated up from the first load, and it won't have to work so hard to dry the clothes. You get the most efficiency by drying several loads in a row.

You'll save money on both electricity and your clothes budget if you don't overdry fabrics. Unless you need to wear a garment immediately, take it out of the dryer while it's still slightly damp, especially in thicker areas such as pockets or waistbands. You'll find less shrinking, wrinkling, and static buildup. But to prevent the danger of mildew, let damp items dry completely in an open area before hanging them in the closet or putting them in drawers.

Make sure you don't overload the dryer. Clothes that tumble freely will have fewer wrinkles, so you may not have to heat up the energy-burning iron. And use the permanent press cycle with its cooling down period. That will also reduce wrinkles.

Top-notch treatment for your dryer

Be sure to clean the lint catcher on your dryer every time you use it. For loads of clothes that have a lot of lint, stop and clean the filter in the middle of the drying cycle. You'll save money, improve the efficiency of the machine, and eliminate a fire hazard.

Clean the exhaust vent system at least once a year. Be sure it is never clogged. Never vent a dryer inside the house. It should always be vented to the out-of-doors.

Never dry items that have been used with solvents or waxes or that carry a warning label saying they could catch fire.

Golden oldie

When damp clothes must be kept for a while before ironing, prevent mildew by keeping them in your refrigerator.

1003 Household Hints and Work Savers, 1947

If using the top of the dryer for treating stains, be sure to protect it with a heavy plastic cover. The enamel paint and plastic parts can be corroded by chlorine bleach, ammonia, solvents, and other chemicals.

Separate the heavyweights

Dry lightweight and heavy clothes in separate loads. Lighter weight items dry faster. And heavy items like blue jeans can damage delicate nylons and such.

Make a note of it

You were really tired when you did that last load of clothes just before bedtime last night. Unfortunately, you forgot about your delicate blouse and tossed everything into the dryer this morning. Too late to save it now. But for future use, put a pad and pencil in the laundry room. Next time make it a written reminder, and leave it on the washer where you won't miss it no matter how rushed or sleepy you are.

Forget the fuzzy stuff

It's best to wash clothes right side out to discourage lint from hanging on. Also dry them right side out in the dryer to prevent lint settling in the creases. When drying them on the clothesline this isn't a problem. So you can hang them inside out to prevent fading.

If you're having a problem with lint on your laundry, consider what things you're washing together. Man-made fabrics such as polyester, nylon, and acrylic tend to attract lint. Avoid washing clothes made of these fibers with lint-producing items made of terry cloth or other fuzzy fabrics.

Disasters in the dryer

Sometimes items like crayons and ink pens go through the wash without causing a problem. But watch out if they reach the dryer. Tumbling a load of clothes with a melted crayon or a leaky ink pen or marker can really stain them. And these substances can coat the dryer's drum and get passed on to the clothes in the next load. So if this happens, it's important to clean the insides of the dryer thoroughly before drying anything more. Remove as much melted crayon as you can with a non-flammable, all-purpose cleaner like Top Job, Mr. Clean, or Soft Scrub. (Read the label to be sure it's non-flammable.) Apply it with a clean sponge or cloth. Do not pour or spray it directly on the inside of the dryer. Wipe it off with rags or paper towels. Put some old rags in the dryer and tumble them until no more residue comes off.

To remove ball-point or felt tip marker ink from the dryer drum you may need to use a household cleaner containing a flammable solvent such as Fantastic, Formula 409, or Pas. Be sure the drum is cool before cleaning. Put some undiluted cleaner on a cloth or pad of paper towel, and rub it on. Do not spray or pour the cleaner into the dryer drum. Wipe the drum with a damp cloth or paper towels. Be sure to remove all solution. Leave the dryer door open for several hours to be sure all the vapors from the solvent have evaporated.

The dryer can also get spotted from starch or tinted items. Moisten a cloth with a diluted bleach solution, and wipe the interior. Remove the bleach with a sudsy sponge or cloth, then rinse and dry.

Watch out for blue stain after washing new jeans. The excess dye can coat the dryer and your next load of whites will give you the blues. To be sure this doesn't happen, after washing new jeans, clean the inside of the dryer with soapy water until no more color comes off. Remove soapy residue with a clean wet cloth.

Lay your money on the line

Most folks these days don't think they have the time to hang loads of wash out to dry. But if you want to save money, or just enjoy fresh air and fresh-smelling clothes, then it's time to string up a clothesline. If you are serious about regularly drying your clothes outside, you'll want to put up a permanent set of lines on metal poles that are sunk into the ground with concrete. You can find the materials you need, and probably instructions for making your clothesline support, at a well-stocked hardware store. You can find cotton rope or plastic cord at a pretty cheap price, but they will sag under the weight of a heavy load of wash. For better support, purchase more expensive but longer lasting 12-gauge galvanized wire.

Golden oldie

Wash clothespins in a salt-water solution before using. They will last longer and not freeze on the clothes when there's ice in the air.

1003 Household Hints and Work Savers, 1947

Place your clothesline where the prevailing wind will blow across the wires, not from post to post. If possible, place it where part of the line is in the shade during the middle of the day. You can hang bright colors out of direct sun where they'll fade less. But avoid putting it directly under trees where bird droppings might mess up a line of clean clothes. And locate it where garments blowing in the wind won't get caught on branches or a fence.

Hints on hanging out

Maybe your only concern about using a clothesline is that you'll have more ironing to do. A quick lesson in how to hang up your wash will help. It's true that clothes hung on a line dry stiffer than those tossed in a dryer. But you can avoid most of the extra wrinkles if you follow these tips.

▶ Always hang the wash as soon as it's done. If you wash them at a laundromat, fold them and place them in a clothes basket rather than stuffing them in a bag or hamper.

▶ For fewer wrinkles, hang skirts by the waist band but pants (including jeans) by the leg bottoms. Shirts will blow in the breeze and dry quicker and smoother if you hang them by the tails. Hang lightweight dresses by the shoulders, but fold heavier ones and hang them from the waist. (Dresses usually require some touch-up with the iron.)

▶ Socks dry quicker when hung by the toes. And underwear benefits from being hung inside-out in the sunshine. Bras and girdles, however, should be dried in the shade.

▶ Bath towels will dry quicker if you hang them from the top (shorter) side. Hang sheets folded in half.

When it's time to take them in, you can fold items directly from the line. And while you are at it, take time to smell the freshness of your clean sheets and towels. You'll be sold on line drying from now on.

Special-care items

Hope for the shrunken sweater

Read the care instruction tag on sweaters carefully before laundering. They are made of a variety of fibers from cotton to wool. And they sometimes have delicate decorative parts that require special care to keep them looking their best.

If you wash a wool sweater and it shrinks, try this: Soak it in lukewarm water with some good hair shampoo mixed in. This may soften it enough for you to be able to reshape it. Dry it flat on a sweater rack or on a clean, dry folded towel.

A warm, relaxing bath — for your blanket

Many blankets, even some woolen ones, can be machine washed and dried. But different fabrics and kinds of construction call for different temperatures and cycles. Others require dry cleaning. So always check the label and follow instructions carefully. Machine wash only one large woolen blanket at a time. And measure it first so it can be stretched to the same size after washing. Fill the tub with cold or warm water and dissolve the detergent in the water.

Stop the machine before adding the blanket. Place it loosely around the agitator. Let it soak for 10 to 15 minutes. Advance the dial so that the water will drain out. Let it spin for about a minute and stop it again. Advance it to the final rinse cycle and let it continue through the final spin.

If your woolen blanket can be machine dried, toss it with two or three dry towels at high heat for 10 to 20 minutes. Warm the towels in the dryer for a few minutes before you add the blanket. They will absorb the moisture much faster this way. Remove the blanket before it is completely dry to avoid wrinkles and shrinkage. Finish drying flat or suspended over two clotheslines. If any shrinking has occurred, stretch to original shape and size.

Shapely sweaters

Knitted woolens should not be tumbled dry. Instead, before washing, trace the outline on a piece of paper. After washing, block it to the original size by pushing it gently with your fingers to fit the outline and let it dry.

Don't let this solution shock you

Laundering an electric blanket is as easy as washing a regular one. Do not dry clean or wash with bleach. For best results, follow the manufacturer's instructions. You can hand wash an electric blanket in detergent and lukewarm water. Let soak for 15 minutes. Squeeze suds gently through the blanket. Rinse at least twice in cold water. Do not twist or wring. If using a machine, dissolve the detergent before adding the blanket to the wash. Limit the wash cycle to under five minutes.

Unless the manufacturer's instructions state otherwise, you can partially dry an electric blanket in the dryer. Preheat the dryer on medium heat, then let the blanket tumble for about 10 minutes. Remove it from the dryer and straighten and shape it. Finish drying over two parallel clotheslines.

Pull a clean punch for pillows

If the label says they are washable, you can launder feather or polyester-filled pillows in the washing machine. You can wash two pillows at a time, or balance one in the washer with some large towels. If they are particularly soiled, let them soak for 15 minutes before washing.

Plumper pillows

Pillows can be dried outside in the sunshine on a windy day. Or dry them on a low setting in the dryer. They take a long time to dry thoroughly, but mildew can be a problem if they are left damp. Shake and fluff them a few times for more even drying and to make them plumper.

Using a front-loading washer for this job is better. It allows them to move more freely and results in less lumping. And there will be less rub, so pillows washed this way should last longer. If you use a top-loading machine, pillows will tend to float to the surface. It helps to push them under until they fill with water. Stop the machine and turn them over and punch them back under again once or twice while washing. Wash for four to eight minutes on the regular wash cycle. Rinse three times.

Use 'kid gloves' on leather gloves

Always read and follow the manufacturer's instructions for care of your leather gloves. Even if the label says they are washable, don't wash them if you have had them dry-cleaned previously. The dry-cleaning process removes the natural oils. Washing now will damage them. Leather gloves with fur linings should not be washed. The same is true for suede gloves.

For leather gloves that can be washed, use warm sudsy water. Work the leather gently with your hands, being careful not to pull on the seams. Rinse away the suds with cool water and blot excess moisture with a towel. Dry flat on a towel away from any heat source. While the leather is still wet, work it with your fingers. The oils from your hands will help to soften it. Do this at least three times before the leather dries. If the leather should dry out before you've finish working it, rewet and rework it.

Love's labor not lost on quilts

Handmade quilts, whether bought new or handed down from your great-grandmother, represent a lot of effort by loving hands. They deserve the best of care but should be washed as little as possible. If you have yours displayed on a wall or rack, you can vacuum it lightly every now and then. Use the soft brush attachment of your vacuum cleaner.

The case for a delicate wash

To wash an antique or delicate item that's heavily soiled, place it in a pillowcase and use long running stitches to close the top. Wash in the washing machine with other clothes of similar color using mild soap. Then take out the stitches from the top of the pillowcase and air dry the delicate piece.

If you use your quilt on a bed, it may need a gentle washing from time to time. If you aren't sure it's been washed before, begin by determining

171

if it is colorfast. Dampen a small area – a red part if it has that color, since that's the one most likely to bleed. Dab it with blotting paper. If it bleeds, you want to take it to a good dry cleaner. You might want to ask the textile curator of a nearby museum to recommend one.

Be fair with fine fabrics

No-fuss whitener

When washable items made of wool or silk have yellowed with age, try whitening them with this solution. Mix a tablespoon of white vinegar with a pint of water. Sponge it on the yellowed areas and then rinse. Wash as suggested.

Silks, woolens, and some man-made fibers require special care. The label may say you can hand wash or use the gentle machine cycle. (Fine wool clothing is generally best washed by hand.) Wash in warm or cold water and rinse in cold. Dissolve powdered or liquid detergent completely before putting delicate articles in the water.

If hand washing, gently squeeze the sudsy water through the garment. Avoid rubbing or wringing. Rinse it thoroughly. Roll it in a dry towel to remove excess water. Dry flat away from direct sunshine.

Battling stains

A simple strategy

If you could just prevent stains from happening, life would be simpler. Unfortunately, accidents happen.

So here are some basic rules for dealing with stains before you attempt to clean them. But be sure you read the garment label first, and pay attention to any warnings from the manufacturer.

▶ **Act fast.** The quicker you deal with a stain, the more likely you are to remove it completely without damaging the fabric. That's because oxidation (the process that makes the cut surface of a banana or an apple turn brown) causes the staining substance to interact with the fibers of the fabric.

▶ **Identify the stain.** This is easy when you notice it immediately. But sometimes you find a spot you can't identify. If you're not sure what it is, rinse or soak washable items in cold water before treating or washing them. But keep an eye on them. Soaking too long can affect the color of the fabric.

▶ **Test the stain removing substance.** Apply it on a hidden place first – perhaps a seam allowance – before using it on the stain. Leave it for two to five minutes and rinse. If it damages the fabric or changes the color, do not use it on the rest of the garment. And never mix stain removers. If you try one that doesn't work, rinse the garment thoroughly before you try another.

Out, out darn spot

Never rub a stain. Doing so can break the fibers on the surface of the fabric and may cause the stain to spread. It can also cause blotching and fading. Use a clean cloth, sponge, or maybe a soft toothbrush. Make a blotting or feathering motion (short, light strokes) to remove as much of the staining substance as you can. If it has soaked through the garment, blot it from both sides if possible with a soft clean cloth.

Work from the underside to move the stain out. When sponging or dabbing on a stain removing substance, place the fabric face down on absorbent cloth or paper towel. By working from underneath, you'll push the stain out, not in. Work from the outside edge of the stain toward the center to prevent making it larger. Be patient. Allow plenty of time for the agent to work before rinsing or laundering.

Fight to the finish

Launder the complete garment after treating it for stains. Check it to be sure the stains are completely gone. If not, repeat the treatment, then wash it again. While you're at it, check the rest of your clothes to see if you spot any stains you hadn't noticed before. You can treat them and wash them again before putting them into the dryer where they might get permanently set.

Air dry the garment, but not in the sun. Heat and bright light speed up the oxidation process, which makes it harder to remove the stain if you didn't get it all the first time. (Never press a stained garment for the same reason.) Look over the dry garment carefully to see if the stain is completely gone. You can treat it again if necessary.

Latch on to an expert

When you discover stains on an unwashable item, get it to the dry cleaner as quickly as possible. Point out the location of the stains. Otherwise it will get a general cleaning, and the heat might permanently set the stains. You'll help the cleaner do a better job if you can explain how old the stains are and what substance caused them. And if the fiber content of the fabric isn't on the label, provide that information as well if you can. If the garment is fairly new, maybe you still have a tag that gives the fiber content. If so, take that with you.

Clearly, it still needs attention

Don't assume a clear liquid doesn't need attention just because it doesn't show. If it contains sugar, it will oxidize and turn brown if you leave it in the garment. So if you spill a clear beverage on your blouse, take care of it right away. You know the saying – out of sight, out of mind. By the time you can see it, it may be too late to fix.

Quick (and cheap) stain removers

For a general stain remover for washable items, try one of these:

▶ Apply a paste made from a powdered laundry detergent and a little water.

▶ Soak in cornmeal and water, club soda, or lemon juice.

▶ For tougher stains, mix dry dishwasher soap in a bucket of water. Immerse the item in the soapy solution. If it floats, weight it down with something heavy like a plastic bottle filled with water.

Clear your table toppers

After you use table linens, always check them carefully for spots and stains. Treat them as quickly as possible. If allowed to set, they'll be harder to remove completely. Soak protein food stains like eggs, meat, and fish in cold water. (Hot or warm water will set stains.) If it needs something more, try a paste of meat tenderizer and water. Dab it on, let it set for 15 to 30 minutes, and wash in cold water.

'Chews' the best gum remover

To get chewing gum out of fabric, first try freezing the material. The gum should become brittle and break or peel off. If you still have some spots remaining, use white wine vinegar.

Wipe the wine at once

It may be hard to leave the stimulating conversation at the dinner table, but if you spill red wine on your blouse, your guests will understand when you excuse yourself. This is a situation you need to take care of while the stain is still damp. Stop by the kitchen for the salt shaker, or take it with you from the dinner table. Blot as much of the wine as possible with a clean cloth. Cover the stain with salt. Wash in cold water.

And the rust is history

For rust stains on white clothes, sprinkle with hot lemon juice, pat it in, then rinse with warm water. Or use lemon juice and salt, and put it in the sunshine. Don't use chlorine bleach on rust stains. It can make the discoloration worse.

Iron in the water pipes or water heater can lead to rust stains in a whole load of wash. If this is a problem, it might help to run the hot water for a few minutes before washing to clear the lines. Draining the water heater from time to time can help as well. If it becomes an ongoing problem, consider installing an iron filter in the water supply system.

Try a little tenderness

To remove blood stains, soak the garment in cold water. Change the water when it turns pink. Make a thick paste of meat tenderizer and cold water. Use a damp sponge to apply and leave for 20 to 30 minutes. When dry, rinse with cold water.

Perhaps you are a vegetarian and don't keep meat tenderizer on hand. You can bleach stubborn blood stains on white fabric with hydrogen peroxide. Pour it on, then wipe away the foam with a dry cloth. Repeat until the stain is gone. Rinse, then wash as usual.

Nail that stain

You are giving yourself a manicure when your cat decides to get friendly, knocking over the fingernail polish in the process. Now how do you get that crimson stain out of your skirt? Quickly wipe up the excess. Then, unless the fabric is acetate or triacetate, grab the nail polish remover. Place the spot face down onto paper towels. Then sponge it with a liberal dose of polish remover. Soak it in cool water. Apply detergent to the stain, and launder.

Hot tips for chocolate

Got a chocolate drink stain on a white T-shirt? Dab on ammonia and wash as usual. Or maybe a little person enjoyed a big slice of chocolate cake, but his sticky hands found their way to your shirt. Take the stains out by soaking with club soda before washing.

The real remover

Did you find a cola stain on a favorite sport shirt the morning after a fun night out? Maybe in the excitement of a fast-paced basketball game you didn't even notice spilling it. Is it too late to get it out? Not if you apply full-strength white vinegar directly to the spot within 24 hours, then wash as usual. It should be spotless for the next time out.

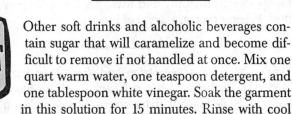

Other soft drinks and alcoholic beverages contain sugar that will caramelize and become difficult to remove if not handled at once. Mix one quart warm water, one teaspoon detergent, and one tablespoon white vinegar. Soak the garment in this solution for 15 minutes. Rinse with cool water. If the stain isn't gone, sponge with isopropyl rubbing (denatured) alcohol. Rinse thoroughly and wash, using chlorine bleach if it's safe for the fabric.

Get fruit stains into hot water

You borrowed a pretty white tablecloth from your Aunt Betty. But a dinner guest spilled fruit compote on it. All you need is some boiling water to keep yourself out of hot water. To remove fruit stains from fabric, dip the item up and down in boiling water. If the stain is on a large item like a tablecloth, place a bowl under the stain, and pour the water through the stain and into the bowl. If the stain is stubborn, try dabbing it with lemon juice.

If you prefer not to deal with scalding water, try this method. Soak the stain for about 15 minutes in a mixture of one quart warm water, one teaspoon detergent, and one tablespoon white vinegar. Rinse it in cold water. If the stain is still there, sponge with alcohol and rinse thoroughly, then launder. If the fabric can take it, add chlorine bleach.

Maybe it's a Rorshach test

The inkblot on your shirt may look like something from a personality test, but you probably don't want to keep it there permanently. You can remove ink stains from clothing by applying alcohol-based hair spray. The alcohol will break up the ink. Blot the stain with a rag to absorb the excess before laundering it. Test in a hidden spot first since some fabrics can be damaged by hairspray.

Don't come unglued

Do your kids come home from day camp with more glue on their clothes than they used on their creative art projects? Never fear. Just soak the clothing in warm water with three tablespoons of vinegar. Rinse well, and all signs of the glue should disappear.

Toothpaste and milk are alternatives you can use. Apply toothpaste to the stain before washing, but soak the stain if you use milk. Fresh will work, but sour milk is faster.

It must be mustard

Your hot dog from lunch has left its mark — you've got a bright yellow stain right on the front of your shirt. As with all stains, act as quickly as possible to remove it. Mix a solution of one quart warm water, one-half teaspoon liquid handwashing detergent, and one tablespoon vinegar. Sponge it on the stain and let it air

Stains are not 'kool'

Kool Aid stains are among the toughest ones your kids bring home from camp. Try sponging with a solution of one tablespoon ammonia to half a cup of water. Or if you need something a little stronger, try dabbing it with hydrogen peroxide.

dry. Then do one of the following: Apply liquid detergent directly to the spot, or dampen the spot with a wet sponge, and apply a paste of water and powdered detergent. Launder as usual, using bleach if it's safe for the fabric.

Per'suede' grease to go

Suede garments are expensive to have dry cleaned. But maybe that won't be necessary. You can remove a grease stain from a suede garment by sponging it with a cloth dipped in vinegar. Dry it and use a suede brush to restore the nap.

Fresh from the medicine kit

A squirming youngster with a cut or scrape can cause you to spill the iodine, mercurochrome, or merthiolate. Quickly soak the stains in a solution of one quart warm water, one teaspoon detergent, and one tablespoon ammonia for 30 minutes. Then wash as usual.

The kiss of death for clothing

Dancing cheek to cheek may be romantic. But trying to get the lipstick out of your best white dress shirt can bring you out of the clouds pretty quickly. Try this process:

▶ Soften the stain first with a bit of petroleum jelly (Vaseline).

▶ Dab it with denatured alcohol or hydrogen peroxide.

▶ Launder as usual.

Now you should be ready for the next formal dance. But you might consider holding the lady at arm's length.

There's a fungus among us

Mildew is one of the toughest stains to get out. It is a fungus that can grow and, in the advanced stages, weaken and destroy some fabrics. If it occurs, treat it as quickly as possible with one of these solutions.

▶ Soak it in white vinegar.

▶ Dab on lemon juice and salt, and put it in the sunshine.

▶ Blot repeatedly with hydrogen peroxide.

▶ Soak overnight in buttermilk or sour milk.

Run rings around an oily collar

Your bathroom has the answer for removal of oily collar "rings." Shampoo dissolves body oils, so it's a natural for this job. Pour the shampoo into a squeeze bottle if it didn't come in one. Apply directly to the stain, let it stand, and then wash it.

Treat other oily or greasy stains on your clothing with a paste of water and cornstarch. Apply, let dry, and brush off.

Strike after the iron is hot

Scorch stains, if not too severe, can sometimes be removed from 100 percent cotton and cotton blends with liquid detergent. If a garment is 100 percent polyester, take it to the cleaners to see if they can save it.

If you find yourself wearing your coffee

If you spill tea or coffee on a favorite shirt or table-cloth, put it in this solution to soak for 15 minutes or so: one quart warm water, one teaspoon detergent, and one tablespoon white vinegar. Rinse. If the stain remains, sponge it with alcohol, rinse and wash using chlorine bleach if the fabric can take it.

What did you say that stain was?

It's best to deal with urine, vomit, and mucus stains right away, so don't be tempted to put it off. Sponge or soak these types of stains in cold water. Then apply laundry detergent directly to the stain and wash. If a change in color occurs, it may be possible to restore it by sponging ammonia on new stains or vinegar on old ones.

Don't sweat perspiration stains

Perspiration stains will usually come out if you dampen them with cool water and rub with bar soap. If the fabric has become discolored, sponge fresh stains with ammonia or old stains with white vinegar. Rinse. Launder with the hottest water the fabric can stand.

Age-defying solution

When white cotton or linen fabrics get yellow with age, use hot water with twice as much detergent as usual.

Wash on the regular wash cycle for four minutes, then stop the washer and let items soak for 15 minutes. Restart the machine, agitate for 15 more minutes, and complete the wash cycle. Repeat if necessary. For yellowed nylon, soak the article overnight in a solution of water and oxygen bleach. Then wash in hot water, using oxygen bleach and twice as much detergent as usual.

No crying over crayons

You always check your kids' pockets before you throw the clothes in the washer. But what happens if you forget? You could wind up with a whole load of wash spotted with crayon wax. Your best bet, in this case, is to scrape off the excess with a dull knife and head for the dry cleaners. Explain what happened and request bulk cleaning. Or you might try doing it yourself at a coin operated cleaner.

Deep freeze it

Sometimes an item of clothing gets stained, but you don't have time to wash it right away. Put it in a plastic bag and toss it in the freezer. Then wash when convenient, and the stain will come out as if it just happened.

If the stains don't come out with dry cleaning, wash them for 10 minutes in hot water. Use the amount of soap, not detergent, for a regular load and one cup of baking soda. If you have hard water, use a water softener as well. If stains still remain, work a soap paste into the stains, return to the hot water solution for five more minutes, then launder as usual.

Wax poetic — but not for long

Candlelight can set the mood for a romantic evening. But it's back to everyday reality when it's

Smoke on the water

There are times when you just can't avoid being in a smoke-filled room. Unfortunately, smoke can penetrate and leave odors on your clothes. To remove the unpleasant smell, hang them over a bathtub. Fill the tub with hot water and add a cup of white vinegar. The steam will make them smell fresh again.

time to get the wax out of your best tablecloth. Begin by hardening it with ice. Then use a dull knife to scrape away as much of the wax as possible. Next, place the stained area between two clean paper towels and press with a warm iron. Replace the paper towel a few times as it absorbs the wax. Now place the stain face down on fresh paper towels and apply a prewash stain remover or dry-cleaning fluid. Blot with clean paper towels and let it dry. Launder as usual. If any stain remains, wash again using a bleach that is safe for the material.

Show shoe polish who's boss

If you spill liquid shoe polish on your clothes, pre-treat the spots with a paste of water and dry detergent. Then wash as usual.

If it's a paste polish spoiling your attire, first scrape off as much of the residue as possible with a dull knife. Then pretreat with cleaning fluid or a prewash stain remover. Then rinse and apply detergent to the spots while it's still damp. Wash with chlorine bleach if the fabric can take it. Otherwise wash using the milder oxygen bleach.

Outdoor challenges

Don't muddy the waters

Southern gardeners who do a lot of digging in Georgia (or Alabama) red clay have learned not to spoil a load of clothes with the red stuff. When they've spent the morning digging in the garden and have some heavy-duty mud on their jeans, they hose them off with the garden hose before putting them in the wash. This is a good idea no matter which region your mud comes from.

If you splash mud on the hem of a good dress or the cuffs of your favorite slacks, try this solution. Let the mud dry completely. Brush off as much as possible. Put a quarter cup of detergent in a bowl of water big enough to hold the muddy hem or cuffs. Let soak for one to two hours, then wash as usual.

Another way to get rid of mud is to brush off the excess, then soak for about 15 minutes in one quart warm water, one teaspoon detergent, and one table-spoon white vinegar. Rinse with cool water. If the stain is still there, dab with alcohol, rinse, and wash as usual. If you still have a rust-colored stain, try bleaching with an oxygen bleach.

Paint stains are a pain

You're always careful when you're painting, but somehow you dripped paint on your clothes. Don't take time to fret about it now. You need to act quickly before the paint dries. If the paint is water-based,

sponge or soak it in cool water. Put detergent directly on the stain, then launder it as usual. You might
want to add some chlorine bleach if the material can
stand it. If it is oil-based paint, sponge it with turpentine and then rinse. Work some detergent into the
stain. Wash it in hot water using chlorine bleach
unless the clothing label warns against it.

The 'resin'able way to clean clothes

Climbing trees can be fun for kids, unless they slip and
skin their knees. But it's getting pine resin out of their
clothes that causes the pain for the adult who does the
laundry. It isn't easy, but it can be done. Dissolve the
resin with turpentine, paint thinner, or mineral spirits.
Rinse thoroughly and launder as usual.

Keep it on the driveway where it belongs

Scrape away tar or asphalt residue from clothing with
a dull knife. Saturate the stain with salad oil and let it
sit for 24 hours. Pour some liquid laundry detergent on
the stain. Wait a few minutes and launder as usual. For
washable items, if this doesn't get rid of all the stain,
work petroleum jelly (Vaseline) into the stain. Let stand
for half an hour, and wash in hot soapy water.

Strike out grass stains

Sliding into home just under the catcher's tag made the
softball game exciting! But now what do you do about
the awful grass stain on your shorts? Apply denatured
alcohol to the spot, and wash in warm water. By the next
game, you'll be ready to step back up to the plate all
clean and bright.

CLOTHING

Ironing

Pressing matters

Along with your iron and ironing board, one of the most useful tools for pressing is a "press cloth." It enables you to get wrinkles out of even the most delicate fabric without scorching or melting it. You can buy one at a fabric store, or simply make your own out of an old cotton handkerchief or a large scrap of muslin. Just be sure you use a white or ivory cotton fabric, about 12 square inches or larger.

To use your press cloth, smooth out the item you want to press on the ironing board, then lay the cloth out flat on top of it. Use the heat setting that is appropriate for the delicate fabric. The heat will transfer through the press cloth to smooth out the fabric underneath. Simply move the press cloth to cover each area as you iron.

Too many irons in the fire

Slight scorch marks in clothing from a too hot iron can be fixed in a flash. Dampen a cloth in white vinegar, and place it over the area to be repaired. Iron, using a low temperature, and the marks should disappear.

It's a scorcher

A piece of clothing that sports a big scorch mark in the shape of an iron will probably become just another rag. But it just might be possible to get the scorch mark out, especially if the garment is made from natural fibers such as cotton or linen. Here's a technique you can try when there's nothing left to lose. To a bucket of warm water, add eight ounces of 3-percent hydrogen peroxide. Mix well and add the scorched clothing. Soak the garment overnight, then remove it and wash separately. You may have saved yourself the time, trouble, and expense of replacing the garment.

Golden oldie

Keep the wax-coated boxes in which crackers are packed, as they make excellent polishers for irons instead of the little blocks of paraffine wax generally used.

Household Hand Book, 1860

Strike while the iron is hot

When ironing several fabrics that require different temperatures, iron the ones at cooler temperatures first. It doesn't take an iron long to heat up, but it takes a while to cool off.

Save electricity and money when you iron. Turn the iron off about five minutes before you finish ironing, and use the retained heat to finish the job.

Smooth move

Letting a hem down can be an excellent way to extend the life of a garment. However, the old hem sometimes leaves a nasty crease in the fabric. Try wetting a clean sponge with white vinegar and pressing it along the line of the fold. Then press with a warm iron, and the crease should be gone.

Recycle the silver

Your heat-reflecting ironing board cover may be worn out, but it has life in it yet. Cut it up, and use the less worn areas to make pot holders, hot pads for the table, or oven mitts. Just combine it with some fabric and batting to make items that can take the heat.

Water works

Keep water handy for your steam iron by storing it in a recycled sports water bottle or mineral water bottle with pop-up top. The small spout is the right size for pouring water into the iron's water tank.

A wrinkle in time

You're headed off to an important appointment, but when you pull your blouse out of the closet, you find an ugly wrinkle in the collar. There's no time to set up the iron — what can you do? Take out your hand-held hair dryer and set it to high heat. Aim the blow-dryer at the wrinkle, pulling the collar smooth with your other hand. Hold the dryer nozzle a few inches away until the wrinkle disappears. Continue to hold the collar straight until the fabric has cooled, and the wrinkle will be gone.

Sewing and mending

Material assets

Make a small swatch book of the fabrics you have at home, and take it with you when you shop for clothing or other fabric. Tape or glue small slivers of your fabrics to index cards (several will fit on one card), along with the amount you have. Staple the cards together with a "cover" card and stick them in your purse. Next time you shop, you can choose new clothing or fabric to coordinate with what you have already invested in. You're more likely to use the fabric if it goes with something else.

A stitch in time

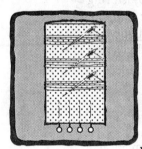

Make yourself a good quality sewing kit so you'll be ready for those unexpected repairs. Cut a three-inch by 10-inch strip of felt, heavy fabric, or paper, and fold it in half to make a rectangle. Thread one needle with a length of white or ivory thread, another with dark gray or black thread, and another with light to medium brown thread. Knot the ends of each thread, and wrap them around the cloth or paper rectangle, sticking the needles in last to hold the thread in place. Add four straight pins to the kit by threading them onto the cloth or paper. Put the kit in a top dresser drawer or on a closet shelf, and store a pair of small scissors with it. Next time you need a quick repair, instead of rummaging around for matching thread and a needle, you can fix it in a couple of minutes and be on your way.

A measurable difference

Measure your fabric before you store it, and write the amount and width of the fabric on an index card cut in half lengthwise. Tuck the card into the folds or roll of fabric. Next time you want to use a certain piece, you'll know whether you have enough yardage without opening the fabric and measuring it again.

The law of averages

Survey your patterns, and figure out the average amount of fabric you need to make a pair of slacks, a skirt, a blouse, a slim dress, a full dress, and any other clothing you make for your family. Write these average amounts on an index card, and stick it in your wallet. Then when you see the right fabric, you can buy exactly the amount you need.

Pretend it's wrapping paper

The best way to store fabric waiting to be made into clothing or household items is to roll it up. An open bookshelf or a box turned on its side makes the perfect storage area for your rolled fabric. Fold and roll the yardage to fit the depth of your shelves or box, then secure each piece with a rubber band. You'll know at a glance whether you have the right green or that perfect shade of pink.

On pins and needles

Save scraps of soap and wrap them in cloth for a pin cushion. The extra lubrication will help the pins slide more smoothly through your fabric.

Get to the point

Having trouble threading a needle? These two tips are for you:

▶ Spray a little hairspray on your fingers, and smooth the cut end of the thread between your fingers. The hairspray will dry immediately and stiffen the thread enough to make a nice, sharp point.

▶ Try holding the thread between your finger and thumb and bringing the needle's eye to the thread instead of putting the thread into the needle. This old embroiderer's trick allows you to hold the thread more firmly in place as it makes contact with the needle.

Shoulder to shoulder

You can recycle unneeded shoulder pads by putting them to good use. Fold one in half, and stitch it along the curved edge to form a carrying case for small scissors or rotary cutters. Or make knee pads to use in your garden by sewing or safety-pinning both ends of a piece of narrow elastic to the sides of the shoulder pad.

Bob-bob-bobbin along

To change the thread color on your sewing machine bobbin, do it the easy way. Place the bobbin in your pocket, and keep pulling on the end of the thread until all of it has been removed from the bobbin. No chance of losing it this way!

Bargain clothes

Discount duds

Get the best deals on clothing by checking out garage sales, thrift shops, and consignment shops. You can often find "gently worn" items, or even brand new clothing with the tags still on, for a fraction of their original prices. The quality of such clothing can be surprisingly good. Or consider having a clothing swap meet with friends or neighbors who wear clothing in sizes similar to yours or your family's.

Wetter is better

Do yourself a favor by buying fewer clothes that have to be dry cleaned. Except for dress suits and overcoats, most items of clothing have washable alternatives you can choose. Also, many items that say "dry clean only" can be gently washed by hand.

That's using the old bean

Consider buying some of your clothing from a catalog company with an excellent return or repair policy. L.L. Bean wins lots of praise from customers for its 100 percent satisfaction guarantee on its products, no matter how old they are. Items are sturdy and well made in the first place, and the company will repair or replace products that wear out at no charge. A good quality winter coat bought from a reliable company will cost more up front but may save you lots of money over a period of years. Be sure to investigate the service policies of any company before you buy.

Just don't put them in the washing machine or dryer. Cutting down on dry cleaning will save you money and keep you healthier by avoiding the chemicals in dry cleaning solution. Some people have allergic reactions to these chemicals while they are evaporating from clothing.

Button up your overcoat

To stay warm and comfortable in a cold climate, choose clothing made of fabrics that are naturally warm. Wool, of course, is the best known for warmth. But cotton is a contender, too, especially if it has a rough texture like corduroy or flannel. Fabrics with more than one layer do an even better job of holding in your body heat.

Clothing care

Top tips for wiser wear

Here are three things you can do to get the most mileage from your clothing:

▶ Make sure your clothes are clean when you put them away. A stain left in a piece of clothing can become a permanent one. Clean spots and spills as soon as possible.

▶ Repair small rips, tears, and pulls when they happen. The more clothing is worn, the worse the rips get, and repairing them can be much harder later on.

▶ Store your clothes the right way. Keep them out of direct sunlight and away from damp, moldy areas. Keep moths away from woolens. Don't hang stretchy clothing on hangers that can pull it out of shape.

Spice up your wardrobe

Here's a spicy sweet alternative to mothballs: whole cloves! Bugs hate them just as much as mothballs. Make a clove sachet with cheesecloth for hanging in the closet, or just put a few individual cloves in the pockets of wool coats and jackets.

It's in the bag

An inexpensive substitute for a cedar closet is lying around the aisles of your local pet store. Just look for a bag of cedar shavings used to fill cages for small pets. Fill several paper lunch bags with the cedar shavings, then staple the tops closed. Punch holes in the bags to let out the aroma, and place the bags around the inside of your closet or drawers.

Spot blotter

Grease spot on your favorite cotton dress or shirt? Take a clean powder puff or cotton ball, and dip it in baby powder or cornstarch. Rub it into the stain. Brush off the excess powder when the stain disappears. For stubborn stains, repeat the process.

Dress for success(ful cleaning)

When you have a messy job to do, dress for it. Have a special "work" wardrobe for messy chores, and keep it in a convenient place. Those clothes that have already been stained or painted are the perfect choice. Save your good clothes from accidental ruin, and you'll have them to wear when you want to look nice.

Zippity do-dah

When your zipper refuses to glide smoothly, try rubbing its little teeth with a candle, a pencil lead, or a bar of soap. The teeth should slip on down their tracks.

Off the cuff

If your favorite sweater has the droopy-cuff-blues, don't assume it has to be relegated to the "work clothes" section of your closet. Dip the cuffs in hot water, and dry with a hair dryer to bring the sweater back to its original look.

Now you see it; now you don't

Did you just notice a sea of lint on your nice black skirt? You don't need a fancy brush or roller to get it off. Just wrap some masking tape or scotch tape around your hand, sticky side out, and lift the lint away.

A dab in time ...

These days, the buttons on ready-to-wear clothing are sewn on with the shortest possible length of thread, sometimes working loose the first time you wear a garment. To avoid losing buttons from your new outfit, apply a little bit of Fray-Check or clear nail polish to the thread on the front of each button. Just be careful not to get any on the fabric. This reinforces the thread to help keep the button in place.

Knit picking

Your new knit jacket gets a pulled-out thread on the sleeve, and you need a quick and easy way to put things right. Get an inexpensive metal or plastic-and-wire needle threader, the kind you can find in any sewing department near the thread. From the inside of the sleeve, push the needle threader to the right side of the sleeve just next to the pull. Stuff the pulled-out thread through the loop of the needle threader, then pull the threader back to the wrong side. The pulled thread will stay on the wrong side of the sleeve and will be invisible from the outside.

Wired up

Annoying static cling is often a problem during cold, dry, winter months. If your skirt is sticking to your slip, try this diverting tactic. Run a wire coat hanger over your skirt or between your skirt and slip. The static energy should transfer from you to the wire. This also works for static-filled hair!

Shoes and stockings

Size up the situation

If you are looking for a pair of shoes and the fit is not quite right, ask to try on another pair in the same size. Each pair, even though the same size, may have a different feel and fit.

Shoelace saver

Threading a frayed edge of a broken shoelace is nearly impossible. Next time, dip the frayed end in clear nail polish and allow it to dry before threading it through again.

Good news for shoes

Afraid to get near your teenage son's smelly sneakers? Let newspaper soak up the smell. Wad up newspaper, and stuff it in each shoe. Leave it overnight. In the morning, the aroma should be greatly improved.

Golden oldie

Here's how to waterproof your shoes and lengthen their life: Melt together a dressing of two parts beeswax to one part of mutton fat. Apply it at night, and in the morning, wipe it well with a piece of flannel. You now have waterproof shoes, at practically no cost to you.

1003 Household Hints and Work Savers, 1947

If the shoe fits

What to do with athletic shoes that are outgrown or worn out? If your teenager outgrew them before they even showed much wear, see if he has a younger or smaller friend who can use them. If the shoes are really worn out, mail them to Nike's special recycling program, where they will be turned into rubber flooring and donated to resurface inner city basketball courts. The address is:

Nike Recycling Center
c/o "Re-Use a Shoe" Program
26755 SW 95th St.
Wilsonville, OR 97070

Shine on

▶ Petroleum jelly makes an excellent "shiner" for patent leather shoes.

▶ For your regular leather shoes, try a little beeswax or car wax left over from waxing your car.

▶ Furniture polish can also give a nice, clean shine to leather shoes.

Resurface your suede

Stains on your suede shoes can be removed with an art gum eraser, available at art supply or craft stores. Then sand the spot lightly with an emery board or very fine sandpaper to bring back the nap of the suede.

Another good way to get grease off suede is with vinegar. Dip a clean, dry toothbrush in white vinegar and brush the spot. It should be clean when the vinegar has evaporated.

An a-peel-ing tip

Don't throw away that banana peel! You can use the inside of a banana peel to polish your leather shoes. Then buff them with a soft cloth.

Less stress

When you buy pantyhose, choose a slightly larger size rather than a slightly smaller one. The fabric will last longer if there is less stress on it when it's worn.

Toe the line

Pantyhose with reinforced toes tend to last longer than the sandalfoot type, since the toe area doesn't get as many holes and snags. If you do buy sandalfoot hose, spray the heels and toes with hairspray for longer wear.

Hazards ahead

Before you put on your stockings or pantyhose, check for hazards. Rings and bracelets can cause snags, as can hangnails or even rough skin on your hands or feet. Take off your jewelry, and put on a little hand lotion to save your pantyhose from snags and runs.

Pantyhose popsicles

You may have heard this one before and laughed. But all joking aside, it really helps prolong the life of your pantyhose. Wash and wring out your hose, place them in a plastic bag and put them in your freezer. After they freeze, thaw them and hang to dry.

Stop runs in their tracks

You have a run in your stocking that is, at the moment, covered up by your skirt. Stop it in its tracks before it makes an embarrassing appearance beneath your hemline. A dab of clear nail polish at the bottom of the run will prevent it from traveling any farther. If you don't have nail polish, try hairspray.

Tie one on

Give torn pantyhose a new lease on life! After machine washing and drying, cut them into wide strips, removing the elastic waistbands, and use them to stuff pillows, soft dolls, or toys. Keep the waistbands for bundling and storing winter blankets and quilts.

Accessories

Screen saver

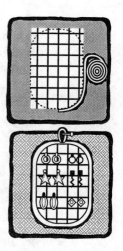

To store pierced earrings, buy a small piece of stiff screening from the hardware store. Round off the corners, and use sticky-backed cloth tape to cover the edges. Push the earring post through a hole in the screen and put the earring back on the other side to hold the earrings securely. Lay the screen in a drawer, or hang it in a convenient location.

Put it on ice

If you have a large number of small, pierced earrings, try storing them in a plastic ice cube tray. Each cube space will hold several pairs of earrings. You can group earrings by color, if you like, so you can tell at a glance whether you have something to match a particular outfit. The trays fit easily into a dresser or vanity drawer and can even be stacked several layers in a deep drawer.

Erase earring disasters

If you lose the back of an earring at work, for a temporary replacement, cut an eraser off the end of a pencil. Take off your earring and push the post into the eraser to make a hole. Then put your earring

back on with the temporary back. It will last until
you get home!

That touch of fashion

If most of your clothes are the classic, durable kind,
you may get tired of wearing them year after year.
Instead of buying new clothes, buy new accessories.
An inexpensive scarf, earrings, pin, pair of shoes, or
hat may give your clothes an up-to-the-minute look
without a lot of expense. Shop discount stores for current accessories at low prices.

Put on your Easter bonnet ...

If you like to wear straw hats but aren't sure how to
clean them, follow these tips:

▶ Brush straw frequently to help keep dirt and dust
off.

▶ Clean light-colored straws with diluted hydrogen
peroxide.

▶ Use a weak solution of ammonia and water for
dark straws.

▶ Bleach white straws with a homemade paste of the
juice of two lemons and two tablespoons of sulfur.
Apply the paste with a soft cloth, and let dry.
Then brush off the dry powder with a stiff brush.

VALUABLES

Paintings and artwork

Your fine art needs a soft touch

Wondering how to keep your artwork in pristine condition? Be gentle with it. Paintings and sculptures should be dusted occasionally with a soft camel-hair or sable paintbrush. Don't use dust cloths or feather dusters, which can trap dirt particles and scratch the artwork.

Don't undo the master's strokes

Resist the temptation to clean an oil or acrylic painting with any kind of cleaner or solvent, including linseed oil, sometimes rumored to be good for oil paintings. If your painting needs anything more than a dusting, take it to a professional. With a valuable painting, you'll save more in the long run by having it cleaned properly and safely. Call a local art museum or artists' supply store to find a person who cleans and restores paintings.

Protecting your Picasso

To keep the environment from creeping in and slowly spoiling an original painting, attach a protective

TLC for your trophies

If you're a hunting or fishing enthusiast, you may be concerned about keeping your wall trophies in top condition. Professional taxidermist Larry Reese of Centreville, Maryland, offers these suggestions.

The best way to clean furred animal mounts is with a vacuum cleaner, Larry says. "They can be vacuumed with a brush-type attachment, or you can use a cotton rag and a spray furniture polish like Endust. Wipe from the head towards the tail."

For fish and birds Larry recommends using a feather duster. Any glass or wooden parts can be cleaned with regular window or furniture cleaner.

backing board to the canvas stretcher (the wooden frame the canvas is stretched onto), not the picture frame. Archival-quality cardboard, which will not cause the painting to deteriorate, is available for this purpose. It will keep out dust and give the painting more stability if you need to move it or reframe it. The archival cardboard should be cut to the size of the stretcher and screwed carefully into the stretcher to seal out dust and other dirt from your painting. You can get this cardboard at an art supply store or frame shop.

3 top tips for hanging pictures

▶ Don't hang paintings or photos where they'll get direct sunlight. It will fade pigments and discolor varnish over time.

▶ Attach small rubber spacers on the back lower corners of framed artwork to increase air circulation and protect walls.

▶ Never hang paintings over the fireplace! Although it's a favorite place to display a landscape or family portrait, it's not a healthy environment.

The heat and soot will wreak havoc on artwork. Likewise, don't hang valued pieces near air conditioning or heating ducts.

Priceless papers

Memories should be seen, not touched

Before you go dig out the old family photo albums or keepsake books to start preservation improvements, look at your hands. Visible dirt can do tremendous harm to paper items, but the invisible oils and acids on your skin can do even more. Always wash your hands well before handling your treasures, and get some inexpensive white gloves from the local photo shop. They're made for handling photos and negatives, but they work well for any sensitive materials.

Hesitate before you laminate

You want to save the family's historic Civil War document so you can pass it on to your children. Should you laminate it for safe keeping? Absolutely not! Laminating can speed up the deterioration process due to its high heat and glue. Here are some sound tips to keep the family's treasure in good condition:

▶ Make a copy for display, but store the original.

▶ Don't use an irreversible process (like laminating) on the item.

▶ Store the item in the best possible conditions. Avoid direct sunlight, high humidity, and storage near the ground or near an outside wall where moisture may be a problem.

Use archival products to store your precious photos and documents. Archival products are made of acid-free paper or additive-free plastics that won't react chemically with the item you are storing. You can buy archival products from specialty mail-order houses, photographic supply stores, art supply stores, craft stores, and frame shops.

A safe alternative to laminating your documents is to use two sheets of mylar (polyester film). Close the edges with double-sided tape such as 3M's product number 415, taking care not to let the tape touch the document inside. Then it will be safe to display and handle the document.

A good read, again and again

Did you know that the typical book is made with paper that will only last about 50 years? Book collections need special care to guard against the ravages of time. If possible, keep books in an area with a constant humidity of 45 to 60 percent and a temperature of 60 to 70 degrees. These conditions rule out storage in basements and attics.

Extra! Extra!
Newspaper clippings require special care

Newspapers were not designed to withstand the test of time, but most of us can't resist clipping something now and then, especially if it's about a friend or family member. The bad news is these clippings don't last when they're stored in the typical scrapbook or envelope. They can even damage other papers and photos they're stored with. To keep your clippings in tip-top shape, put them in mylar (polyester film) folders, and put sheets of alkaline buffered paper behind each clipping. Store the film folders in acid-free boxes in a cool, dry room, away from direct light. Then someday your great-grandchildren can enjoy looking at them.

Save your books, come humidity or high water

If a valuable or treasured book becomes damp, move it to an airy place where it can dry gradually. Stand the book on end and fan out the pages so air can get to them. If the book is very damp, you can sprinkle baby powder between the pages. Let it sit for several hours and then brush it off the pages with a clean, soft cloth.

If a valuable book or paper develops a bad odor from being wet, dry it first; then seal it in an airtight box with a bowl of cat litter or baking soda. Let it sit for several days to absorb the odor.

Low light is right

Sunlight is one of the worst things for paper – it quickly damages inks and dyes and makes paper brittle. But it's not always practical to store valuable paper treasures in the dark. To help guard against the UV rays in sunlight and fluorescent light, keep your books and papers out of direct light and use heavy draperies in the rooms where they are stored. Keep individual papers in acid-free file folders away from direct light.

Kill mold with bright light

Sometimes storing things in the dark can lead to mold growth. If you find dry, loose mold on a treasured paper item, remove it very gently with a camel's hair brush or soft cloth. Then let it sit out in the sunlight for about an hour to kill any mold that is left.

Keeping out dust is a must

When framing precious documents, make sure they are completely sealed inside the frame. This will keep out pollutants and protect the paper from dust.

Frame it up for posterity

You might want to display some of your paper valuables in frames. This not only gets them out where they can be enjoyed, but also gives you the chance to encase them in the proper materials to keep them safe. Acid-free boards can be used to mat and mount documents and artwork. You can even get special plexiglass or acrylic materials that filter UV(ultraviolet) light. Just make sure these materials don't touch the actual paper you are preserving. There should be small spacers between the paper and the glass. Ask the experts at a frame shop for the latest tools in paper preservation.

Keep your cool, save your page

If a treasured book gets soaked with water, don't give up and throw it away; simply put it in the freezer! Use layers of wax paper to separate the pages so they won't stick together, and wrap the book in wax paper. This will buy some time until you can get on the phone to a paper specialist or conservator to find out what to do next.

Silver and other metals

The tin commandments

Tin is often added over other metals to prevent rusting. If you see rust on tin, it's probably where the tin has worn away, exposing the metal underneath. You can brighten up tin-coated objects with regular silver polish, but be gentle. Rub very lightly to keep from wearing off the tin coating.

Rust on or rust off?

Before you try to clean the rust off iron keepsakes, find out whether the object will keep its value if it's cleaned. Heavy rust should be evaluated carefully. If rusting is really severe, sometimes the item is best left as it is. Once cleaning is started, it can't be undone, so be sure of what you want.

You can remove rust from iron with a soft abrasive. Use bronze wool and mineral spirits or very fine emery cloth to remove light rust. Once the object is free of rust, you'll need to do something to protect the exposed surface. Beeswax or silicone can be used to coat iron objects to prevent future rusting. Iron farm tools and machinery may be cleaned and painted with a rust-preventive paint.

Rubber robs silver of its shine

A silent enemy of your silver flatware, trays, and bowls is anything made of rubber. Rubber can actually corrode silver through a chemical reaction, sometimes so badly that it will need repairs. Don't wear rubber gloves when cleaning or polishing silver; they often leave an imprint of the glove's textured fingers. Don't store silver items on a shelf lined with a rubber mat or in the same cabinet with rubber bands or rubber seals.

Silver is sensitive

A silver bowl or tray laden with fruit or a silver pitcher holding a bouquet of flowers can add a touch of elegance to your table. But if you want to keep your silver pieces looking lovely, be careful what you fill them with. Foods containing acids, such as fruit, salad dressing, or vinegar, can damage the surface of silver. So can eggs, salty foods such as olives, and even fresh flowers. If you're going to serve any of these foods on silver, be sure to use a plastic or glass liner. Inexpensive clear plastic trays and bowls can usually be found at a party supply or paper goods store. If your vase or pitcher is large enough, try lining it with a small glass jar or plastic cup before adding the flowers.

De-salt your shaker for silver safety

If you like to use your treasured silver salt and pepper shakers for special occasions, be sure to remove the salt from the shaker before putting it away. If you leave the salt in the silver shaker, it will cause tarnishing and eventually damage to the silver.

Flatter flatware with tender treatment

For the best results when washing your silver flatware, wash it by hand with mild soap and dry it with a soft towel. If your flatware is silver plated, do not put it in the dishwasher. The finish will be damaged, and may wear off completely after a number of washings. However, you can safely wash your sterling silver flatware in the dishwasher if you follow these tips:

▶ Put your silver in a separate section of the silverware basket, away from your stainless steel flatware or utensils, making sure they don't touch each other. The silver could be damaged by exposure to other metal, especially under high heat conditions.

▶ Don't wash hollow-handle knives frequently in the dishwasher. The heat and detergent can loosen the handles.

▶ When you fill the dishwasher with powder detergent, don't spill any on your silverware. It can cause dark spots to form on the surface of the silver.

Spot polishing

Silver pieces should be polished gently after every third or fourth use. If they aren't tarnished all over, just polish the tarnished areas and leave the rest of the piece alone.

Go light on the elbow grease

Even regular silver polish that you buy at the store can be too abrasive, so clean very gently. You might try making your own polishing paste of denatured alcohol and very fine precipitated chalk, available through some jewelry and drug stores. Just realize that no matter how gentle you are, a tiny bit of silver is removed with every polishing. Thin areas can develop in old pieces that have been polished frequently over the years.

211

Post-polish precautions

Always rinse your silver pieces well with water after using silver polish, then buff them dry with a soft cloth. This helps remove any residue from the silver polish that might cause damage if it isn't washed off.

Silver protection is all wrapped up

After you clean and polish your silver, try an ounce of prevention, too: wrap your silver items in acid-free tissue paper. Make sure the pieces are clean and dry, then place the wrapped silver in a plastic bag.

For extra help in preventing tarnish on your silver utensils and serving pieces, you can line your silver drawer with Pacific cloth. It is specially made to absorb tarnish-promoting chemicals in the air. Buy it by the yard at a fabric shop and cut it to fit your storage areas. Get enough fabric to have a piece to put on top of your silver, too.

Another way to prevent tarnish is to wrap your silver pieces tightly in plastic wrap such as Saran Wrap.

Age mark or beauty mark?

Like many metals, pewter forms a "patina," an outer coating that results from chemical reactions with other elements. Before trying to remove the patina on your valuable pewter pieces, get the advice of a professional. The object might retain its value better if the patina is left alone as a sign of its age. If cleaning is advised, use a very fine abrasive such as the combination of rottenstone and mineral oil. Harsher abrasives might leave scratches. You'll find rottenstone at better hardware stores and through woodworking supply catalogs.

Choose copper cleaners carefully

Avoid using cleaners containing ammonia on your copper and brass pieces; they can corrode these surfaces. As with any other metal valuables, consult an expert before removing the tarnish on very old pieces, since it could decrease their value.

The pewter polluters

Pewter, silver's first cousin in the metal family, is vulnerable to the same substances as silver. In addition, it can be damaged by oil or cheese. Be sure to use glass or plastic liners for your pewter pieces. Keep pewter items away from heating elements or flames, since pewter has a low melting point.

Does your lacquer lack luster?

Some of your brass items may be lacquered, or might once have been. Lacquer is a glossy protective finish that helps prevent tarnishing. If the lacquer is still in good shape, don't use a polish on the piece. Simply wash it gently in lukewarm soapy water, rinse it in lukewarm water, and dry it completely.

If the lacquer finish on your brass item is flaky or spotty and needs to come off, try soaking the piece in soapy water for about 15 minutes, then rinse with hot water. Rub with a soft cloth until what's left of the lacquer begins to peel off. You can also use denatured alcohol applied with a soft cloth. Remember that once you completely remove the lacquer, the exposed surface is going to tarnish more quickly, so it will require more frequent care.

Blow dry your 'hair'looms

When cleaning silver, copper, or brass, use a hand-held hair dryer on the low or cool setting to help dry hard-to-reach spots.

Glass heirlooms

Avoid a shattering experience

Believe it or not, glass actually reacts to the environment it is stored in. It might seem that light, heat, and moisture wouldn't affect glass, but they do. Be particularly careful to protect your antique glass from any big changes in temperature – it is brittle and can shatter in response.

Golden oldie

Add glisten to your copper or brass by moistening rottenstone with sweet oil, apply with a soft cloth and rub vigorously. Polish with flannel or chamois. Rub with dry whiting or tripoli. This gives a much richer, deeper finish than when acid is used.

1003 Household Hints and Work Savers, 1947

Through a glass darkly

Some glass reacts chemically to excessive ultraviolet light by changing color. Clear glass from the turn of the century may turn pink or violet because of its manganese dioxide content. Pieces from the World War I era up to the Depression may contain selenium, which causes them to turn amber when exposed to too much light. These changes are permanent, so prevention is the only cure. Keep antique glass out of direct sunlight as much as you can.

Don't dunk it!

Glass pieces that have been repaired should not be immersed in water when cleaning. It can soften or loosen the glue holding the pieces together. You'd do better to simply clean them with a damp cloth.

Calgon, take these water spots away

If you live in an area with hard water, you'll need to take precautions to keep hard water spots from forming on glass heirlooms when you wash them. Adding a bit of water softener such as Calgon to the rinse water will do the trick.

Get the dirt on antique glass

Found an antique glass medicine bottle in the old privy? Here's how to clean it. Soak it for a full day in a solution of water, detergent, and water softener. After soaking, pour out half the water in the bottle and add a couple of tablespoons of uncooked rice grains or fine sand. Shake and swish it around for a

Insurance for butterfingers

When washing your prized glass possessions, line the bottom of your sink with a thick towel. This will soften the blow if you happen to drop a piece. It will also contain all the glass if something should get broken.

few minutes to help scour the inside surface.

To remove stains from inside old glass containers, try a solution of water, ammonia, and deionized soap such as Orvus. You can also try soaking it in a solution of one part hydrogen peroxide to four parts water.

Fragile — handle with care

When storing your antique glass items for the long term, take care to wrap them carefully in acid-free tissue paper. If they must be stacked in boxes or on shelves, put layers of bubble wrap between the wrapped pieces.

Wrap any lids or stoppers separately from their containers. If you find that a lid or stopper has become stuck, put the item in the refrigerator. The glass will contract very slightly, allowing you to remove the stopper. After taking both pieces out of the refrigerator, wrap them in a towel so that they will return to room temperature slowly and safely. A rapid change in temperature might cause the glass to shatter.

Crack the secret of china

You won't believe it till you see for yourself, but there's a miraculous milk cure for cracked china!

Make a solution of milk and sugar – lots of sugar – in a large saucepan. Immerse the piece of china in the milk solution. Gradually heat the milk and let it come to a slow rolling boil. Keep it on low heat for about 45 minutes. The solution will heal and harden the crack.

Jewelry

Rings on your fingers

Some people are allergic to some of the cheaper metals used in jewelry making, especially nickel. If you notice that a piece of white gold or 10-carat gold jewelry leaves a dark mark or ring on your skin, replace it with a nickel-free piece. Your jeweler can direct you to pieces that don't contain nickel, although they may be more expensive. You can also paint the inside of the ring with one or two layers of clear nail polish, and you should be able to wear it again without a reaction.

Strange drug side effect

The prescription drugs you take can actually discolor your jewelry. Antibiotics, in particular, can change the chemical properties of your sweat and cause tarnishing. So you might want to take off your rings while you're on antibiotic treatment.

Clean getaway

Is your ring stuck on your finger? Spray your finger and the ring with window cleaner. The ring will be cleaned and will come off easily at the same time.

Put your jewelry where your mouth is

Here's a jewelry cleaner you may not know about –
denture tablets. Put your rings in a glass with a tablet
of denture cleanser. After soaking for an hour or
two, scrub them gently with a toothbrush, just like
you would scrub your teeth. Then rinse well and dry
them with a soft cloth.

Platinum keeps a tighter grip

If you have a family diamond or other heirloom
stone you want to pass on to your descendants, consider getting it reset in a platinum setting. Although
it's more expensive than gold, it's very resistant to
wear and it's hypoallergenic. For extra security, you
can get the platinum prongs retipped every few
years. Your favorite diamond ring will still look
beautiful on your great-granddaughter's hand.

Sweat and solder

Did you know that your body sweat is bad for your
silver and gold jewelry? The acids in sweat actually
weaken silver solder and can cause cracking in some
gold. Wash these items once in a while in a mild
alkaline soap or detergent to
remove the acids.

Baby your opals with the oil treatment

To keep your opals from drying out and cracking, wipe
them every week with a small
amount of baby oil or olive oil.

Precious care for emeralds and opals

Never clean your emeralds
or opals in an ultrasonic jewelry cleaner! Liquid can seep

into these stones and cause them to shatter. Instead, wash them in warm soapy water and gently clean with a soft toothbrush.

A clean diamond is a girl's best friend

Diamonds may be forever, but they still get dirty. Keep your diamond jewelry sparkling new by treating it to a good cleaning now and then.

▶ **Ammonia soak**: Mix half a cup of cold water with half a cup of household ammonia and put it in a teacup. Soak your diamond pieces in the mixture for half an hour. Then very gently scrub with a soft toothbrush. Give them one more rinse through the mixture and let them dry on a soft cloth.

▶ **Detergent bath**: Swish some dish-washing liquid into warm water in a teacup and carefully drop your jewelry into it. After soaking for half an hour, scrub gently with a soft toothbrush. Then rinse thoroughly with clear water and let your diamonds dry on a soft cloth.

▶ **Ultrasonic cleaning**: You can buy one of these jewelry-cleaning devices or have a jeweler use one. High-frequency waves pass through water and agitate the grime off your jewels, kind of like a pressure wash for diamonds.

Pampered pearl protection

To keep your pearls from losing their natural luster, never wear them when you are spraying hair spray or perfumes. Even tiny amounts of chemical products

219

will dull their shine and will never come off. After wearing them, wipe the strand with a damp cloth to remove any skin oils or other residues. Let them dry thoroughly before putting them away. If you wear your pearls often, get them restrung yearly.

Golden oldie

Men think beads are just gimmicks. Women know what they can do to beautify the neckline. Don't risk losing your beads through breaking of the string. A good idea is to re-string the beads with dental floss. Your beads will be safer and they'll hang gracefully.

1003 Household Hints and Work Savers, 1947

A knotty problem

To get a tight knot out of your gold chain necklace, try this method. Lay the necklace on a piece of wax paper, and put a drop of oil (salad or household) on the knot. Then use two straight pins to pull and loosen the knot until it comes undone.

Beware the bleach

Be careful not to get household chlorine bleach on your white gold jewelry. It can cause it to turn yellow. Wearing white gold jewelry in a swimming pool with highly chlorinated water might have the same effect.

Clean your silver jewelry in a flash

Here's how to clean jewelry with a chemical reaction. Put some short strips of aluminum foil in a small jar, fill it with cold water, and add a tablespoon of salt. Let your silver items sit in this solution for a few minutes, then rinse them off and let them air dry. Keep the lid on the jar between uses. One word of caution: Be sure the jewelry isn't plated silver and that it doesn't have any dark, oxidized areas that are part of a decoration. This technique may strip off the silver plating or lighten all the dark areas.

Don't let your handyman manhandle your jewelry

He may be great with needle-nose pliers, but your dear husband could accidentally destroy your favorite necklace if he tries to fix it. Any time a piece of jewelry needs mending, take it to a reputable jeweler who guarantees his work. Don't go to one of those jewelry stores in a mall – mall stores often send broken pieces out to other jewelers to be repaired. Find a local jeweler you can talk to if you need something fixed.

Avoid a tangled web of chains

To keep chains from tangling up in the jewelry box, undo the chain and run one end through a plastic straw; then reclasp it. You may need to cut the straw into sections to fit your jewelry box.

Quick cleanup

Clean your jewelry while you're getting dressed. For gold jewelry, add a little toothpaste or shampoo to a soft toothbrush and scrub gently. For sterling silver,

sprinkle a little baking soda on a washcloth and polish until it shines.

A story with the ring of truth

Did you ever wonder how the tradition of giving a diamond
ring as an engagement ring got started? Well, here's the story.
It seems that in 1477 Maximilian, the Archduke of Austria,
was engaged to Mary of Burgundy. To show his love for her,
he gave her a wedding ring with a diamond in it. And the rest,
as they say, is history.

Cameras

Canned air does the trick

One of the best things to keep around for routine
cleaning of your camera is a can of compressed air
or carbon dioxide. Clean the inside of the camera
first with compressed air or a soft brush designed
for cleaning cameras. Then clean the outside and
then the lens. Do this each time you load a new
roll of film.

Fuzz-proof your pictures

Remember that a dirty lens will make a fuzzy picture. The film will actually record the grime on the
lens as though it's in the scene you're photograph-
ing. So keep your lens clean by spraying it with
compressed air or wiping it with lens cleaning fluid
and a lens cloth before you take pictures.

Good batteries gone bad

Camera batteries can leave invisible chemical deposits inside your camera. Clean the batteries and the contacts regularly, and replace batteries once a year.

Bag it or box it

The best place to store your camera for the long term is in the original box it came in. If you don't have it anymore, use a sturdy cardboard box or camera bag. Take out the batteries and store them in a film canister and mark the date on the canister. Remove batteries from the flash unit, too. When you take your camera out after it's been stored for a long while, clean it first and then put the batteries back in.

Appliances and electronics

Lightning only needs to strike once

If you have a typical selection of home appliances and electronic devices, you are vulnerable to two very expensive little accidents that can occur, one natural and one man-made. The first is a lightning strike and the second is a power surge that comes from your electric service. Either can cost you hundreds of dollars and numerous headaches to deal with. To protect against both, you need to plug all your vital appliances and expensive electronics into surge protectors. Even your refrigerator can become a victim.

Conduct a surge purge

Surge protectors come in various sizes and with many optional features. They are designed to stop any kind of increase in electrical energy from passing into the machines that are plugged into them. They can cost up to $100 or more, but they are worth the investment. Some even have guarantees that the manufacturer will replace the surge protector and anything plugged into it that is ruined by lightning or a power surge. That's quite a claim! But if you value your computer, your large screen television, or your fax machine, to name a few, you should keep them safe from the ravages of runaway electricity.

If it's not turned on, it's not working

If you want your surge protector to keep your electronics safe, it has to be turned on. Just having a machine plugged into a surge protector is not enough to protect it. Usually they come with a switch and an indicator light to show that they are on and working properly. Check your surge protector monthly to make sure the light is on and it's doing its job.

Professional protection

The very best way to protect your appliances and electronic devices from lightning is to unplug them. But that's not always a convenient option, particularly when you're talking about refrigerators or freezers. And what about storms that come up when you're not home? There is a solution. Some local power companies will provide a special surge protection service for all of your home's appliances and electronics. For a small monthly fee, they will install a whole house surge protector at your electric meter. These systems don't have to be

Calling all power surges

Don't forget about your telephone when planning for protection from power surges. Lightning can travel through your phone lines and your computer's modem and zap your phone and your computer at the same time. To protect your phone and your modem, get a special telephone surge protector.

turned on and off, and you don't have to worry about unplugging anything during electrical storms.

A message to thieves: This is mine!

To make your valuables easier to find if they should be stolen, give them your personal mark. Contact your local police station to find out what numbers to use to mark your valuables. It is likely to be your drivers' license number preceded by a state identification code. Your police station should also have an electric engraving pencil you can borrow to engrave the number into some of your belongings such as power tools or electronic equipment. Put the numbers in an obvious place so that they can be seen without taking the item apart, and put them on a permanent section that can't be discarded.

Computers

Defending your disks

To keep data safe, don't let your floppy disks become too hot or too cold. If they do, let them come back to room temperature before putting them in the computer.

———————————

Keep floppy disks in disk storage boxes, away from anything magnetized like televisions or computer monitors. A magnet can damage the information on your disk.

———————————

The hard disk in your computer is very sensitive, and data can be corrupted if the unit is jostled or jolted. Always keep your computer on a very sturdy table top or desk.

Help your computer keep its cool

The vents on the sides and top of your computer components are very important, since they allow for escape of the heat that builds up while the computer is running. If your computer is frequently overheated, it's probably going to have a shorter life and frequent bouts of corrupted data. So always provide plenty of free air space around the vents so they can cool things properly. Leave at least a foot between a computer and a nearby wall or cabinet.

Nobody here but us dust bunnies

Open your computer's CPU (central processing unit) once a year and what do you think you'll find? A whole litter of dust bunnies! Computers are dust magnets, and dust buildup can cause a variety of problems. Heavy dust buildup inside the CPU can cause overheating; if it's never cleaned out, it can even cause a fire. So give it a regular dusting with a bottle of compressed air, and wipe off the vents with a clean soft cloth. Just be careful not to disturb any of the components inside the unit.

Keys to a clean computer

Your computer keyboard can harbor all sorts of filth and germs if it's not cleaned regularly. Dust buildup can lead to keys that stick and won't work anymore, which means you'll have to take it to a professional. Cleaning it yourself is tricky – you can't just dunk it in the sink! You should never get it wet with any kind of cleaner. Instead, use a lightly moistened cloth for wiping off grime, and use a bottle of compressed air to force all the dusty stuff from between the keys. If you spill a drink on it, unplug the keyboard and take the screws out of the back. Take the top off and use a slightly damp cloth to clean off the spill. Let it air dry and then put it back together.

Videotapes

Nothing lasts forever, especially videotape

Even though it's so easy to tape your family members and friends, keep in mind that videotape has a short life span compared to other media. Even under the very best conditions, it won't last more than about 20 years. To preserve your images for posterity, have your videotapes copied onto clean,

Some like it hot — videotapes don't

Never store your videotapes in the attic! Videotapes should be stored in a cool location with low humidity, out of direct sunlight. If it gets too hot, the tape inside the boxes will stick to itself and be ruined.

new videotape every five years, and watch for technological breakthroughs in the future.

Book 'em

Always store videotapes on their ends like books. Give them their own shelf, away from the magnetic fields produced by televisions and other appliances.

Keep a clear head

To keep your VCR running smoothly, get a special dust cover for it, and keep it covered when not in use. Regular use of a tape head cleaner will keep grunge from building up on your VCR's delicate inner parts. If these parts become too dirty, it can damage or even ruin your VCR and your videos.

Loosen up

For the best quality recordings, fast-forward your new blank tape to the end and rewind again before recording on it. This will help relax the tape a little, letting it record more accurately.

Cut the cardboard

Keep your treasured home videos in individual plastic storage boxes. These boxes will protect the tapes much better than the cardboard ones they came in.

Antique textiles

Mind the mothballs

To discourage insects like moths and beetles from making a meal of your antique textiles, you can use moth crystals or mothballs. Put them in an old sock and hang it in the top of the closet. But use this method only for short-term storage. Both forms of moth repellent contain para-dichlorobenzene, a strong chemical that should not directly touch valuable textiles. It must be kept out of the reach of children and pets, too. Cedar chests and cabinets provide a more natural solution, although they won't repel all kinds of insects.

The great put-up

Store antique fabrics and clothing flat, if you possibly can. Quilts can easily be stored by laying them flat on a bed several quilts deep, if necessary. If items must be stored folded, take the time once a year or so to unfold them and refold them in a different

---

Keep your treasures in the dark

Light, humidity, and extreme temperatures are the enemies of all your textile treasures. Vintage clothing, quilts, embroidered items, linens, needlepoint, and lace should all be protected from any extremes of humidity and temperature, doing best at 50 percent humidity and a temperature of 60 to 65 degrees. Fluorescent and ultraviolet light will fade colors and damage fabrics, so take the time to store your valuable textiles out of the light.

place. Put acid-free tissue paper between the folds before you store them again.

Another way to store antique textiles is to use a cardboard tube like the ones that blueprints are stored in. First wrap the tube in acid-free tissue paper or plain unbleached muslin. Then wrap the item around the covered tube with the design or decoration to the inside.

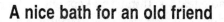

A nice bath for an old friend

Old quilts must be handled very carefully to preserve their colors and stitching, so never wash one in a washing machine. Instead, wash it in a bathtub. Immerse the center of a clean white sheet in a tub of water to act as a support under the quilt when it gets very heavy with water. Then wash the quilt on top of the sheet with a mild laundry soap like Ivory Snow or a special quilt soap like Orvus paste. After washing and rinsing well, use the sheet to lift the quilt out of the tub. Lay it out on a flat surface. Pat the quilt with towels and reshape it. Don't dry it in the dryer or on the clothesline as both can stretch fabrics and break stitching.

Gentle dusting for hanging quilts

Antique quilts look beautiful as wall hangings, but they gather dust just like everything else on your walls. Gently clean off dust by vacuuming with a piece of nylon hosiery over the brush attachment. The top of the quilt will likely be dirtiest, so focus your efforts there.

Safe storage secrets

Where you choose to store your textile treasures will make a big difference in how long they last. Several things that should never directly contact your textiles are wood, cardboard, plastic, and colored gift-wrap tissue paper.

You can store textiles in cedar chests; just make sure they don't actually touch the bare wood. The inside of the chest can be sealed with polyurethane so that textiles can be stored safely.

Plastic storage boxes don't provide a healthy environment for antique textiles. They can trap moisture, which promotes mildew, and they also break down chemically over time, giving off harmful gases.

Acid-free storage boxes and acid-free tissue paper are available for storing delicate antique textiles. Replace acid-free items every three years or so to ensure ongoing protection.

Unbleached muslin fabric that has been washed to remove excess chemicals makes an excellent, stable wrap for protecting old textiles.

HOME EXTERIOR

Protecting the exterior

Partner, pick your paint

Picking a paint to beautify the outside of your house?
The color is a matter of preference, but the type of paint
you use is important, too. Latex paint is almost always
the best choice for your exterior. It is easy to apply,
dries quickly, and cleanup is a breeze. And because of
its flexibility, latex paint is really durable. Your best
choice is 100 percent acrylic latex, not vinyl latex.

That stubborn undercoat

Old oil-based and lead-based paints may bleed through
the new latex paints, especially if you're trying to cover
a dark color with a light one. Test a small area and let it
dry for 24 hours before you invest a lot of time in painting. If the new paint doesn't cover well, seal the old
paint with a primer before painting. Make sure you get
a primer made specifically for this purpose.

And you thought geometry would never come in handy

To estimate how much paint you'll need to paint the
outside of your house, measure the perimeter and

the height from the foundation to the roof line. Multiply the two figures. If your house has a triangular-shaped gable end, add two feet to the overall height of the house. If you're painting a masonry surface, you'll need more paint than for wood. Take your numbers and surface conditions to your paint dealer. He or she can then determine exactly how much paint you'll need.

Clean feet are a shoe-in

To protect your shoes from drips while you're painting, slip a large pair of old socks over them. When you're done with painting, you can just throw the socks away, or save them for the next time you paint.

Feels like paintin' weather

The temperature can make you sweat or shiver while you are painting your house, but did you know it can also affect your paint job? Latex paints usually need about 24 hours of temperatures above 50 degrees Fahrenheit to dry properly. Walls that are exposed to a lot of sun can absorb heat in the summertime and cause your paint to blister. Your best bet is to paint when it is cool to warm outside, and to avoid painting during temperature extremes.

Off with the old

The first step in repainting your house is to wash it thoroughly. Painting over dirt will just cause the paint to peel off easily. If your house exterior is particularly dirty, you may save time and effort by renting a pressure washer. Besides leaving you with a clean surface to paint, it will help lift off old, peeling paint.

Scraping off loose paint is an important part of your preparation to paint, but don't scrape off any paint that is still firmly attached to the surface.

An old-fashioned puncture-type can opener is ideal for scraping old paint or caulk from hard-to-reach crevices.

And on with the new

Painting a clean, flat surface is pretty easy – it's the corners and funny angles that will give you problems. A few things to remember:

▶ Use the correct size brush; it will take more than one. You can't get into every little crack and crevice with a thick, wide brush – you need a small, skinny one. For wider areas that a roller won't paint well, use a medium or large brush.

▶ For a professional-looking finish, use sandpaper to smooth any rough edges that formed when you scraped.

▶ If you use a high-quality roller, you shouldn't have a problem with "roller fuzz"– loose fibers from the roller that get stuck in your paint. To be sure, wrap some masking tape around your hand, sticky-side out, and dab it all over the dry roller before you paint.

Hey, who invited the drip?

To keep your painting area clean, glue a paper plate to the bottom of your paint can. It will catch stray drips and dribbles, and when you move the paint can, your splatter-catcher moves along with it.

Put paint in its place

Don't want to go around with speckles of house paint on your hands? To make washing paint off your hands easier, try rubbing on some petroleum jelly before you start.

When you're painting windows, don't worry about getting paint on the glass. It will clean up easily with a razor scraper and some window cleaner. By painting along the edges between the wood and the glass, you're more likely to seal out moisture that could damage your windows over time.

Paint on the wall is better than you in the bush

Nothing ruins a nice paint job quicker than a single, arcing brushstroke all the way down the side of the house because one of your ladder's feet sank into the soft ground and sent you flying into the bushes. It's not good for the bushes, either. Take a couple of empty coffee cans or old paint cans and put them on the feet of your ladder like shoes. Their flat bottoms can give you a bit more stability and keep you out of the bushes.

Hosing down the hacienda

To keep your paint job bright and fresh-looking, wash your house once a year. Mix one cup of extra-strength detergent and one quart of chlorine bleach in three gallons of water. Use a long-handled mop to scrub the siding, and rinse well with your garden hose.

Through paint-colored glasses

If you wear eyeglasses, protect them from stray spatters and still be able to see what you're painting. Just cover them with a layer of clear plastic wrap; it will stick to the lenses without tape. Replace the wrap as needed until your paint job is all wrapped up.

Siding style and savvy

When choosing your siding, remember that different kinds have different advantages. Wood siding looks more natural, but it must be painted regularly. Aluminum siding color is already painted on, but if it is damaged, the metal may show through. Vinyl siding is usually the same color all the way through, so scratches won't reveal a different color. But vinyl siding may seal an exterior so tightly that moisture may build up underneath it and damage the wood. Before you choose siding, look at all the angles and decide which type will last the best on your house.

But I thought I didn't have to paint siding!

You chose a house with vinyl or aluminum siding because you didn't ever want to hoist another paint can onto a ladder. However, now your siding is showing some signs of wear, or perhaps you're just sick of the color. You don't have to rip your siding off and start over. As much as you may hate the thought, you can paint vinyl and aluminum siding.

As with any paint job, the first step is to wash your siding. If you see signs of rust or a chalky residue, use a medium or fine grade steel wool to remove it. You only have to use a primer if the original siding is in poor condition. If you do use a primer, choose a primer and paint from the same manufacturer, since they are designed to work together. To make sure your paint job lasts, use a top-quality acrylic exterior latex paint.

Don't fence me in

Ever since Tom Sawyer, people have recognized that painting fences is not a lot of fun. But using a tool that gets the paint on the fence efficiently can make the job much less painful. To paint a picket fence, use a paint roller. You'll cover the surface in half the time it would take to use a brush. To paint a wire fence, use a sponge. It will put a thin layer of paint exactly where you want it.

You talk the talk, but can you caulk the caulk?

You want your house to be snug and warm in the winter and cool in the summer. You also want to pay as little as possible in energy bills. One way to help accomplish these goals is to make sure your house is tightly sealed. Caulking around windows, doors, siding, and trim will help. Here's how to caulk your home:

▶ Before adding new caulk, remove as much of the old caulk as possible. Wash the area with soap and water. Use chlorine bleach if mildew is present. Rinse and let dry thoroughly. The caulk will

stick much better to a
clean, dry surface.

▶ Stuff some scraps of insulation into wide or deep
cracks before caulking.

▶ Check the weather fore-
cast before starting. If it
rains within 24 hours after
you caulk, all your hard
work may be washed away.

Cap it off

If your ladder doesn't have
plastic caps, wrap the ends
that lean against the house
with rags. This will keep them
from marring your siding
while you work.

▶ Cut the nozzle of your caulking tube off at a 45-
degree angle, and use a coat hanger or nail to
pierce the seal. Apply steady pressure, holding
the caulking gun at a 45-degree angle to your
work surface.

▶ Smooth the caulk down with a wet finger or
damp sponge, but don't push it in too far. That
might cause it to shrink too much as it dries and
not fill the crack.

Mildews and don'ts

Have you ever left something in the refrigerator too
long, and it started to grow fuzzy green stuff? The
mildew on your house is similar. It is a fungus that
thrives and grows in a damp environment. Besides
making your house look ugly, it can also damage the
surface it grows on. Mildew needs nutrition to grow,
and it can get that nutrition from the grime that accu-
mulates on your house. So in areas that are prone to
mildew, keep things clean. A little laundry detergent,
a bucket of water, and a scrub brush can do wonders
in thwarting mildew's growing efforts.

Secrets of a good climb

A good ladder is an essential tool for exterior house repair and maintenance. It can also be a potential source of danger, so use good ladder sense when working on your house. If your ladder is old and rickety, invest in a new one. You may save yourself from a painful injury.

An aluminum ladder is lighter and lasts longer than a wooden one. However, keep in mind that aluminum conducts electricity, so don't use it while doing electrical repairs or when there is lightning in the area.

Steady as she goes

Keeping your ladder level and steady is your number one priority. For added safety and steadiness, use stabilizer bars that attach to your ladder.

Put a board or other firm, flat object beneath the feet of your ladder before you climb. It will help keep the ladder level and prevent it from sinking into soft ground.

The roof

What's in a roof?

When adding a new roof, remember the most important features are protection and appearance. Consider carefully the style of your house, the amount of roof that will show, and even the roof colors of other houses in the neighborhood. Be careful of light-colored roofing if you live in an area with lots of overhanging trees. Trees can make unsightly stains on a light roof. Try to put all roof vents and flues on the back slope of your roof, if possible. Paint them the same color as the roof so they won't be so visible.

Carry that weight

Be careful of adding a heavy roof, such as cement or clay, to a house built in the 1940s or earlier. Have it checked to be sure the frame will support the additional weight.

Roofing recommendations

Trying to decide whether to patch or reroof? Making your choice is easier if you look at the lifetime of your roof in the following four stages.

Stage 1: Tiny pieces of your roof that look like fine gravel gather in gutters and below downspouts.

Stage 2: Bare patches of black tar become visible as the roof sheds the tiny pieces.

Stage 3: Shingle tabs curl up and become brittle.

Stage 4: Curled shingles break off, tar patches wear, and nail heads and seams are exposed.

If your roof is in Stage 1 or 2, patching will probably do the trick as a short-term solution. By Stage 3 and certainly Stage 4, the more cost-effective solution is to reroof.

When more costs less

If you have only one or two layers of roofing on your house, consider adding a third layer without removing the other two. In most areas, it's permitted to have up to three layers of roofing. Adding a new layer costs about half as much as removing the old ones and starting from scratch.

Water, water everywhere

A drippy leak in your ceiling can drive you crazy. Locating the source of the leak can be almost as maddening. Keep in mind that the leak usually isn't located directly over the drip mark in your ceiling. Water enters your roof, then runs downward before dripping onto your ceiling. During a steady rain, go into your attic and find the drip. Then follow the "drip trail" until you find the original entry point for the water. Mark this spot by pushing a nail upward through the roof. When the sun shines again, you or your repairman will be able to see the precise location of the leak by the nail sticking through the roof.

Inspection and detection

Inspecting your roof regularly can help avert some drippy disasters. Pay special attention to the flashing around chimneys and roof vents, because that's where most leaks begin. If you're not comfortable walking on a roof, inspect it from a safe distance, using binoculars.

While you're up there

While you're up having fun on your roof, you might as well take the opportunity to make sure everything else is fastened down and in good condition. Chances are you won't be back up there for a while. Here are some additional things to check:

▶ Check the stability of your TV antenna, weather vanes, skylights, and anything else that sticks up.

▶ Inspect the roof shingles for any damage. Loose or broken shingles can obviously cause leaks, but they can also break away and create barriers in your gutters.

▶ Examine the seams and corners of your roofing. The crown of the roof, the corners around the chimney, and the edges are areas that may weaken easily.

▶ Look at the trees around your house. If possible, you should remove any overhanging tree limbs. Even if they never break off and damage your roof, they will be a constant source of litter for your gutters.

Gutters and downspouts

It's a bird, it's a plane, it's ... something from your gutter

Gutters may not be the most attractive part of your house, but they perform a useful service, directing water down the corners of your house instead of letting it pour off in all directions to slowly wash away your foundation. Unfortunately, they're also a magnet for anything else that might blow around on your roof, including leaves, sticks, and acorns. This leads to clogged downspouts, backed up rain-

What's the scoop on gutters?

A plastic sugar scoop or a garden trowel makes an excellent tool for scooping up leaves from your gutters. When you're done, install a leaf strainer into each downspout opening to help eliminate clogs that cause water backup.

water, and eventually a rotting mess on your roof. Gutters should be cleaned at least twice a year, particularly after autumn leaves have accumulated.

Good gutters gone bad

You can tell if your gutters are overdue for a cleaning by a few telltale signs. Walk around your house, checking the gutters and downspouts for twigs and debris sticking over the top or out from between cracks. The places where gutters turn or change direction are common problem areas for clogs. Water marks and discoloration on your siding are signs that rain has backed up and leaked into the wrong places. On the ground, check for erosion around the foundation of the house. Also, pay close attention to any leaks that appear in your basement. Water seeping into the house should tell you that rain is not being properly directed away from the foundation.

Up on the roof

Spring and fall are good times for inspecting your gutters. The best way is to use a ladder or actually get up and walk around on the roof itself. This gives you the best view, but can also be dangerous. Remember, put safety first. If your mobility is limited, this is not the time to test your limits. Get someone else to do it for you, or hire a professional service to inspect and clean your gutters.

Guard them well

You can buy mesh guards for your gutters that will let water through, but catch the debris. However, most experts say these don't eliminate your need for cleaning. They may even make cleaning more difficult than in unguarded gutters.

Golden oldie

Areaways should be cleaned out frequently lest they become so clogged with trash that they fill with rain and flood the basement.

1003 Household Hints and Work Savers, 1947

Fiddling on the roof

If you are able to move safely on your roof or get to problem areas with a ladder, you should be able to clean your gutters yourself. Some things to remember:

▶ Clean all your gutters, all the way around. Debris that is not causing a blockage now could move in the future, so make sure you get everything out.

▶ Clear all the downspouts after you've cleared the gutters. To make sure they're flowing smoothly, drop a marble from the top and listen to its progress. Better yet, run water from a hose through the downspouts to clear any small, remaining particles.

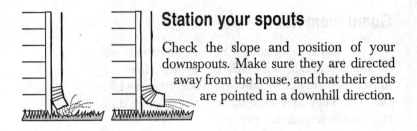

Station your spouts

Check the slope and position of your downspouts. Make sure they are directed away from the house, and that their ends are pointed in a downhill direction.

Windows and doors

Simple solution to a sticky situation

Frustrated with sliding glass doors that stick? Look to see if your door has an adjustment screw near the bottom roller. You can use this to raise the door frame up from the track. If you still have a problem, clean the top and bottom tracks with soapy water and a stiff-bristle brush. When the tracks are dry, grease them with white lithium grease. Your sticky door problems should be solved.

Easy as pie

You probably thought your pizza cutter was only good for your Friday night dinner, but it has at least one more use. To open a stubborn window that has been painted shut, run a pizza cutter along the crack.

Golden oldie

Don't waste your anger on a sticky window. A thin coating of beeswax on the pulley stiles will make it slide like ice.

1003 Household Hints and Work Savers, 1947

Don't buy a hole new screen

Don't trash that window screen yet. Here are two quick fixes:

▶ Small holes in a screen can easily be patched using a few thin coats of clear nail polish. Dab it on lightly, letting it dry between coats. This will prevent clumping and dripping, and make the repair job almost invisible.

▶ If you have some extra screening on hand, you can repair a small hole in a screen by gluing a small piece of screening over the hole. Use a permanent, waterproof glue that dries clear.

Garage door danger

Automatic garage door openers are a great convenience, but they can also be dangerous, especially to children. Most are designed to reverse if they hit a solid object, but may not reverse if they hit the soft body of a child. Test your door by closing it on a roll of paper towels. If it doesn't reverse, consult the manufacturer to see if it can be adjusted. If not, replace it.

Home remodeling

The house of your dreams

Adding on or remodeling your house can be a dream come true or a nightmare. Here are some important tips to keep in mind:

▶ Take the time to really think through what you want. Everything should be planned in detail before you actually begin any demolition or construction.

▶ It is often just as expensive to make a small addition to your house as it is to make a larger one. Make sure the addition will really meet your needs for space and comfort.

▶ Don't build an addition that will give you the most expensive house in the neighborhood; it's bad economy. You might want to simply move to a house that better suits your needs.

▶ Be sure you have checked on any zoning or building regulations in your area and know which permits you need. The time to find out whether your addition will be allowed is before you begin it.

▶ Understand that remodeling is a slow process, and you will need to be patient to get the results you want. Don't plan an important function, like a wedding reception, at your home soon after the target date for completion.

▶ Throughout the process, communicate clearly with your architect and builder.

How to co-op with the contractor

If you're going to have major work done to your house, consider hiring out only part of the job and doing part of it yourself. For instance, if the remodeling includes painting the exterior of your house, perhaps you could do the prep work such as washing, scraping, and sanding. Then a professional could step in to do the painting. Your cost would be much less, and you would still get an excellent job. Some contractors will agree to this arrangement, and some won't. Be sure to check before starting on the prep work. One word of warning: Make sure the guarantee of the contractor's work still applies even if you do part of the preparation work yourself.

Keeping ahead of dangerous lead

Until they discovered it to be a health hazard, paint manufacturers often used lead in their paint. Even though this practice has ended, millions of gallons of lead-based paint still cover the walls of American homes and businesses, particularly older ones. People who breathe in lead paint dust or children who eat the chipped paint may develop a variety of ailments. If you have to make repairs to an area that you suspect might contain lead-based paint, use caution. Don't let children or pregnant women come anywhere near your work area. Try to contain the mess you make, and always clean up thoroughly

Getting the lead out

If your house was built before 1978, it might have lead-based paint, and if it was built before 1960, it almost certainly was painted with a high concentration of lead-based paint. If you think your house might be harboring this dangerous substance, avoid:

▶ Scraping, sanding, or blasting old paint off before repainting

▶ Making holes in the walls for pipes or wiring

▶ Tearing out walls for remodeling

afterward, using wet rags or a mop. Don't sweep or vacuum the area, because it could spread the lead particles through the air. A solution made with powdered dishwashing detergent that contains phosphate is most effective in cleaning up lead dust. Dispose of your cleaning water carefully, and thoroughly clean any rags or mops before using them again.

Backyard decks

Stacking the deck in your favor

Moisture from below can cause problems for your porch or deck. Help keep moisture down by covering the ground underneath it with polyethylene sheeting, topped with about two inches of sand.

Swab the deck, matey, but not too hard

Pressure washing your deck is quick and easy, but high-pressure washing may cause live mold spores to be forced into the wood, causing decay. Using a sprayer is OK, but use a lower pressure setting, around 750 psi (pounds per square inch).

On your side

When washing your deck, protect the siding of your house from strong cleaning solutions, which may cause spotting. Take old pieces of plywood or leftover siding and lean them against the walls of your house while you clean.

Moisture barrier

Potted plants can make your deck lovely and lush looking, but make sure they don't also damage it. Most planters have drain holes to prevent excess water from rotting the plant's roots. The problem is that moisture draining from the planters can't evaporate between the planters and the deck. This can lead to decay of the wood. Use plant stands or place blocks of lumber between the pots and the deck. Moving your plants frequently is also a good idea.

Deter deck decay

Clean and reseal your deck at least every other year to keep it protected from the elements. If your deck isn't mildewed, you can just use a mild detergent. To get rid of mildew, use a water and bleach solution or a commercial deck wash. Be sure to rinse thoroughly and let the deck dry completely before sealing the wood.

Stand in the gap

Be sure to keep the gaps between your deck flooring free of dirt, twigs, and leaves. The gaps are intended to prevent standing water and keep air flowing around the wood so it won't decay.

Driveways and sidewalks

Make a clean sweep of it

You work hard at making your house look attractive. So why settle for that "permanent" grease or oil spot on your concrete driveway? Get rid of it by pouring mineral spirits or paint thinner on the dirty area. Make sure it covers thoroughly. Then take a bag of cat litter, sand or a large box of baking soda (even corn meal will work – you just want something dry and absorbent) and spread it on top of the spot. Leave it there for 12 hours or so and then sweep it up. The oil spot should be "gone with the litter." Get up final traces of the mineral spirits with warm water, regular detergent, and a mop. You can use this method with dry cement, too, but in that case, let it sit for a couple of days before sweeping it up.

Better safe than scar-y

If you're not sure what surface material you're dealing with, it's best to play it safe. Many commercial products are available for cleaning concrete, blacktop, and various types of patio surfaces. These can be bought at hardware and some paint stores, and should tell you right on the bottle if they can clean your surface without scarring it.

Foil that dripping oil

Oil is a tough enemy to face in the trenches of stain warfare, particularly when it has soaked in good and deep. But here's a secret weapon that just might carry the day. Fix up a solution of one part TSP (trisodium phosphate) to four parts of water. Soak an old towel in the solution, lay it over the sinister stain, and allow it to sit. From time to time, you can work the solution into the stain with a scrub brush, but the best results will come from the towel leaching the stain out. Even if this does not completely remove a deep stain, it will reduce it.

A spot of trouble

For a stubborn grease spot, try scrubbing it with concentrated detergent suds. Use a very stiff brush, and then hose it down with water. Or you might try automatic dishwashing detergent. Spread the powder onto a dampened surface and allow it to stand for a while. Take a bucket of boiling water and rinse the area, then scrub it and rinse it again.

Slick snow removal

To make snow shoveling easier, coat your snow shovel with car wax. Snow slides right off. If you don't have any wax handy, try using nonstick cooking spray.

The squeegee is mightier than the snow

A snow shovel is fine for the sidewalk, but can be pretty awkward on steps. Use a rubber floor squeegee to remove a light dusting of snow from your porch or steps. The soft rubber is much gentler than a rough shovel for clearing the surface of your deck as well.

Home security

Help prowlers to see the light

Darkened yards are an open invitation to intruders. No ne'er-do-well wants to commit a break-in on a brightly-lit stage. A few well-placed exterior lights can do wonders for correcting this problem. Many stores sell reasonably-priced outdoor lights that are activated by motion. These light up your yard when something is moving, but keep you from having to live in the spotlight.

The ins and outs of door safety

Doors that lead to the outside should have the hinges located on the inside to prevent burglars from simply taking the door off its hinges to get in. These doors should be solid and well mounted. Check them periodically to make sure the frames and hardware are sturdy and have not come loose. The same goes for windows and sliding glass doors. Be sure to check the screws and bolts that hold these items in place. Anything that could be easily unscrewed or tampered with should not be accessible from the outside.

Keep security tight

Outdoor security lights should be fitted with some sort of bulb protection, such as a metal grill over the bulb. You don't want prowlers to be able to turn off your lights by some simple tampering such as loosening a light bulb.

Neatness counts

Sometimes a messy yard can be more than an eyesore — it can be a security risk. Never leave yard tools, shovels, or other items lying around if they could be used as weapons. Even if a prowler doesn't use these as weapons, he might use a well-placed garden shovel as a tool to break in. If you don't have a garage or shed with a lock, keep these things in the basement or in a closet inside your house.

Good fences make good ... fences

Fences are good for keeping people out, but they're also good at hiding people once they are in your yard. For this reason, see-through fences are your safest bet.

Help the police help you

Your address numbers should be visible day and night, so police, firemen, or ambulance drivers can locate your house quickly in an emergency. Small digits on your mailbox are not enough. Almost any hardware store carries a full line of reflective address numbers, which are inexpensive and easy to install. Place your house number in a visible location. It's for your own protection.

That all-important lived-in look

If you go away for a few days, don't let mail or newspapers collect. You might also collect a burglar. Have someone go by your house now and then to empty your mailbox and pick up anything that's left on your doorstep. This friend should also take out your garbage and bring in the trash cans afterward.

Lights, camera, crime!

Don't turn out all the lights when you go on vacation. A house that is dark for several nights in a row is a pretty attractive lure for thieves. For a few dollars, you can pick up a timer device that turns lights on and off for you while you are away. Plug a few well-chosen lights into your timer, and set it for an irregular pattern. This should keep any sinister watchers guessing.

HOME WORKSHOP

The toolbox

When things get a little screwy

One of the hardest things for the amateur wood-worker to do is get a screw to go in straight. Fortunately, one of the handyman's oldest tricks takes care of this problem. Before applying the screw, rub the threads with a bar of soap. The soap helps the screw go into the wood more smoothly, and hopefully, in a straighter line.

Heads up

Fixing a screw or a washer directly over your head is tricky business. Next time you're working on the ceiling or an overhead fixture, try coating the screw, nut, or washer with a slight film of a sticky substance, such as crazy glue or rubber cement. This will keep the hardware on your tools and out of your eyes. Once you're done, wipe away the excess glue with a rag.

Bang the lid slowly

Tired of putting dents or holes in your wall because you missed a nail with your hammer? Never again.

Instead of panicking over the condition of your wall, get yourself a plastic lid off a coffee can or an old Tupperware bowl. Drill a hole in the center that's large enough for your nails to go through, then place this guard around the nails as you pound them home. Now if your aim misses the mark, the plastic shield takes the blow, not your wall.

Survival tactics for fingers

Little nails can mean big pain for large fingers. To keep from hammering your fingers when dealing with a small nail, stick the nail through a small piece of thin cardboard first. Holding the cardboard by an edge, pound the nail home. Now tear away the cardboard and you're all set, safe and sound.

Another way to handle small nails and tacks is with a comb. Put the nail in position between two of the comb's teeth. The plastic should serve the double purpose of holding the nail in place, and protecting both the wall and your fingertips from unfortunate swings of the hammer.

Don't get stuck by drywall

If you're surrounded by drywall, try this to keep the drywall plaster from chipping away when you nail into it. Place a little bit of masking tape or cellophane tape on the spot where you're going to put the nail. After your nail is in, just peel away the tape from around it. But go slowly. Tape can get a pretty sticky grip, and you could peel away some of the paint if you're not careful.

What goes in must come out

When it's time for the picture to come down, sometimes the hole left behind is the least of your problems. If you yank the nail out using a hammer claw, the head of the hammer can really do a number on your paint job. Prevent this by placing a magazine or a paper towel folded in quarters flat against the wall, then tilt your hammer against it when pulling out the nail. A spatula will also work and has a handle built right in.

Got a screw loose?

Here's an easy fix for a loose screw. Get yourself a "twist-tie" or two, the kind used to keep bread fresh. Cut the ties or fold them over so they are about as long as the hole is deep. Next, take the screw out of the wall and insert the twist ties into the hole. When you put the screw back in, it should mash into the twist-ties, and the extra width created should make the screw fit tightly.

A bolt out of the blue

That bolt just won't budge. The problem could be many things, but the most likely one is rust. To convince it to move, dab a little bit of WD-40 oil down into the threads. If that doesn't work, try a few drops of ammonia. Finally, some folks swear by soda pop. Wrap the bolt in a rag that has been soaked in any kind of carbonated beverage, and more often than not, that rusty bolt will stop being so stubborn.

Another one bites the rust

Moisture is probably your workshop's worst enemy, especially where tools are concerned. A little bit of rust can go a long way toward ruining just about everything in your toolbox. For this reason, stainless steel tools are usually a good choice when they're available. Although stainless steel resists rust better than other types of metal, you still need to take care of it.

Clean your tools after each use, especially yard and garden tools or tools that are exposed to water and soil. Dry them off well and keep them in a clean, dry place. Don't leave yard tools out in the yard or leaning against the side of the garage. Staying one step ahead of rust is the best way to beat it.

Know the drill

Breaking a drill bit while boring a hole is not only frustrating, it's dangerous. To prevent this, spray your bits with a touch of silicone before you begin. The added lubrication will keep your bits sharper, too.

Headlights for hard-to-reach places

You're putting a hole in a shadowy, remote spot, and you can't quite see the target area. What do you do? Improvise. With a piece of masking tape, attach a penlight to the drill's casing, and viola! This tip will work with any tool that has to reach into a dark corner.

Laying rust to rest

If you'll be storing a particular tool for a while, spray it with WD-40 before putting it away. A very fine coating will help protect the metal from moisture. If you have a tool that is frequently exposed to water (especially salt water), or is constantly used in harsh conditions, coat its metal parts with petroleum jelly before storing.

If you find rust on your tools, don't panic. Remove the rust by rubbing it down with sand-paper. Start with the finest grade you have, and work up to coarser grades if the finer ones don't work. Steel wool will also work for certain types of rust. Make sure you get every last bit of rust – don't be afraid to sand all the way down to the metal. It's better to remove a little of the surface with sanding than to leave even a small trace of rust, which will continue to spread and cause deterioration.

Stretching your dollar

Who says a dollar won't go as far as it used to? Actually, a one-dollar bill will go just as far as always – about six inches. Actually, any U.S. bill will work as a mini-ruler; they're all the same size. Remember this little fact the next time you're caught without a ruler.

The long and the short of it

When you need to measure objects that are round or curved, a ruler usually won't cut it. Take a tip from people who sew. In any fabric shop or sewing department of a discount store, you can get a cloth tape measure that's ideal for such jobs. In a pinch, you can wrap a piece of string around an object the same way you would if you were using a tape meas-ure. Then hold the string along a yardstick to get a fairly accurate measurement.

Give your ruler a hand

How big is your hand? Don't laugh. If you know the span of your hand, you can get a reliable, if rough, measurement when you're caught without a ruler. Probably the best way to measure is to flatten out your hand as wide as possible, then measure from the tip of your thumb straight across to the tip of your pinkie.

Working with wood

Lumber party

Leaving lumber on the ground is a carpenter's first no-no. Always keep your wood off the floor or ground to protect it from dirt, insects, and its arch-enemy, water. A little bit of moisture can quickly turn a fine piece of wood into a warped, discolored, decomposing mess. Store your lumber at least an inch or so off the ground. A couple of old tires make a fine platform for this purpose.

The devil is in sanding the details

Small objects present special sanding challenges. Often, the best way to attack a small item is to simply tape down your sandpaper and rub the item against it, instead of the other way around. For small corners and little detail jobs, twist your sandpaper onto a pencil or a popsicle stick. And remember: What's an emery board besides sandpaper on a stick? There's no law that says you have to use it on your fingernails.

Sanding is a delicate art. To find a spot you've missed, slip the leg of an old pair of pantyhose over your hand like a glove and pass it back and forth over the surface. The nylon will catch on even the slightest roughness in the wood, and you can zero in on any spots that still need sanding.

Happy sandings

Wrapping sandpaper around a small block of wood gives you something more substantial to hold onto while you're sanding large objects. If you practice this common technique, be sure to dampen the back of the paper before you wrap it. This will help keep the paper from tearing, so it will work better and last longer.

Sink your teeth into it

Handsaws are a lot like a smile: their most important part is their teeth. Protect your saw's teeth by covering them when not in use. A good trick for this is to cut a slit along one edge of a piece of garden hose, then affix this to the edge of the saw blade. This little precaution will also protect something else – your fingers.

A working wedge

When cutting with the grain, wood can start to pinch your handsaw, causing it to bend or even break. If this happens, insert the face of a flat head screwdriver into the end of the cut. Wedging it open this way will give you a cleaner cut and an easier time of sawing.

Masking tape therapy

Working with plywood can be tricky. The wood has a tendency to split and fray at the ends and along the edges, especially when you saw into it. Put the kibosh on this troublesome trait by sticking a piece of masking tape right at the place you plan to saw. The sticky substance gives the wood a little reinforcement until you're through cutting.

Staying organized

Little items, big messes

A clean shop area is a shop that works, but you've got too many tools, parts, and mismatched screws lying around. Don't get behind in cleaning up your workspace, or pretty soon you won't be able to find anything when you need it. And what happens then? That's right – nothing.

The stay-put solution

If you're taking apart something with lots of tiny parts – a watch, for instance, or a model – stick a piece of double-sided tape to your work table, and place the pieces on it as you remove them. This way, they won't go wandering off and you'll know just where they are when you need to put them back in place.

Baby your bolts and screws

Keep screws, tacks, and other small items sorted and stored in their own jars. Baby food jars are a good size for this, and their lids can be nailed into the underside of a shelf so you can hang each jar and have quick access to them while keeping them out of the way.

The world's squishiest labels

If you prefer cabinets to hanging jars, invest in one with lots of little drawers. Separate your nuts, screws, tacks, nails, and bolts among the drawers. Then, stick a small piece of a putty-like hanging compound (the kind you hang posters with) on the front of each drawer, and embed one of each drawer's residents in the clay. You'll never scramble through 16 drawers looking for the right washer again, and the adorned cabinet looks rather interesting.

Your eggs in all the right baskets

For certain repair jobs, it's not only important that you not lose any of the small parts as you take them off, but also that you can put them back in the right order. For such challenges, use this nifty trick. Number the sections of a standard egg carton from one to twelve, then store each part that you remove in one section. The first part off goes in section one, the second in section two, and so on. No more scratching your head over which bolt goes back in first. Use as many egg cartons as you need to give you a cup for each piece.

An absolute corker of an idea

Paperwork seems to accumulate everywhere, and the workshop is no exception. Keep your notes, measurements, patterns, or instruction sheets in view but out of the way by putting up a strip of cork board on the wall above your workbench. Foam block works well for this, too, and is a good way to recycle the Styrofoam packing from new appliances.

General maintenance

Home is where the hard work is

Over the years, you've probably done a lot of work on your house, and probably had others in to do some of the work. If you haven't already done so, start keeping records of all that work today. Just keep in a notebook a list of any repairs done to your home, when they were done, by whom, and how much they cost. Having this information handy will make it easier for you to contact the responsible party if a repaired part of your house has an unexpected problem. And if you ever sell your house, it will be an impressive record of your careful maintenance, as well as a tax record of the "basis" (financial investment) you have in your home.

This old or new house needs you

It sure would be nice to walk up to that loose banister or busted door, look it right in the eye, and scare it into submission with your master-craftsman tool belt. Sadly, we can't all wield the home-fixing arsenal of Bob Vila. Fortunately, we don't have to. For a reasonable price, you can put together a respectable army of your own. Focus on the basics, and start with the items you know you'll need more often than any others. A decent home tool kit should include most of the following:

▶ Carpenter's hammer

▶ Flat-tip screwdrivers and Phillips screwdrivers in assorted sizes

▶ Nails and screws in a variety of sizes, hollow wall fasteners, adhesives

▶ Slip-joint pliers, needle nose pliers, 12-inch adjustable wrench

▶ Variable-speed drill and drill bits

▶ Machine oil, penetrating oil, C-clamps

▶ Hacksaw, cross-cut saw, butt chisel, utility knife, scissors, single-edge razor blades

▶ Block plane, rasp, sandpaper and sanding block, steel wool

▶ Paintbrushes, putty knife, 5-in-1 tool, interior and exterior caulk

▶ Combination square, level, retractable steel tape measure, pencils

▶ Clean rags, broom and dust pan, wet-and-dry vacuum (optional)

▶ Workbench, toolbox, step ladder, heavy extension cord, clip-on light, flashlight

The rent is overdue

If you are planning to do a project that will require expensive tools, consider renting instead of buying. Estimate how long you'll need to rent a tool and how much the rental is per day. If this is less than the cost of the tools, you'll do better renting. Or rent for a day to see how you like the process and then decide whether to buy.

Is it a keeper?

A good question to ask yourself when you need a tool for a specific task is this: How many times will I have to do this in the future? Particularly for a very specialized or expensive tool, you should think long and hard about your likelihood of ever using it again. If it seems unlikely, you're better off renting it.

Roll out the 'barrow,' and we'll have a 'barrow' of fun

Tired of buying a new wheelbarrow every few years because your old one rusted out? All you need to do is store it on end when not in use. Any rainwater will run right out.

A good neighbor policy

When large or complicated jobs come along, don't overlook your "tool network." Having friends who share your fixer-upper interests is not only fun, it can save you money. Your neighbor across the street might have just the hammer you need, and you might have the drill he needs for his next project.

Getting a handle on the situation

Ever had a wobbly push broom? You know the type – the head is so loose that you spend half your time sweeping and the other half screwing the thing back on. Well, never again. Keep the work ends of all your tools – brooms, shovels, fireplace tools – firmly in place with the help of some black electrical tape. Just wrap the threads of the handle before screwing it in, and you'll never again have to worry about "losing your head."

Grate expectations

Sharpen a dull pair of scissors quickly and easily by cutting through a folded piece of fine grade sandpaper several times. Be sure to have the rough side on the outside of the fold.

Has that old razor blade seen better days? You're not finished with it yet. Give your old razor blades new life with a few sweeps across the striking surface of a matchbook.

AUTOMOTIVE

Routine maintenance

Tune up for the long haul

Did you know? Keeping your car properly maintained translates into a more efficient, safer car that will last up to 50 percent longer. That means thousands of free miles! Something as small as a misfiring spark plug can reduce your gas mileage up to 30 percent. But you can prevent such a problem with regular tune-ups. Check your owner's manual to see how often you should have a tune-up. Then mark the dates on your calendar and keep the appointments.

Battery not included

Batteries can fail any time of year, and they will. Many of the maintenance-free batteries available today have to be checked by a professional. You can do routine care on most batteries, though. Clean corrosion off the posts and cable connections, wipe down all surfaces, and tighten up all the connections. If you can remove the caps to check fluid levels, do so monthly. Wear protective gear for these jobs, including eye protection.

An idling engine is the devil's playground

What's one of the worst things you can do for your car's engine? Idling. Or at least frequent or long-term idling. If you have to stop your car for more than a few minutes, turn it off. And on cold winter mornings, keep "warming up" to just a minute or so; today's cars are designed to warm up quickly. This will save on gas as well as protect your engine.

Oil's well that ends well

After changing your oil, most professionals will put a little sticker on an inside corner of your windshield. This tells you when you're due for another oil job, 3,000 miles down the road. If you do the job yourself or if your mechanic doesn't provide this service, just note your car's mileage at the time you make the change, then add 3,000. Write this number on a small piece of masking tape and stick it on your visor, and you're all set.

And you thought they just liked writing tickets

That 55 mph speed limit isn't just for safety. It makes a big difference in your fuel economy to drive at 55 or less. Gas mileage decreases sharply above that speed.

Drive safe, drive clean

For the sake of both you and your car, keep a box of moist towelettes in your glove compartment. Use them to clean the grease off your hands after checking the oil or messing around under the hood, and to wipe up spills inside the car before they become stains. They also come in handy when one of those annoying gas pumps "burps" up a little extra after you're done filling the tank. Wipe the gas spill off your paint with a paper towel, then finish cleaning the spot with a towelette.

Golden oldie

When driving, shift gradually from low to high. Increase the speed by degrees up to 10 miles per hour before going into second, gradually up to 25 before shifting into high. Run car slowly, the first 10 minutes of driving, before attempting to pick up speed at all.

1003 Household Hints and Work Savers, 1947

Air out your engine

If you want to make a difference in how much gas your engine uses, start by making a difference in how much air it gets. A dirty air filter doesn't allow enough air into your engine for it to burn gas properly. This translates into more trips to the gas pump. Check your air filter as often as you check your oil. If it looks clogged or very dirty, replace it. You know it's time for a new air filter when you hold the filter up in front of a light and you can't see your fingers through it.

You get out of it what you put into it

Sometimes spending money is actually the best way to save money. If your car's coolant hasn't been changed in several years, it's probably time to have it flushed out. Draining and replacing the coolant helps remove any rust or dirt that could cause problems in the system later.

Waxing nostalgic before you hit the oldies station

Probably the last part of your car you're worried about is the antenna. But wouldn't you know it, that can wear down too. Help keep your antenna from sticking or catching by waxing it every now and then. Just rub a piece of wax paper up and down its length. That little bit of protection will help keep your antenna running smoothly and your tunes coming in loud and clear.

A slick drip trick

What's filthier than a garage floor? Nothing, if you've got an oil leak. Even a tiny drip can cause a

The road best travelled

If you want to know just how long your car can last, pay a visit to Bill Desch. As a refurbisher of old cars, Bill is delighted to show people that, in most cases, it's not the car that quits on the owner, but the other way around. So how do you keep that from happening?

"Change your oil," Bill says. "Every 3,000 miles, no matter what your manual says. I don't care if it's just off the showroom floor or a classic in your garage. That's the number one thing you can do to lengthen your car's life." And don't forget to replace the oil filter when you change the oil, he adds. That's where the gunk collects that will cause your engine problems.

So take it from an expert. Just like you watch what you eat, take care of what goes into your car. It's the best way to keep it healthy for the long haul.

major stain in a pretty short time – a stain that's very easy to track into the house. Head this problem off at the pass by making a drip pan. Place a few sheets of corrugated cardboard in a cookie sheet and arrange this pan under your car's drip. You can also use cat litter, oatmeal, or sawdust in the pan. If you already have a major oil slick in your garage or driveway, spread one of these thirsty substances all over the spot, wait for a while, then sweep up and discard it.

The old switcheroo

Have you ever had your tires rotated? You should. Rearranging your tires' positions on the car exposes each one to the same wear and tear and gives you an even ride. Get your car tires rotated about every 5,000 miles for the best, most even wear.

Can you handle the pressure?

Here are some tips for keeping your tire pressure in check.

▶ Use a reliable pressure gauge when checking your tires. Don't use the one at the gas station; you don't know who's been mistreating it or how well it works.

▶ Here's something that's often overlooked. When you check the pressure on your four tires, check your fifth one, too. What good is a spare if it's not properly inflated and ready to roll when you need it?

▶ Always check tire pressure when tires are "cool." If your tires are warmed up from a long period of use, the heat can cause a false reading. Be sure to check tire pressure at least once a month. Make it a natural part of your service routine, every three or four times you fill up, to give your tires the once-over.

Golden oldie

Keep speed low. High speed is much more harmful to tires in hot weather than in cold. Go especially slowly on roads with sharp projecting stones. Take curves and turns slowly. Speeding around curves multiplies tire wear – as much as 10 times in some cases.

1003 Household Hints and Work Savers, 1947

Less is not more

Here's a common mistake to avoid. Although you may hear people recommend it, never let air out of your tires in order to get better traction in icy or snowy conditions. In addition to not working, this trick will damage your tires and could cause them to explode.

The tire that came in from the cold

Another cold-weather caution: Try to avoid putting air in your tires when it's extremely cold, particularly if it's below 10 degrees. Under such freezing conditions, the air valve could stick and, in a matter of seconds, let all the air out of your tire.

Another round for my tires

To avoid problems, remember to check your wheels and tires regularly. Your tires should contain their recommended amount of air pressure to work properly; underinflated tires waste gas, make your engine work harder, and wear out faster. Wheels that are out of alignment also make the engine work overtime and can wear out your tires. Having your wheels and tires checked and realigned if necessary isn't an expensive proposition, but it will pay big dividends.

No rust for the weary

Remember, the hood and bumpers aren't the only parts of your hard-working car that need attention. Rust can creep up where you least expect it or where you're least likely to look for it. Salt, dirt, and road oils can build up on the exposed underside of your car and do some serious damage. Keep rust away by flushing out the undercarriage of your car every so often. Toss the sprinkler underneath and turn it on, moving it around every now and then so that each part gets good and clean.

> ### It's not heavy; it's my junk
>
> What's in your car's trunk? Tools, a baby stroller, and a few bricks for your garden? Bet you didn't know that they're robbing you of gas mileage. Lighten the load, and your gas gauge will thank you. And on trips, use the trunk rather than stowing gear in a car-top carrier – it just creates extra drag and wastes gas.

A manicure for your car

Ouch! A shopping cart took a nip out of your car's beautiful finish. Doesn't look too bad, but how do you keep it from getting worse? Nail polish. That's right. A quick coat of clear fingernail polish will help prevent rust from forming and keep that small scratch from getting worse.

Show the next guy how much you loved her

It's always a good idea to keep a close record of all maintenance and repair work that's done on your car. Keep it with your auto files or in the glove compartment. Having the names of those who have worked on your car handy will be very useful if

New life for old wheels

Bill Desch knows a thing or two about getting the most out of an older vehicle. An avid car restorer, Bill spends much of his time under the hood of his 1972 Chevrolet Chevelle. He advises would-be auto enthusiasts to be patient and cautious when picking out a car to restore.

"Find an unpainted car if you can," he says. "That way, you can see all the rust and whether or not it is worth rebuilding. Fork over a couple bucks and take it to a garage where you can put it on a lift, so you can look at the undercarriage for rust, rot, and other problems."

You don't need to own a garage to get started in restoration, says the self-taught grease monkey, and you don't need to spend a fortune. "Your starter tool kit should include just the basics. Buy reliable tools that have a lifetime guarantee." Like what? "Pick up a 3/8-inch dry socket set, and a combo set of open and box wrenches 7/16-inch to one-inch, and you're on your way."

something goes wrong with the repair. This can also help you out when it comes time to sell your car. If you have saved your receipts for such things as oil changes and new batteries along with this log, you will have a record that proves you kept the car in good shape – a very comforting and attractive bonus to potential buyers.

In the garage

Your car's castle

Your garage is as important to your car as your house is to you. Storing your vehicle in a spot where it is protected from the elements can improve the performance, preserve the appearance, and extend the life of your car. Rain, snow, wind, hail, extreme heat, and extreme cold cause damage that can be prevented by keeping your car in a sheltered place. If your garage is full of things other than your car, clean it out and use it for storing this very important possession.

This zone is for lawnmower parking only

Of course, your car is usually not the only resident of your garage. Lawnmowers, bikes, tools, and all sorts of things can start to clutter up your car's safe haven, and make parking difficult. To prevent this from getting out of hand, try this simple trick: Create parking zones. Paint lines or boxes on the floor to help children and grandchildren (and maybe yourself) remember to put things back where they belong. This will also keep you from having to search for a place to put that mower, especially if you paint a parking spot for the mower, too.

And you thought bumper cars were fun

Of course, no one's perfect. Accidents will happen from time to time in a crowded garage. If this is a problem for you, try this solution. Use foam rubber, strips of an old tire, or pieces of carpet to pad surfaces that your car doors might collide with if you accidentally park too close.

Keeping your car in line

To help guide your car into perfect parked position, paint a stripe down the middle of the back wall of your garage. This bearing will help you center your car when you pull into the garage, and should keep you from ramming your door into something because you parked too far left or right.

A little more light on the subject

These days, most garages are fixed with automatic door openers, and most of these come equipped with an automatic overhead light. However, if your garage or carport doesn't have a light, there's no need to avoid your garage. Simply put a couple of pieces of reflector tape on the things you don't want to run into. These include walls, garbage cans, and any items that have a tendency to get in your way when you pull into the garage.

Cleaning the car

Hey ... you clean up nice

For a shine that looks like it just came off the showroom floor, rub down the vinyl and hard plastic parts of your car's interior with aerosol furniture polish.

Not only does it look great, the coating helps keep dust from gathering, too.

When your bumper sticker has stuck too well

Get an ugly old bumper sticker off your tail with a little WD-40 or lighter fluid. Simply moisten the sticker (or the gummy remains of one), let the fluid seep in, then gently rub it away. You may have to do this more than once to get all the stickiness off. Be sure to clean up any trace of the oil or lighter fluid afterward. It can damage your car's finish if you leave it on too long.

A dirty car's best friend

There's nothing quite like picking flattened bugs off the grill and headlights with your fingernails. Avoid this unpleasant task with the magic of baking soda. Apply this mild abrasive with a nylon net, and watch the splatter marks disappear. Baking soda also works wonders on chrome and enamel.

Just when you thought it was safe to put your baking soda away... your windshield wipers need cleaning. A good rubdown with baking soda and water will get those wipers in clear working order in no time.

Low tar, no tar

Ugh! Road tar on your beautiful paint job. Makes you almost wish they wouldn't fill those potholes in front of your house. But calm down, you've got a secret weapon. Laundry pre-wash sprays successfully remove tar from car surfaces.

Getting down to the nitty gritty

Dirt doesn't seem to have much trouble getting into all the nooks and crannies of your wheels, but it can be pretty tricky to get out. Cleaning your wheels and hubcaps is a lot easier with a large, stiff paintbrush. Just dip it in sudsy water and get to work.

A clear and simple solution

If you wash your car in direct sunlight, you're just begging for streaks. Avoid this problem by sudsing up the sedan in the shade.

For special detail jobs, make yourself a little close-order tool kit. You'll need a small foam paintbrush, a medium-size bristle paint brush, and a few cotton swabs. Use these helpers to reach into the nooks and crannies of your dashboard, down into your cup holders, along seams in the upholstery, ledges and tiny surfaces of your knobs and radio display. If you can't whisk dirt out with a brush, dampen a cotton swab and use it like a liquid magnet. You'll have your car's interior ready for the white-glove inspection in no time!

See the road clearly

Even if you don't have time to wash the whole car, at least keep your windshield clean. A dirty windshield causes eye fatigue and can pose a safety hazard.

Want to get a like-new sparkle on that hazy windshield? Simply give it a good wash with white vinegar, rinse with water, and dry it off.

If your windshield has a tendency to fog up on the inside, try this simple solution. Keep a common blackboard eraser in your glove compartment. If your car's "defrost" setting won't do the trick, this little helper will wipe away the fog quick as a wink.

Your windshield isn't the only glass that needs a clear view. Headlights can collect dirt, mud, salt, snow, dead bugs, and other muck from the road. Any object stuck to your headlight reduces your ability to see the road, so keep those headlights clean and clutter-free.

Roadside trouble

Remember to keep your coolant

The most frequent cause of summertime breakdowns is overheating. Have your cooling system checked, flushed, and refilled every 24 months. Periodically check the level of coolant just to make sure you don't have a leak.

If your car begins to overheat in traffic, don't panic. Put it in neutral, then rev the engine a few times. This should get the coolant moving again. If this doesn't work, try running your heater at full blast.

This will push more of the heat away from your engine. You might want to roll your windows down first, though.

Membership has its privileges

Ever wanted to join a club? A motor club might be a good one to start with. Groups like AAA (American Automobile Association) offer roadside assistance to their members. Usually, all you have to do is call the club at an 800 number, and they will arrange for a tow, a jump start, or other minor services.

Shop around before you join. Check prices, and see what benefits each club offers. Often, memberships will be offered as promotional incentives to buy other products — tires, for instance, or cellular phones. If you are in the market for something like this, check out the possibility of getting an auto club membership out of the deal.

This little light of mine

Keep a pen light and a couple of rubber bands with your emergency tool kit. If you ever need to go under the hood at night, you can rubber band the light to whichever tool you're using, which is a lot easier than trying to balance a regular flashlight in your mouth or under your arm.

Map out your plans

It's always a good idea to plan ahead before you travel. Maps are pretty inexpensive and can save you time, trouble, and terrible headaches down the road. Always buy a map if you are traveling to a new area by car. But what about your hometown? If you live in a large urban area, it's likely you don't know your way around every neighborhood, so a few local maps are good to have along, just in case. You can photocopy local maps at

> ## Hang your maps out to dry
>
> If you want a real challenge, try getting a parking stub out of your pocket with your seat belt on. If you want to do it the easy way, snap a big clothespin on the visor over your steering wheel. It makes a convenient holder for parking stubs, toll tickets, maps, or that list of forgotten items you've gone back to the grocery store to get.

the library or out of the front of the local telephone book and keep them in your glove compartment.

Let your fingers do the driving

Want a great glove compartment reference? Try this little project. Go through an old telephone book, cutting out maps, emergency information, and important telephone numbers. Place these pages in a small folder and keep this reference file in your glove compartment.

How about this for useful recycling? If you've got the room and don't mind toting a little extra weight, why not throw last year's Yellow Pages in the trunk or back seat? You'll never be at a loss for a number when you're out on the town.

Drive like a Boy Scout: Be prepared

Other than gas, what's the most important thing to keep in your car at all times? An emergency kit. You can design your kit to contain whatever you think you'll need most often, but a few essentials should never be overlooked. Be sure to include:

- Spare tire
- Flashlight
- Tool kit
- Jumper cables
- Fire extinguisher
- Road flares
- Gallon of water
- First aid kit
- Blanket, towel
- Stand-up emergency reflectors
- Umbrella and waterproof parka

Customize your kit

A complete emergency kit cannot only save your life in a critical situation, it can also provide you with peace of mind from day to day, knowing that you are prepared for most anything. Of course, you should adapt your own kit to the needs of your car and your environment. If your car tends to overheat a lot, for instance, maybe you should carry a couple of gallons of water and extra coolant. If you drive in an area where there is often extreme weather, tuck away an extra set of dry, warm clothes.

Jump right in

You hope you'll never be in the situation where you have to jump-start your car. But if the worst happens, a little knowledge about the proper procedure can save you towing or service charges and possibly some expensive car damage. Here are the steps:

▶ Ask someone with a car engine larger than yours, if possible, to help you out. Line up the cars so the jumper cables can reach both batteries. Make sure the cars are not touching. Do not smoke or allow any open flame near the area.

▶ Start the car with the good battery, and let it idle.

▶ Connect the red (positive) cable to the positive terminal (the post with the "+" mark) on the idling car's battery. Then attach the black cable to the negative terminal. Make sure the jumper cable is not in the way of any moving parts.

▶ Holding the remaining metal clamps away from each other, hook the red one to the positive battery terminal in your car, and the black to the negative terminal. Be careful. If you make a mistake and hook a positive to a negative (called "reversed polarity") you could cause some serious and costly damage. Also, if you touch the metal clamps together, you'll cause severe sparking and could injure yourself.

▶ Try to start your car's engine. Once it's running, let your motor idle for a few minutes to recharge the battery, then disconnect the jumper cables.

▶ If your car won't start after a few tries, it's time to call for service.

Cold weather travel

Let it snow, let it snow, let it snow

After a good night's snowfall, the best way to clear away the flakes is with a broom. A tiny window scraper doesn't pack much muscle, and a snow shovel could easily scratch your windshield or paint job.

Keep a sawed-off broom in the trunk of your car for those heavy snow days, but keep an extra one in the house. After a really cold night, there's bound to be more than just snow on your car, and that sawed-off broom won't do you much good if the trunk is frozen shut and you can't get to it.

Just pop the cap

Caught in a snow drift with no shovel? Improvise. If you really need to dig yourself out – whether it's snow, sand, turf, or mud – simply pop a hubcap off one of your tires and set to work. It'll do surprisingly well in a pinch.

When it's OK to litter

If your car gets caught in the snow, sprinkling a little sand under your wheels can be a lifesaver. But sand is not always available, and it's heavy to carry around. Try a bag of cat litter instead. Cat litter is a very gritty substance that can give your tires some much-needed traction, and get you out of a tight winter spot.

A little idle gossip

If you simply have to idle your car in winter to warm it up, don't do it for more than five minutes, and always do it where there's plenty of ventilation. It's best never to idle your car in a garage that's attached to a house, because the carbon monoxide can creep inside without your knowing it. And never ever warm your car with the garage door closed.

Pull the curtain on Old Man Winter

Discouraging winter task number one – scraping off your frozen windshield every day. Make this morning chore nothing but a memory by using this crafty cover. Cut a shower curtain to fit the size and shape of your windshield. Sew magnets along the edges to keep it stuck to the car, and then place it over your windshield each night. No more early morning ice walls and hands too chilled to grip the wheel.

Weather or not

Remember to replace your windshield wipers during warm weather if you own the new kind of windshield wipers that have rubber coverings. The covers help prevent a build-up of snow or ice during cold weather, but they may cause unnecessary wear and tear on your windshield wiper motor because of their weight. It will serve your car better to take them off during hot weather.

Stick to it

Slush and melted snow can make your floor mats slide around so that they're not protecting your floor very much. Fix this problem by attaching Velcro strips to the corners of the mats. That way, they'll stick to the carpet and stay in place where you need them, but will still pull out easily for cleanup.

Buying a car

Why the lemon is nobody's favorite fruit

You're ready to buy that used car − it seems to run OK. But how do you know if it's actually a lemon? One way is to figure out if the car has ever been recalled by the manufacturer. To do this, simply copy down the VIN (vehicle identification number). A metal plate with this number is usually located somewhere on the dashboard. Have your local dealer

287

check the VIN; he can tell you if the car has ever been called in for major reworking or repairs. If it has, you might want to think twice about buying it.

Facing the man in the polyester suit

Most people fear buying cars, probably because of the unfortunate stereotype of the sleazy, dishonest car salesman. Whether or not this mythical creature has any basis in reality, there really is no reason for anyone to fear buying a car. All you have to do is take an informed, intelligent, no-nonsense approach to the process. If you feel you are being treated with anything short of total honesty and fairness, simply walk out and take your business elsewhere.

Your secret weapon

There is one golden rule of car buying, and you should always keep it in mind. The salesman's greatest fear is that you will get up and walk out without buying a car. For this reason, the willingness to do so is your greatest strength. Never forget that you carry this powerful weapon. But you also must be willing to use it, if necessary. If a salesman thinks you are going to leave, he will usually do most anything to get you not to, like lowering the price of the car.

Don't get stuck with the sticker price

When you're in a showroom, don't pay too much attention to the sticker price of a car. The sticker reflects the MSRP (manufacturer's suggested retail price), which is what the car manufacturer thinks the car should sell for. Most cars are sold for much less than what appears on the sticker, so don't be too impressed if your dealer offers you a "great deal" just under the MSRP.

Dealing with dealers

The factory invoice price is an important number to find out. This figure reflects what the dealer actually paid for the car, and it is the same for all dealers. It is not their actual cost, however, so even if you paid this price, the dealer would still make money. There are dealer hold-backs and incentives in place that allow the dealer to haggle with smart shoppers. Because it can be pretty tough to keep all these figures straight in your head, the best way to go about buying a new car is to get prices from several different dealers. If a dealer thinks he's in competition with other car dealerships, he's much more likely to give you a competitive price.

Hold your ground

Very little is hard and fast in the car-selling business. If the salesman believes he has to deal and dicker with you, he will do that. If you are calm, well-informed, and willing to walk away at any time, he will recognize you as a smart customer and treat you accordingly.

Fix your car for free

More than 500 secret automobile warranties are deliberately being kept from the public, according to the Center for Auto Safety (CAS) in Washington, D.C. These warranties cover defects in specific cars that the manufacturer knew about – but didn't necessarily tell you about – when you bought the car. And the manufacturer should fix those problems for free. Why are these valuable warranties kept secret? Because, in all but four states, there are no laws requiring the automaker to tell you about them. That's where the Center for Auto Safety comes in. The Center is a nonprofit organization that fights for your rights as a consumer. They have a record of every secret warranty out there and will gladly share this information with you whether your car's gone kaput or not.

To find out if your car company is keeping secrets, check the CAS website at <www.autosafety.org> or send a self-addressed, business-size envelope (stamped with 55 cents postage) to CAS Consumer Packets, 2001 S Street NW, Washington, D.C. 20009. Include a note that lists the year, make, and model of the car as well as a description of the problem your car is having (if any).

If you discover that your car's problem is covered by a secret warranty, talk to your dealer, show him the report, and ask him to fix it for free. If your dealer refuses, call the manufacturer's customer service number.

If you feel you haven't been treated fairly, contact The Center for Auto Safety for additional assistance. Or try one of the car manufacturing customer service numbers listed below. You may have more coming to you than you think.

Buick	1-800-521-7300	Nissan	1-800-647-7261
Cadillac	1-800-458-8006	Oldsmobile	1-800-442-6537
Chevrolet	1-800-222-1020	Pontiac	1-800-762-2737
Ford	1-800-392-3673	Saturn	1-800-553-6000
GMC	1-800-462-8782	Toyota	1-800-331-4331
Lincoln	1-800-521-4140		

Car insurance

Play the policy game

One of your biggest expenses as a car owner is automobile insurance. It's almost never cheap, and there are so many companies and policies out there, it can seem impossible to figure out just what you need and just what to pay. Every day, thousands of people pay too much for their car insurance. So shop around. There's usually a wide range of prices for similar policies. Don't get stuck with a company just because you're used to it or because it has a famous name. Check out the competition, too.

Look smart behind the wheel

Buy a sensible car, not a flashy one. Low profile cars are less likely to get stolen, less expensive to repair, and less expensive to maintain. So guess what? That's right, they're almost always less expensive to insure.

It pays to get that 'A'

Look for discounts. Most insurance companies offer discounts for safety features, those that are built into the car and those that come with the driver. Having air bags, automatic seat belts, or anti-lock brakes can often get you a better rate. Driver-based incentives often include reductions for low annual mileage and good student discounts.

Watch for overlap

Check your health insurance against your car insurance to make sure you're not paying twice for the same coverage. If you're covered for certain auto injuries by your health policy, you might want to drop similar provisions from your car insurance.

The gamble of the confident man

If you consider yourself a low-risk driver, consider raising your deductible. The higher your deductible, the lower your rate. Of course, you'll pay more if you have to file a claim, but for safe drivers, the trade-off is sometimes worth the risk.

Sentimental value doesn't count

Don't go overboard. If you drive an old or inexpensive car, don't buy too much insurance for it. Insure an older car only for what it is worth. Why pay more for potential repairs to a car that would be less expensive to simply replace?

LAWN AND GARDEN

The war on weeds

Quick tips for using herbicides

The first step in fighting weeds is to know your enemy. Get a county extension agent to help you identify the weeds in your yard, or get a field guide to common weeds and grasses and identify them yourself. Then follow these simple steps for killing weeds:

▶ Pick an herbicide that is right for your particular weeds.

▶ Always wear protective clothing, safety glasses, and gloves when you apply herbicides.

▶ Use weed killers on days when the wind is not blowing.

▶ Don't mow your lawn just before or just after applying herbicides.

The soda bottle technique

When you're applying herbicide to individual weeds, you want to keep it off everything else growing nearby. So try this idea to make your herbicide stay put. Cut off the bottom of a plastic two-liter soda

bottle. Put the bottle over the weed you want to kill. Insert the spray nozzle of your chemical sprayer or garden hose into the top of the soda bottle and spray away. Wait a few seconds for the chemical to soak in, then move on to the next weed.

Can you dig it?

If you have a problem with perennial weeds, don't try to kill them with a rototiller. All you'll really do is break up their root system and give their runners a chance to spread. It's a lot of work to dig them up, but if you have the patience, it's as effective as herbicides. You just have to do it carefully and thoroughly. An old apple corer does a good job of digging up weeds. It will dig down deep and cut the roots at the same time.

How low can you mow?

Take care not to mow your lawn too closely. If you cut it too short, too much sunlight will reach the soil surface and help weed seeds to germinate.

6 ways to deep-six weeds

▶ Maintain your lawn with regular feeding, watering, and mowing.

▶ In flower beds, use a mulch that's two to four inches deep to help prevent weed seeds from germinating.

▶ Plant shrubs in dense groupings and seed over your grass to choke out weeds.

▶ Don't water too much; give just the amount needed according to what's planted.

▶ Remove weeds from root balls of trees and potted plants that you bring into your yard.

▶ When you see a weed, carefully take it out by hand, roots and all.

Natural weed warfare

Weeds can often be killed, at least temporarily, by boiling water. Just heat up the tea kettle, take it outside, and pour generous amounts directly on the weeds. Another easy, earth-friendly method of weed control is to pour vinegar and salt directly over bothersome weeds.

Countdown to a weed-free lawn

▶ In spring, apply a pre-emergent herbicide before weeds start to grow. It's time to do this when the dogwoods are in bloom.

▶ In summer, check to see what weeds survived your initial attack. Apply more or different herbicides on individual weeds or pull them by hand.

Petroleum product alert

Don't be tempted to use gasoline or kerosene to kill weeds. You'll poison your soil and the local water table.

▶ In fall, after your final trip around the yard with the mower, do one more application of a general weed killer. Pull up by hand any weeds that slipped through your defenses.

▶ Next year, you should have a weed-free lawn!

Handle with care

If you use herbicides or pesticides in your yard, you'll have to be very careful not to contaminate yourself or your clothing. Always wear a long-sleeve shirt and long pants, protective eyewear, and gloves. If you do get any spray on your clothes, you'll need to wash them separately from the rest of your laundry. Don't handle them with your bare hands – wear rubber gloves. Keep the clothes in a plastic bag until you can wash them. Use the presoak cycle and then do a regular wash cycle with liquid detergent and hot water. Dry the clothes on the clothesline to let the sun and wind help finish the cleaning process.

Flying and crawling pests

Organic pest control

You can make a natural pesticide with the rhubarb leaves left over from making fresh rhubarb pie. Cut up the leaves and boil them for about an hour. Cool and strain the liquid and add it to a spray bottle. Then spray it on your plants for natural pest control. Never use this spray on herbs, fruits, or vegetables, since rhubarb leaves are poisonous to people, too.

Smoky solution

Get rid of mealybugs around your plants with this nasty brew. Soak the leftover tobacco from cigarette butts in water, then use it to water the plants.

Sweet treat has bugs beat

If you're having trouble with ants, roaches, and other outdoor bugs coming into your home, try this remedy. In a disposable container, mix borax and sweetened condensed milk, using a plastic spoon or knife. Put on rubber or plastic gloves and roll small globs of the mixture to form sticky little balls. Put these around your house's foundation, doors, windows, basement entrances, and crawl space. Pesky insects will think they've found a tasty treat – and you won't be bothered with them again. Be sure to dispose of the container, plastic spoon, and gloves, and keep this homemade poison away from pets and children.

Get 'em with garlic

Repel aphids with this "terrible tea." Mince two cloves of garlic and put in a jar with a pint of boiling water. After cooling, strain out the garlic and put the remaining liquid in a spray bottle. Spray new shoots and flower buds to protect them from aphid assaults.

Slug solutions

Here's a sure cure for those nasty slugs that slime through your garden at night. Put some jar lids or other shallow containers here and there in your garden and fill them with beer. Next morning, carry a small bucket out to the garden and dispose of the slugs in warm, soapy water. Each night fill the lids again with beer until your slug problem subsides.

Epsom salts is a substance that's toxic to slugs. Try sprinkling it lightly around their favorite plants to keep them away. Just watch out for any signs of leaf burn from using too much. The magnesium in the salt is good for your soil but will build up over time and can damage plants.

Collect egg shells and crush them finely. Then sprinkle them on the ground near the base of the plants the slugs are attacking. They don't like the feel of the sharp, prickly shell fragments and will leave the area alone.

Sunny side up

Here's a great way to get rid of earwigs and woodlice. Grow one of the giant varieties of sunflowers with the really big heads. Once the birds are finished with them, lay the flower heads on the ground anywhere you have dead plants, branches, or leaves. The bugs will be attracted to the sunflowers. Let them sit for a few days and then throw away the sunflower heads, bugs and all.

Bug-busting combinations

When you're planning your next garden, consider these "companion plantings" to help keep down the bug population:

▶ Plant radishes with your squash plants to keep away squash bugs.

▶ Marigolds repel aphids, Colorado potato beetles, whiteflies, and even rabbits.

▶ Grow basil around your eggplants and tomatoes to keep away pests.

▶ Try sage, rosemary, and thyme with cabbage to repel cabbage worms.

▶ Onions keep bugs away from beets.

'Companions' help each other out

The practice of growing certain plants together started long ago, before there were any ready-made chemical treatments for the garden. Native Americans planted corn, squash, and runner beans together. The squash leaves provided shade, tall corn acted as stakes for the beans to grow on, and the beans added nitrogen to the soil to benefit the other plants.

Flowers and herbs are often used for companion planting. When they are planted together, the scent of some blossoms and the aromatic oils in certain herbs repel insects from nearby fruit and vegetable plants. Whatever their special relationship, companion plantings make it easier to grow an abundant, healthy garden without the use of harmful chemicals.

▶ Borage will defend your tomatoes against the dreaded tomato horn worm.

▶ Garlic will keep aphids away from almost anything.

Cats on patrol

When birds are becoming a nuisance around the garden or in your fruit trees, attract your cats to the area by planting catnip – the birds will seek out safer ground.

Sneaky snake trick

Discourage birds from taking up residence in your garden or yard by creating a "snake" with some garden hose. Cut a section about six feet long and paint it with a bright pattern and two beady eyes. Wrap it around a nearby fence post or lay it out on the open ground; they'll get the idea pretty quickly that it's not a friendly environment, and they'll move on.

Four-legged pests

Get rid of rodents

Is your garden overrun with pesky mice? Make them an offer they can't refuse: put pumpkin seeds in your mousetraps for bait. Mice can't resist this yummy treat.

Recycled repellent

Try this trick for getting rid of moles. Dig up one of their tunnels and plug it up with cat litter. Fresh litter will do the job, but used litter might make a more lasting impression.

Turn up the heat on garden pests

Teach rodents to stay out of your vegetable garden with a mixture of one gallon of water and three ounces of cayenne pepper. Mix it up and pour it over the plants you want to protect.

Hit them with your best shot

A sure-fire way to shoo the neighbor's cat from your yard: Get one of the long-range water guns and fill it with a solution of water plus a tablespoon or so of vinegar. If the cat strays into your yard, spray him with the water gun. Most cats really don't like to get wet, and the smell of vinegar discourages them even more.

Cats won't cross this line

If cats are on the prowl in your garden and using it for a litter box, here's a safe, natural trick to try. Surround your plants with a border of orange peels and used coffee grounds to keep cats out.

'Hot' dog repellent

Trouble with the neighbor's dog urinating on your lovely plants and shrubs? Keep him away by whipping up a batch of this naturally pungent brew. Drop a few cloves of garlic and hot peppers (the hotter the better) in a blender and puree them. Add a little water and pour this concoction around the edge of the area you want to protect. Dogs will get the message and stay away.

Smelly soap scares away strangers

Hotel-sized bars of soap or left-over pieces of used soap bars can keep deer out of your yard or garden. Hang soap bars from a string or just place them in trees, as close to ground level as possible, to work as a repellent. Informal studies show that fragrant soap bars scare away deer because the smell disturbs them and may warn then that a predator is near. The soap repellent seems to work best under wet conditions rather than during dry weather.

Beautifying the garden

Barter with buds and branches

Look around your yard. Maybe you have too many of one kind of plant and not enough of another. If you live in a big neighborhood where lots of people have gardens, you might want to organize a "plant exchange" day. Have everyone bring extra plants, trees, and shrubs and swap for other plants they would like to have. Encourage even swapping to cut down on money handling. Kids can make some extra pocket money by starting their own seedlings to swap or sell at the event. You'll improve your garden and your neighborhood for almost no cost at all.

Simple stepping stones

Here's an inexpensive and easy way to make your own garden stepping stones. Use any kind of plastic or disposable container about a foot in diameter, such as a frozen food container or a plastic bucket, then follow these steps:

▶ Put a thin layer of petroleum jelly on the inside surface of the container.

▶ Mix up a bag of concrete according to package directions in your wheel barrow.

▶ Using a small bucket or plastic cup for a ladle, fill each container about two inches deep. Stir the concrete gently to get rid of air bubbles, and smooth over the top.

The shade-tree gardener

Under most conditions, grass doesn't grow well under large trees. Instead of struggling with unwilling grass, try something different that will spruce up your yard and keep down your frustration level. Shade-tolerant plants like hostas, ferns, columbine, and impatiens, and vines like ivy and periwinkle will fill in those bare areas under your trees with color and texture that grass just can't match.

▶ After an hour or so, add decorative touches like trinkets, stones, writing, or leaf imprints.

▶ Let the concrete set up for a couple of days before removing your stepping stones from the containers.

Measured moisture

Here's a technique that will make your flowers look like they've just been watered even in the toughest drought. Take a gallon milk jug and cut off the bottom. Punch some holes in the sides and in the cap. Turn it upside down and plunge it into the ground a few inches from your plants, preferably hidden in the back row of the flower bed or behind a larger plant. In large beds, space the jugs about 12 inches apart. Fill the jug with water every couple of days. It will slowly dispense the water and spread it evenly throughout the soil. You won't have to water with the hose, and there will be less waste from evaporation and runoff. If you don't have any extra milk jugs around, you can use old coffee cans.

Attract beautiful butterflies to your garden

If you want to enhance the beauty of your garden with the presence of butterflies, plant stinging nettles in an unused corner of the garden. Butterflies will light there to lay their eggs.

Free fertilizers

A 'mulch' better way to mow

If you use a "mulching mower," your mower is designed to pulverize the grass clippings and fallen leaves and spread them back over your yard to recycle nutrients. If you have a regular mower, you either use a bagger to catch the debris or you may rake it up after mowing. Either way, yard wastes are a ready source of natural nutrients like nitrogen, so don't throw those grass clippings away! Let the grass fall as you mow it, spread the clippings over your lawn, or let them become free fertilizer in your compost pile.

Clip, collect, and compost

Compost enriches and conditions your soil and gives you a great way to recycle some of your yard and kitchen waste. You can start a compost pile with a variety of different organic materials, like leaves, grass clippings, animal manure. You can buy a fancy

---

Things you should never put in your compost pile

Animal meat or fat scraps, cooked or raw

Raw potatoes or potato peels

Animal bones, skin, cartilage, knuckles, or organs

Dairy products like cheese, milk, ice cream, butter, margarine

Garlic cloves

Animal or vegetable food scraps that contain butter, margarine, sauces, seasonings, marinades, or glazes

---

composting bin, but with just a pile of grass clippings and a pitchfork, you can make all the compost you want. Simply add the tough outer leaves of lettuce and cabbage, those nectarines that spoiled in your vegetable bin, the dried-out carrots from your sack lunch. You can use an empty flower bed or any space in your yard where you can bury organic scraps. Set up a composting system and your yard and kitchen scraps will turn into "black gold," food for your flowers and vegetables.

Mighty manure

A good material for composting in your garden is farm animal manure. Check your local area for farms that might give you free manure if you're willing to haul it away. Manure is high in nitrogen, one of the three most important nutrients for anything you grow. Horse manure is highest in nitrogen, followed by chicken and then pig manure. Chicken manure will cause a gradual buildup of salt in your compost or soil, so don't use it for too long in one place.

Hairy helper

Even better than manure, human hair is a rich source of nitrogen for your garden plants. If you have a friend in a barber shop or hair salon, see if she will collect hair trimmings for you. Spread them on loose garden dirt and work them well into the soil. This will also help keep deer from foraging in your garden.

Seed starters

After you finish the donuts ...

Don't spend good money on expensive seed starter kits at the gardening center. They're just fancy plastic. You can make a very simple "mini-greenhouse" for starting seeds with recycled plastic containers from baked goods. Find one that is clear plastic and has a hinged top. Open it up and fill both sides with seed starter mix if you want, or use just the bottom and close the lid to retain moisture. Look for this bonus product next time you buy baked goods from your grocery.

Egg-cellent seed starter

Another ideal seed starting container: empty egg shells. Put seed starting medium in half of an eggshell, plant your seed, and put the shell back in the carton.

Place the carton in a sunny window. When the seedling is ready to plant, crack the shell in several places and put it directly in the garden soil for a nutritional boost for the growing plant.

Window treatment

Got a spare sunny window, a sponge, and a plate? Then all you need are some seeds and water, and you can start a garden. Just wet the sponge and put it on the plate, spread out the seeds evenly on the sponge, and put the plate in the sunny window. Keep the sponge damp by frequently adding water. As soon as your seedlings have a nice healthy root and

Give seedlings a bubbly boost

Here's a cheap and simple starter solution for your seedlings: Mix a teaspoon of baby shampoo into a quart of water and use this mixture regularly to water seed trays and peat pots. The mixture keeps the soil surface soft and moist so seedlings can break through easily.

baby leaves, pot them up in peat pots to get ready for life in the garden.

A warm, cozy spot

A good place to keep your seed trays is on top of your refrigerator, where it's a constant 70 to 75 degrees. Keep the trays in this cozy environment to help seeds sprout sooner. On cloudy days and at night, keep already-sprouted seedlings up there for an added boost before transplanting outdoors.

Kinder, gentler watering

Once your seedlings are up and growing, they may look vigorous but they're really still fragile. Don't pour water from a pitcher or watering can directly on them. Instead, use the "bottom-up" method of watering. When planting seeds in individual planting cells, leave one cell empty near the center and always pour your water in it. It will slowly dispense the water into the tray underneath, and it will gradually spread throughout the soil to all the seedlings. If you're using a recycled food container without cells, just don't plant any seeds right in the center of the container and add water there.

Preserve and protect your plants

Once your little seedlings have been planted, they are much more vulnerable to the elements and to garden pests. You can use recycled pint-size cherry tomato or strawberry baskets to protect newly planted seeds in the garden. Just push them down into the soil over a planted seed. You can also recycle your old plastic milk jugs as seedling and transplant protectors. Just cut off the bottom of the jug and remove the cap. Press the jug down into the soil over your tender young plants. These plastic "dome homes" help retain heat and protect plants from the elements while they're getting established.

Cost-cutting techniques

Think big

Many local nurseries will give you a sizable price break if you buy a large number of the same plant. Consider this before designing a garden full of individual specimens. It will also greatly simplify upkeep if you have large plantings of the same species.

Pasta for your plants

Don't dump out that water from the pot when you cook noodles or potatoes. Instead, let it cool off, take it outside to the garden, and pour it on your plants. They'll love the starchy boost of nutrition.

A spot of tea

Recycle used tea bags as seed starters. Cut a tiny slit on one side, put in a seed, and "plant" the tea bag in a peat pot. Keep it moist until the seed sprouts and is ready to transplant. Then mix the leftover tea leaves from the bag into the soil of a houseplant or potted plant. Ferns especially love tea.

There's always room for fertilizer

Got a spare box of unflavored gelatin in the pantry? Keep it around to fertilize your plants. Just mix up one envelope in a quart of water and douse your houseplants or garden for a healthy nitrogen boost.

Stake your claim

Locate a local stand of bamboo and cut some stalks to use as stakes for tender, long-stemmed plants. The bamboo looks much better than metal poles or strings, and is sturdy enough to last for several seasons.

Don't hose away your garden budget

Those plastic garden-hose holders are nice but costly, especially when you can make one for free. Instead of giving away your tire rim (the metal part that holds the rubber tire) next time you get a new tire, save that rim! Your garden hose will curl up nicely around the rim, and will unroll easily without tangling. Hang one on the wall near the spigot. You can even paint it to match your house. Your hose is easier to use, and you can spend that money elsewhere.

Another inexpensive way to store your garden hose is to use a sturdy, metal, five-gallon bucket. Mount the bottom securely to the side of your house or shed, with the open end facing outward, and wrap the hose around it. Use the inside of the bucket to store hose nozzles, fertilizer sprayers, and garden gloves.

Much mulch for free

For free mulch, check your local landfill or a tree removal service. Many communities now have facilities that create mulch from yard debris and give it away. If yours doesn't, call a tree removal service. These companies have to pay to unload debris at dumps, so they will be happy to let you have it. With a chipper/shredder machine, you can turn the stumps and branches into usable mulch. Even if you have to rent a chipper/shredder for the day, you can create a mountain of mulch for a fraction of the cost of mulch you buy in bags.

Save those last few veggies

Don't want to waste the last of your vegetable crop as the frost approaches? Put some aluminum foil on the ground under them to speed up ripening.

Seed survival secrets

If you find an old packet of seeds lying around, try this test to see if they are still usable. Moisten a paper towel and spread the seeds out in a single layer. Lay another moist paper towel on top. Gently put the whole thing in a plastic bag and leave it alone for three days. Then open up the bag and see what has happened. If only one-third of them have germinated, throw them away. If roughly half have germinated, go ahead and use them but plant the seeds close together. If three-fourths have germinated, plant them as usual.

Share and share alike

Share tools with your neighbors and they'll share with you. Maybe you need a special hoe that your neighbor has, and he needs a fertilizer spreader that you own. Work out a tool exchange with neighbors who garden and you won't have to buy so many expensive gardening tools.

Aid for failing ferns

Here's an inexpensive tonic for your ferns: mix one tablespoon of castor oil and one tablespoon of baby shampoo into two pints of lukewarm water. Give your fern about three tablespoons of tonic, then give it a drink of plain water. Your plant should be perky soon.

Flowerpots for free

If you drink your milk from waxed cardboard cartons, you have a free source of flowerpots. Rinse the
carton well and cut off the top half. Cut slits in the
bottom of the carton or snip off a little of the corners
for drainage. Add soil and your plant.

For starting seedlings or small plants in your garden,
another free alternative to purchased pots is papier
mâché pots that you make your-
self. Mix up some flour-and-water
paste (don't use commercial glue)
by adding one-fourth cup of water
to one-half cup of flour and mixing
until it's smooth. Gather some
newspaper and a drinking glass.
Turn the glass upside down and
paste short strips of newspaper
about one and one-half inches
wide to the bottom half of the
glass, covering it to form a pot
shape. You may want to add one
or two more layers of newsprint to
make a sturdy container. When the
paper is completely dry, remove the glass and add
the soil and the plant. Put the papier mâché pot
directly into the ground. It will protect your seedling
while it gradually disintegrates into the garden soil.

> ### Low-cost landscaping
>
> Check out local agricul-
> tural colleges for students
> of landscape design or
> horticulture. They might
> be willing to come to
> your home for free or a
> reduced cost and design
> a garden scheme for you.

Stay sharp

One way to make new plants from existing ones is to
make cuttings. Just be sure that you use a very clean,
sharp knife. Anything less may cause a nasty wound

on the plant that could become infected and harm both the "mother" plant and the "baby" plants.

Height does not make right

Don't waste your money choosing the wrong plants from the nursery. Though they might catch your eye first, tall "leggy" plants with flowers aren't the best choice. Instead, look for plants with bushier, thicker growth and fewer flowers. The bushier ones will get established faster and will probably have more blooms later on.

Re-tire in your garden

Instead of investing all the money and time in constructing raised beds to grow melons and other vine plants, just collect some old tires and make smaller, round versions of the same thing. Cut the sidewall off one side of the tire, lay it on your garden soil with the cut side down, and fill it with rich compost or soil. Plant your vine seedlings inside and they'll grow quicker in the warmer environment created by the tire. In far northern areas, this trick may make it possible to enjoy melons in areas where the growing season is really too short.

Give 'em a fighting chance

When you buy plants from a nursery or greenhouse, remember that they've been in a very special environment with optimum light and food. Don't just set them out right away and expect them to start growing. Give them a week or so in a sheltered place where they can adapt to outdoor life, and gradually move them to where you'll be planting them. They'll have a much better chance of survival.

Know your zone

Before you let yourself fall in love with a particular shrub or flower, make sure you live in the right part of the country to grow it. You'll waste money and effort on cold-loving plants if you expect them to survive the heat of the Deep South, and plants meant for hot climates won't survive New England winters. Many plant catalogs and seed packets give information on appropriate growing zones. Double-check this information so you don't put the right plant in the wrong place.

Small-space gardening

Double-duty dirt

When you have very little space to plant your tulips and crocuses, try planting them in the same space. Plant the tulip bulbs eight inches deep and the crocus bulbs four inches deep, above the tulips. The crocuses will come up as usual and a few weeks later so will the tulips, keeping the garden colorful and thick with growth.

Portable planting

If you live in an apartment, you can still grow vegetables and herbs – just grow them in containers. Pie tins and other lightweight baking pans make simple, inexpensive planters for shallow rooted plants like herbs and strawberries. As the seasons go by and the sunlight changes on your patio or porch, you can move the containers to take best advantage of the light and warmth. Growing even a few vegetables and herbs will save you money and give you food of the highest quality.

Planters with pizzazz

Looking for inexpensive but creative garden planters? Try these creative substitutes:

▶ Cinder blocks laid on their sides

▶ Tin cans with holes punched in the bottoms

▶ An old bathtub with a working drain opening

▶ A used wheelbarrow with a few rust holes

▶ An old pair of shoes sprayed with outdoor paint

Baby seed sitters

To start tomato plants, sprinkle a few seeds in the soil of your houseplants. The mature plants will shelter the tiny ones, and when you water you'll be nourishing both at the same time. When they're ready to make it on their own, remove the seedlings gently and replant them.

Be wise to size

When choosing planters for container gardening, be sure to consider how heavy the object will be when it's full of moist soil and plants. Think small and light. If it's too big or heavy, it may become impossible to move once it's home to a plant. If your heart is set on a barrel or other large, heavy container, place it on a wagon or platform with wheels before planting it so you can move it when you need to.

Smaller means drier

Remember that the smaller the flowerpot or planter, the more often you'll need to water your plants. It helps to use saucers underneath pots or gather several small pots together on a tray filled with pebbles. The tray or saucer should be able to hold an inch or so of water.

Trees and shrubs

Planting pointers

Buy the largest tree you can, preferably five to eight feet tall, for the best chance of survival. When you get the tree home, soak the root ball for about eight to 10 hours. Dig the planting hole a little deeper than the root ball so that it can start to grow quickly. Make the hole about two feet wider than the root ball.

After the tree is in the ground and the soil has been packed in around it, make a small mound of extra soil in a circle about two to three feet out from the trunk. This will help prevent ground water runoff in rain storms and while watering.

Mulch the area around, but not touching, the trunk to help prevent runoff and protect the tree's roots from hot sun. Check on the availability of cypress mulch in your area – it has the added benefit of discouraging insects.

Sapling secrets

Don't prune saplings (young trees) for the first few years. They need all their leaves at first to get enough food to build a strong root system.

Keep your sapling stable by staking it. This will help it grow straight. Staking kits are available at lawn and garden stores, or you can use old pantyhose and tent stakes.

Keep your saplings shapely

Lawn mowers and string trimmers can permanently scar the bark and alter the growth of your young tree, so protect it with a tree girdle. You can get one from a lawn and garden store, or you can make one with an old rubber shower mat or a thick, rubber-backed bath mat. Just wrap the mat around the trunk at ground level, secure it with a piece of string, and mow your lawn or use your string trimmer near it. Then you can untie the tree girdle and move it to the next tree.

Defeat a drought

When the heat of summer sets in, there are often long periods without rain. Be sure to mulch well around your trees to cut down on weeds and slow down the process of evaporation. When you water, don't just dampen the top layer of soil, or you'll risk injury to the roots near the surface. Water well and deeply about once a week.

Prune when the time is right

For the healthiest bushes and shrubs, don't start pruning until late in the spring when you see at least a few inches of new growth. You might even want to wait until early summer. Evergreen bushes and shrubs prefer a June pruning. In the fall, stop pruning at least six weeks before the usual date of the first frost.

Shrubs that bloom in the fall like to be pruned in the spring. Likewise, those that bloom in the spring like to be pruned in the fall. Exceptions are those plants that bloom on last year's growth, such as lilacs.

Don't prune your lilacs after the Fourth of July. By that time, they've started forming flower heads for the next year. If you prune, you'll cut them off and won't see any of next year's blooms.

Ship-shape shears

Always use freshly sharpened shears or clippers when pruning hedges. Dull blades can lead to split or broken branches and can open the door to diseases and pests.

Rose-saving secret

If you're tired of watching the Japanese beetles devour your lovely floribunda and grandiflora rosebuds in midsummer, try this trick. Go ahead and enjoy the first flush of late spring blossoms, then give them a good trimming. Though you'll miss them for a couple of months, by September they'll start blooming again without danger from the beetles. An added bonus: this technique also controls black spot disease, which also tends to strike at midsummer. But don't try this clever trick on roses that bloom on old wood, like climbers, because it will remove the very branches where blooms would form.

Watch the edges of those hedges

Trim your hedges in a pyramid shape, leaving them a little wider at the bottom than the top. If you trim away too much at the bottom, the lower branches won't get enough light and will get scraggly looking.

Just a trim, please

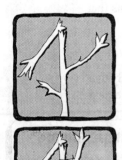

Most hedges and shrubs should be pruned about once a month. However, some appreciate even more frequent shaping up. Privet, hemlock, holly, juniper, and boxwoods can all be pruned more often with good results.

Follow the leader

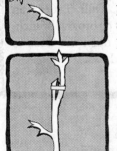

If the leader (the central growing point) of a young tree in your yard is damaged by a storm, you may be able to save it with a couple of simple tools. Take some electrical tape and create a new leader by bending the nearest healthy branch up toward the damaged leader and tape it in place. Leave the tape on for the rest of the year. The new leader will start to grow up and will eventually take over the job. Then the next spring, prune the damaged leader just below the tape.

Lawn care

Become a collector

If you're aggravated by litter, pine cones, and other debris that gets in the way while you're mowing, don't just throw it out of the way. Instead, try this tip. Tie a heavy-duty garbage bag to the handle or push bar of your mower. Whenever you see a piece of trash or debris, just pick it up and pop it in the bag. It saves the time and trouble of going back to pick it up later.

Many holes in one

Don't throw out your old golf shoes – they make great soil aerators! Just wear them every time you mow, prune, or clean up. The tiny holes they punch in your yard let rain, nutrients, and air down into compacted soil. Here's a great item to buy at a yard sale if you don't already have some.

Let them drink tea

If you need to spot seed a couple of places in your lawn, give the seeds a boost by soaking them in tea in the refrigerator for a day or two. Let them dry out on paper towels, then spread them as usual.

Let 'em lie

Old-fashioned push mowers would let the grass fall where it was cut. Then someone decided that grass clippings should be vacuumed up like dirt from carpet, and bagging mowers became popular. Now the

Water well

It's time to water your lawn when can see your footprints where you just walked across it. If your lawn is healthy and well-watered, it will spring back immediately after you walk on it. Never water your lawn in the heat of the afternoon sun. Always do it in the morning or late evening when the evaporation rate is lowest.

pendulum has swung back to the old way again. Instead of bagging your grass clippings, let them stay on the lawn. They will provide insulation from the heat, hold in the moisture, and provide nutrients as they decay.

Oh, my aching back!

If mowing is starting to wear you out, consider a native grass rather than a high-maintenance turf lawn. Buffalo grass grows well in warm Southern states; it only needs mowing a couple of times a year and requires very little water.

The lawn ranger

Self-taught mechanic and lifelong tinkerer Bill Desch has owned the same lawnmower since 1985. And it still runs like new. His secret? He treats his mower right. "Preventive maintenance is the key to a long life for anything with a motor," says Bill. "If you take care of your tools, they'll take care of you."

Babying your lawnmower is as simple as an annual check-up. Each spring, Bill changes his mower's oil, installs a new filter, and makes sure the plugs are still in good firing order. "And sharpen the blade," he adds. "It wears down just like anything else."

Even if you don't have Bill's mechanical ability, you can always find a repair shop that will tune up your mower, usually for about $25. And your mower will thank you for it – the engine will last longer and perform better.

Gardening tools

Brighten it up

It's easy to misplace your small garden tools when you're working in the yard. Paint the handles of your garden tools a bright color, like yellow or hot pink, so they'll be easier to find if you lay them down in tall grass and shrubs. No more replacing lost tools!

Wheelbarrow woes

Why is the tire on your wheelbarrow always going flat? Because most of the time wheelbarrows are fitted with tubeless tires. They stay on the rim by the pressure of the inflated tire. But if the tire gets a puncture from going over a bump or landing too hard, it goes flat in a hurry. And it's next to impossible to reinflate at home with a bike pump. The solution? Get a tire inner tube at the hardware store or home center. There are tubes made specifically for wheelbarrow-size tires. Inflate it properly and it may last longer than the wheelbarrow.

Slick, quick, pruning shears

Before you start pruning, give your shears a spritz of vegetable oil spray. Plant sap will wipe right off when you're finished pruning.

Infection protection

Just like people, plants can get infections that make them sick. It's especially easy to spread problems from

No-rust sand trap

Trowels and other small gardening tools will scar and rust quickly with frequent use. Here's how to prevent the problem. Fill a small bucket with sand and a quarter cup or so of motor oil. Each time you use your tools, clean them off and then stick them down in the sand. Store tools this way and they'll last years longer.

one plant to another when you're cutting into them with pruning shears. Regularly clean your pruning shears with a solution of 10 parts water to one part bleach to prevent the spread of disease.

What's at stake?

Tie up fragile plants in your garden with plastic-coated wire such as telephone cable. It won't deteriorate like string or cloth, and it's kinder to soft plant stems. An even gentler, stretchier tie is cassette tape – so recycle your next tape that breaks for garden duty.

For a kinder, gentler way to stake tomato plants and other tender vines, cut the legs off old pantyhose, and tie up the branches. The stretchable fabric will give as the plant grows and gets heavier with fruit or flowers.

Dig soap instead of dirt

Digging the garden dirt out from under your nails is one job that there's no good tool for. So how do you prevent it? Gently dig your nails into a bar of soft soap before you go gardening. The soap will block dirt from getting under your nails and you won't look like you've been digging in the garden.

PETS

A lifelong playmate

Choose the perfect puppy

When checking out a puppy for a pet, first take him to a quiet place and put him down on the floor. The dog will probably freeze at first, which is perfectly normal. Before too long, though, he should begin to explore and get friendly. If the animal never moves from its initial spot, or tries to hide or run you down, keep looking. After gently petting the puppy, stand up and walk around the room. A friendly dog will follow you. If the dog wanders off as you pet him or is only friendly for a second, he may be too aloof.

Uh, what's up doc?

A rabbit can be a good pet if it's healthy and well-cared for. Follow these tips to find one that you can enjoy for a long time:

▶ Make sure the rabbit is alert and active. The rabbit should come to the front of the cage when you open the door.

▶ Beware of a listless look. The eyes should be bright, the nose dry. The front paws shouldn't be matted – that's a sign the rabbit has a cold.

▶ Rabbit droppings should be hard and round. If not, the rabbit may have stomach problems.

▶ Rabbit ears should be clean.

▶ Stroke the fur from the rump toward the head. The fur should quickly return to its original position.

▶ Examine the teeth. Upper front teeth should barely overlap the tips of the lower front teeth. If the teeth overlap too much, the rabbit will have trouble eating.

Creative play time

What interesting, amusing things occupy your puppy's time? They can be the key to finding an inexpensive toy for your playful pet. Does he like to chew or carry around bones? Try cutting a piece of hard plastic tubing from the hardware store as a replacement. Is tug-of-war the game of choice? Many rubber belts from the hardware store will work well for the wrestling match. The replacement items will probably last much longer than expensive, store-bought toys.

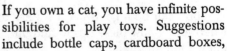

If you own a cat, you have infinite possibilities for play toys. Suggestions include bottle caps, cardboard boxes, straws, plastic rings from milk jugs or water containers, ping pong and tennis balls. An especially clever homemade toy is a shoe box with a golf ball inside. Tape the lid on and cut holes in the top and sides large enough for a cat to get a paw in but not big enough for the ball to fall out. Your cat will enjoy hours of entertainment.

Canine cuddles

Give your dog a special treat. Next time you're at a garage sale, check out the stuffed toys. You can probably get poochie a toy for just $.25 or $.50 – a fraction of the cost of new ones in the pet store. A spot or stain won't bother your dog. Just be sure to look for toys that are sturdy and don't have parts that could be chewed off.

Those rascally reptiles

Iggy the iguana or Sam the snake may be your choice for an interesting pet, but keep in mind that reptiles can carry *Salmonella* bacteria, which can trigger an unwelcome bout of food poisoning. To protect yourself and your family, make sure you wash your hands thoroughly after handling your pet or cleaning its cage, and don't allow it in the kitchen.

Pesky problems

Shake, rattle and roll

To stop a dog from misbehaving, put a few coins or pebbles in an aluminum can. When the dog acts up, shake the can. The noise will make the dog stop, and eventually he will learn to stop his bad behavior.

How about some Chinese takeout?

If you have problems with dogs constantly digging in your garbage, place a paper or plastic bag inside the garbage pail. Mix up a concoction of Chinese mustard, Tabasco sauce, and vinegar. Spread liberally around the inside of the bag. One lick and the dog will learn to stay out of your garbage cans for life.

Recycle those plastic bags

Neat and simple poop scoop for dog owners — plastic grocery bags! Take them along when you walk the dog; just put the bag over your hand and pick up the waste. Then turn the bag inside out, knot it, and throw it out at home.

Lemon fresh breath — and peace and quiet too!

If your dog barks constantly, here's a tip to save your sanity (and perhaps your neighbor's)! Squirt lemon juice into the dog's mouth and say "Quiet."

Vinegar to the rescue

Pet urine on a concrete basement or garage floor can be a hard-to-remove odor. Along with house-breaking Fido, the answer to your problem is as easy as mixing equal parts of water and white vinegar and soaking the floor with the solution.

Vinegar also removes pet urine from carpet. Follow this three step process:

▶ Absorb as much liquid as possible by putting layers of paper towel over the spot and stepping on them until each stack of papers is soaked. (Blot gently; never scrub.) Repeat until the papers come up virtually dry.

▶ Spray or sprinkle on generous amounts of vinegar, either straight or diluted, and absorb the same way as before.

▶ If further cleaning is needed, use a solution of liquid dishwashing detergent and water or a commercial carpet cleaner. This treatment should remove the urine's odor so well that the animal will not return to the spot again based on the familiar smell.

Rx for cat attacks

If lumps appear on your neck, armpits, or groin area, try to remember if you have been scratched by a cat recently. You may have cat scratch disease, which is spread by germs on the cat's claws, and causes swelling of your lymph nodes. Children are more likely to be affected than adults. Cat scratch usually goes away in a week or two without treatment, but see your doctor if your lymph nodes become enlarged.

Cat bites may not be as painful as dog bites, but they can still be dangerous. If you are bitten by a cat, see a doctor as soon as possible. Eighty percent of cat bites become infected, compared to only 5 percent of dog bites.

A piece of wood for peace of mind

If you have an indoor cat that's driving you crazy scratching your belongings to shreds, you can make a simple, sturdy scratching post from items you usually have around the house. Using old scrap wood, make a square base. (Make sure it doesn't have any chemicals on it that could harm your cat.) Use a long thick piece of wood for the actual scratching post. Make the post taller than your cat when he's standing on his hind legs so he can stretch while he's scratching. Also be sure the scratching post is sturdy enough so it won't tip over. One tip is likely to turn your cat off to that post forever. For extra support, you can attach the post to a floor or wall.

If you want to get fancier, you can add shelves to the post for the cat to sleep on. Wrap old carpet or sisal rope around the post for the cat to scratch on. Old bluejeans also work well. In about an hour, you'll have a good sturdy scratching post that will last for years. It won't tip over like the discount-store models that most cats disdain anyway, and it won't break your bank account like most luxury models.

A sweet no-no

You may be a chocoholic, but make sure you keep your pet out of the Hershey's kisses. Chocolate can be toxic to them.

Tempt tree-climbers with tuna

Need to get a frightened cat out of a tree? Before you fret or call the fire department, try giving the cat a little time to calm down. Most cats will eventually come down on their own. You may be able to persuade it to come down a little faster if you open a can of its favorite food (or even better, tuna fish) and put it at the bottom of the tree.

Tender loving care

Natural flea remedies

Make a lemon tonic to get rid of your pet's fleas. Slice a whole lemon, and place it in a pint of almost boiling water. Let it sit overnight. Next morning, apply it to the pet's skin with a soft cloth. Repeat daily as needed for bad infestations. (Don't use this remedy on irritated or broken skin from too much scratching.)

Try a natural castile soap to shampoo your pet. Dr. Bronner's almond castile soap is very gentle and helps your pet's skin stay soft and supple. It supposedly repels fleas too.

For a homemade, environmentally safe flea trap, rig a lamp with a low-watt bulb (60 watts or less) so it shines all night on a light-colored pan of water on the floor. Add a tablespoon of dish detergent; fleas will jump or fall in, sink, and drown. Keep in place until you no longer find dead fleas in the dish in the morning, then move to another room. Repeat until no more fleas are collected.

Ice it down for heat relief

In the summertime, help your pet beat the heat by putting a few ice cubes in his water in the morning. They will melt throughout the day to keep your pet's water fresh and cool.

Oil just 'mite' be a cure

Is your pet scratching or pawing at its ears a lot? It may have ear mites. Here's a great natural remedy for ear mites in cats and dogs: mineral oil. Just apply with a dropper or well-soaked cotton ball. Fold outer ear over ear opening and massage gently to get oil down into ear canal. Repeat every four or five days for a few weeks in order to kill newly hatched mites.

Temperature alert

Never ever leave your pet in a parked car, even with the windows rolled down. During summer, the temperature inside a car sitting in the shade can rise to 105F in just a few minutes.

The doctor is in

Giving medicine to a cat can be messy, and you may end up getting scratched or bitten. To make it a little easier, try soaking a small piece of bread with liquid medicine, or coat a pill with butter.

You may think a medicine that helps you can't harm your pet. Not true. Some over-the-counter painkillers like acetaminophen (Tylenol) and ibuprofen (Advil) can be deadly to cats and dogs. Never give your pet any medication without consulting your vet first.

Dry and crunchy does the trick

When it comes to dog food, your best bet is usually dry. It's the cheapest, the easiest to store and the easiest to feed your dog. If you must scoop poop for your dog, dry food also makes the most sense because it produces the firmest stools. Canned foods normally cause a soft stool, which is no fun to clean up.

Surviving the water bowl battle

Does your dog constantly knock over his outside watering dish then give you reproachful looks when you come home because he's out of water? Try using an angel food cake pan for your angelic pet. Put a stake in the ground through the hole in the middle of the pan, and his efforts to turn it upside down will be thwarted.

Home beauty salon

Save money by using a woman's rubber-tipped hairbrush for brushing your cat. You'll find it works better than the expensive "cat" models.

If brushing is a chore, try this unusual technique. Vacuum your pet to get rid of loose hair and dander before it falls to the floor. Use the upholstery or round brush attachment, and be careful not to vacuum near the pet's head. This won't work for all pets, but some of them love it!

Soothe your pet's dry, itchy skin with gentle, all-vegetable Murphy's Oil Soap.

Litter alert

Are you using your daily newspaper as a cheap, plentiful source of cat litter? It's not a good idea if you have kittens in the house. Newspaper may contain dyes that are toxic to small animals. Also, the ink may come off on your cat's paws and get tracked onto your carpet, so if that's a concern, you should stick to regular litter.

Greasy kid stuff

Hairballs can annoy your cat and make your life harder when you have to clean up the aftermath. Help lessen your cat's chances of having hairballs by adding a teaspoon of bacon grease or vegetable oil to his food once a day.

Every pet should have a loving home

Spay or neuter your pet! Eight to 10 million unwanted animals are put to sleep in animal shelters every year in the United States. And it's not just your average mutt that's being euthanized. About one-third of the dogs destroyed are purebreds. If you truly care about animals, you'll take this important step to help stem the tide of unwanted pets.

TRAVEL AND RECREATION

Cutting travel costs

A deal of a lifetime

Don't be taken in by travel scams! Watch out for these danger signals when someone offers you a free or low-cost vacation deal:

▶ A price that's too good to be true. It is.

▶ Pressure to make a decision right away.

▶ A request for your credit card number.

▶ Vague or unnamed hotels, airlines, or other travel services.

Credit card delay — a warning signal

Another travel scam to avoid: If someone offers you by phone or mail a vacation deal of a lifetime, take note if they say you can't take the trip for at least two months. If the trip is going on your credit card, they may be scamming you. Why? Because there's a 60-day deadline for disputing credit card charges, and they probably know it. If something goes wrong, you won't be able to deny them payment.

Beware the early bird

The early bird sometimes gets the best deal, but you won't always get the cheapest airplane seat by making your reservation far in advance. Airline prices rise and fall with demand, and tickets often go on sale after you have made your reservation. That's why it's important to ask if you can re-book your ticket later in case prices drop. Often you can re-book even restricted and discounted seats. It may cost you $25 to $50 to re-book, but you can save twice that much on a sale ticket.

When 'bumping' pays off

Know your rights if you are bumped from a flight. You are entitled to one-half the cost of your round-trip ticket (up to $200) if you arrive at your destination between one and two hours later than your original flight, or the entire cost of your round-trip ticket (up to $400) if you arrive more than two hours late (four hours for international flights).

Champagne and caviar with that seat?

Don't think you have to pay first-class prices to get good seats on an airplane. When you buy your ticket, just ask for the seat you prefer. Usually, seats in the first row and by the emergency exit doors are more comfortable because they have more leg room. An aisle seat also gives you room to spread your legs, but a window seat may be safer because it's farther away from hijackers and any other dangerous action that may be happening in the aisles. Ask for a boarding pass, which locks in your seat assignment. If you can't get the seat you want when you buy your ticket, check in early and ask to be put on a waiting list for a better seat. And once you're on the plane, make sure you count the rows from your seat to each of the exits so you can feel your way there in an emergency.

ATM card: Don't leave home without it

Here's a surprise: ATM cards are your best bet for currency exchange, especially if you want to avoid the 12 percent commission you'll often pay at a currency exchange center plus the 1 percent you pay to buy traveler's checks. Currency exchange centers may advertise a great exchange rate, but may secretly charge outrageous service fees. You can find ATMs in almost every country in the world these days and they'll link you directly with your own checking account at home so you can get the cash you need without paying an exorbitant exchange rate. However, be sure to take a few traveler's checks with you just in case an ATM isn't handy when you need cash.

Next flight to Cancun, please

Did you know that if your flight is delayed or canceled, the airline has to comply with an industry rule called Rule 240? The rule says the airline has to put you on another flight – whether on one of its own planes or on another carrier. The airline won't necessarily provide alternate transportation automatically – the passenger may have to ask. If the airline refuses, ask to see its "Terms and Conditions of Carriage." The airline must prove to you that it has no obligation to put you on another flight.

Cost-cutting travel clubs

Cut your travel costs by becoming a member of a travel club. Even if you're only an occasional traveler, travel clubs can save as much as 50 percent of your travel costs. Some clubs only offer hotel discounts, but others even include bargain deals on airfare. Membership costs vary, and every club offers something different. To find the best membership for you, find out if the club provides deals on your favorite vacation spots.

Sign up with the airline's frequent flier program when you book your flight. Not only will you become eligible to earn free miles, you're less likely to be bumped from your flight.

Don't forget to cancel the newspaper

Before you leave on vacation, especially if it's going to be an extended one, be sure you know what's required by your insurer to protect your unoccupied house. Some companies require a certain level of attention if you're away for an extended period. For example, turning off the water or having a neighbor check your house daily. Others will refuse to pay any claims for damage from vandalism if you've been away for more than 30 days.

Reserve your weekend

The best time to call for airline reservations is evenings or weekends. Reservation agents aren't as busy then and can give you more time and better service.

It pays to ask

You know to shop around for good deals on airfares and car rentals, but did you know you should also shop around for hotel rates? Besides comparing hotel prices, ask about discounts. Every hotel offers them, but they won't tell you about them or give you a better rate unless you ask.

Travel safety

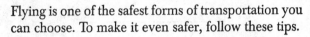

Fly the friendly skies

Flying is one of the safest forms of transportation you can choose. To make it even safer, follow these tips.

▶ After boarding, locate the nearest emergency exit door, and count the rows of seats to it. In an emergency, the lights may go out, and you may have to feel your way to the exit.

▶ Pay attention to the preflight instructions, no matter how often you've heard them before. Make sure you know how to operate the emergency exit.

▶ Keep your seat belt fastened whenever you are seated.

▶ If an emergency does arise and you have to evacuate the plane, don't attempt to take your luggage with you. Your luggage can be replaced. You, however, are irreplaceable.

Passport to a great vacation

When you travel with a passport, be sure to keep it safe and secure either on your person or in the hotel safe. You may need it to check into your hotel, get your mail, or visit consulates or embassies. One person shouldn't carry the passports of everyone in your group. If you lose your passport while overseas, you can expect some delay in getting a new one while all your records are checked.

Foil pickpockets' plans

Women should carry a handbag that will fit under their arm. Put your arm through the strap, and carry the bag close to your body.

Men should carry their wallets in a front pants pocket or carry their money in a money belt. Wrap the wallet with a rubber band to make it harder for a thief to slip it out of your pocket.

Leave your bleeding heart at home

When you're traveling, especially in a foreign country, watch out for vagrant children. They may be pitiful and heartbreaking, but they also may be thieves. Unless your mission is to save them, steer clear.

Foreign exchange

When traveling to a foreign country, exchange some of your money before you leave. Criminals often watch for people exchanging large amounts of money at airport banks and currency exchange windows.

Remember when traveling in foreign countries and using your credit card, you need to keep careful records of your expenditures. People have actually been arrested for unknowingly going over their credit limit! Keep a list of your credit card numbers and cancellation instructions in case of theft, and store it in a safe place during your trip.

Losing money is not funny

What would you do if you were traveling in a foreign country and lost all your money? Answer: You would get money wired or transferred to yourself from your hometown bank. So always keep the phone number of your bank with you when you travel. If you find yourself broke and have no bank to turn to, find the nearest U.S. embassy or consulate and arrange for a family member or friend to send you money.

When traveling abroad, never cash large amounts of cash. Instead get traveler's checks. In case of trouble, keep a written record of the serial numbers and denominations of the checks as well as the date and the name and address of the bank where you got them. Store the list in the hotel safe or other secure location. That way you can get replacements quickly and easily.

Avoid malaria and other maladies

Planning a vacation to exotic locales? Call the Centers for Disease Control (CDC) at least six weeks before you depart for current health information on the areas you plan to visit. (404) 332-4559.

Traveling to the mountains can cause altitude sickness in people who live at sea level. Symptoms include headache, shortness of breath, and nausea. To avoid altitude sickness, spend a day at a lower elevation before traveling higher, and drink plenty of fluids, especially water.

Hold the ice, please

When traveling outside the country, protect yourself from "Montezuma's revenge" – traveler's diarrhea. Drink only bottled beverages, well-cooked foods, and peeled fruits. If you have access to a stove, boiling water for three to five minutes will ensure its safety. One source of contaminated water that many people overlook is ice cubes. Putting ice cubes made with local tap water into your bottled water can defeat your efforts to defend your stomach.

Save your sight

If you wouldn't drink the water when traveling abroad, you most certainly shouldn't store your contacts in it. Contaminants in water may cause eye

---

If you love garage sales

Getting a good deal in a foreign marketplace is one of the thrills of traveling abroad. Bringing home a jade jewelry box from Tibet or a painting from Paris can be a triumph, especially when you paid next to nothing. Here are some tips for better bargaining.

▶ Never say how much you like or need an item. Instead, point out its flaws, say you want to shop around, you think you saw it much cheaper elsewhere, or you want to think about it.

▶ If the merchant won't agree to your price, ask him to throw in an extra item instead.

▶ Carry small bills to pay for your purchases, and count your change carefully.

infections or even blindness. Make sure you take your sterile contact solution with you when you travel.

When in Rome

Remember this rule for saving money when traveling overseas – do as the locals do. Especially when it comes to meals, you can save big bucks by following local examples of when and where to eat. You'll eat better and spend less.

On the road

You mean I have to pay for that dent?

When renting a car, remember that optional waivers like loss or collision damage waivers are not insurance. All they do is release you from responsibility if the vehicle is damaged or stolen while you have it. Check with your homeowner's insurance and regular car insurance to see if you and your passengers and possessions are covered under their policies before you buy any insurance from a car rental company. If you decide against the waivers, remember that you will probably be responsible for paying the deductible on your regular insurance as well as any "loss-of-use" fees charged by the rental company.

I'll take the Cadillac, please

Your homeowner's or regular car insurance may put limitations on what type of rented vehicle they'll cover. Check with your insurance company before committing to a specific vehicle.

Fill 'er up

Check into refueling options at the end of your rental. Watch out for refueling service by the rental company; it may charge a per-gallon service fee. You'll probably save if you do it yourself.

On the road security

While traveling by car, make sure you carry the following items along for comfort and safety. In the glove compartment, stash your maps, owner's manual, car repair/service log, copy of your car registration and insurance card, pocketknife, and sunglasses. In the trunk, be sure you have a jack, spare tire, jumper cables, first aid kit, fire extinguisher, heavy-duty gloves, and reflector triangle (to warn other drivers if your car breaks down).

Picnic in the park

A picnic kit is a handy item to carry along on car trips. In a small bag or picnic basket, include paper plates; plastic knives, forks, and spoons; can opener; bottle opener; salt and pepper; premoistened towelettes, paper towels, or napkins; and a few extra plastic bags for trash. With your prepacked picnic kit, you can stop anytime and enjoy a feast when you run across any specialty food shops or fresh fruit stands you just can't resist trying.

Are we there yet?

When traveling with children, bring along some things for them to do that will keep them occupied and happy. Markers, pencils, and paper will please the budding artist. Encourage him to draw things that he's seeing on the trip. Playing cards can keep several children happy; bring a board game to double as a card table. Bring along your child's favorite action figures or dolls. Play-do can make for hours of fun, even for adults.

Luggage

Packing pointers

When traveling by car, leave your clothes on hangers, and slip a large plastic trash bag over them. Lay them flat in your trunk. This makes unpacking easier and uses less trunk space.

If you iron your clothes before putting them in the suitcase, they'll lie flatter and you'll have more room to include other stuff.

Snap snaps, button buttons, and zip zippers on all clothes before putting them in the suitcase. That will help them maintain their shape better.

A little squeeze'll do it

You probably already know that you can save space on bulky essentials, such as shampoo, conditioner, and body lotion, by transferring the contents to smaller plastic containers. Here's a neat trick you may not know: Once the contents are inside, squeeze a little air out of each mini bottle and reseal. This creates a vacuum that cuts down on messy spills and leaks.

Golden oldie

Old hot water bottles should not be thrown away. They make excellent traveling bags for toothbrushes or round mats to put under house plants.

Ladies Home Journal circa 1920

No fuss, no muss

Make dressing on vacation easier and faster for young kids by packing each day's outfit plus socks and underwear into separate plastic resealable bags. With no decisions to make about what to wear with what and where something is, dressing is a snap. Put dirty clothes back into the same bag. No more confusion about what's clean and what's not.

The heartbreak of lost luggage

You can help prevent your luggage from being lost if you watch attendants carefully when you check your bags. Make sure they attach the right routing slips. If you don't recognize the code for the airport at your destination, ask. Also, be sure you remove all old flight tags before the attendants attach the new ones. This will prevent confusion about the destination.

Even worse than losing your luggage is having it stolen. To increase the odds your bags will make it to their destination, follow these rules:

▶ Avoid overly expensive luggage. It attracts thieves.

▶ Pick up your bags as soon as possible. The longer they sit in the claim area, the better the chances of them being stolen.

▶ Never, ever leave bags unattended. Thieves move fast.

In case your suitcase ends up in Siberia

When packing for a family vacation, don't pack a separate suitcase for each family member. Instead, pack at least one change of clothes for everyone in each suitcase. Then if one piece of luggage gets lost, everyone still has something to wear.

Playing 'tag' with your bags

Tag your luggage with your business address and phone number, but don't use the company name. Use a folding tag with a cover.

Put an address label inside each piece of luggage in case the outside tag falls off.

The perfect combination

If each piece of luggage has just one combination lock, set a different combination for each piece. If

Luggage leave-outs

Don't pack your medications or extra glasses in your luggage. In an emergency you may need them. You're better off keeping them in your carry-on bag or purse.

your luggage has two combination locks, set a different combination on each of the two locks. To further strengthen luggage locks, run a strip of nylon filament tape around the suitcase to keep it from opening accidentally if it's mishandled or dropped.

Low-cost recreation

Free fun

You can enjoy your free time without spending a fortune. Begin by making a list of free activities in your area: libraries, parks, your city's recreation department, museums, or municipally supported concerts.

Oliver Twist online

Wish you had a good book to read but hate to spend the money or make a trip to the library? If you have a computer and access to the Internet, making your wish come true is as easy as hopping online and heading for a site called Project Gutenberg (www.gutenberg.net). This site and several others, including the Online Book Initiative and Internet Wiretap, store complete copies of many literary classics. You just make your selection, download, and enjoy your free reading experience.

The great outdoors

The care and cleaning of sleeping bags

Keep your sleeping bag clean and help it last longer by placing a folded sheet inside the bag to sleep in and by putting a ground cloth under it when using it outdoors. During camping trips, it's a good idea to hang up the bag and let it air out every day. Always be sure your sleeping bag is completely dry before you roll it up for storage.

Most sleeping bags are safe to wash and dry at home, but check the label just in case. For really large bags, use the larger washers and dryers found in coin-operated laundries. Wash in warm or cold water on a gentle cycle. When drying a down sleeping bag, place some clean tennis shoes in the dryer with the bag to help the down fluff up better. Down bags take a while to dry, so be sure they are completely dry before taking them out of the dryer, or you're likely to have a problem with mildew.

Small-fry safety signal

If you have small children, the great outdoors can be a source of fascination and danger. When you are hiking or camping, attach a small whistle to their clothing, so they can blow it if they get separated from you.

Double-duty deodorant

Do you love to hike but hate the blisters that result? Try applying antiperspirant to your feet for several days before you go out. The antiperspirant dries out the skin, reducing friction from your shoes or boots.

However, the ingredients may cause other irritations, so if you find that happens, stop using it.

Tips of the bird trade

If you want to take up bird watching but aren't sure where to begin, start with one or two good bird guidebooks so you'll know what you're looking at. You can either buy the books or check them out at a local library. Choose a book with colored drawings instead of photographs. People who believe the camera never lies will change their minds when they've had some in-the-field experience. Light and shadows, angles, positions, age of the bird, season, background – all these may be distorted in a photo but not in a well-drawn picture. The handiest books have illustrations opposite descriptions and maps of where you can find the bird.

Here birdie, birdie, birdie

Want to encourage a bird to come closer so you can get a better look? Try "pishing." Experienced bird watchers regularly rely on this technique, which consists of whistling air through the teeth, somewhat explosively, making a "pshhwshhwshh" or a soft "tchtt-tchtt-tchtt" noise. The sound apparently resembles a scolding or alarm call, and most birds can't resist coming to see what's going on.

PERSONAL CARE

Beautiful skin

Egg on your face

You can make a quick and effective facial mask with nothing more sophisticated than an egg white. Just beat one egg white until it's frothy, and then apply it directly on clean skin. Let it dry and then rinse. It will tighten your skin as it dries like a mini-facelift.

Don't hold the mayo

Try this mayonnaise mask for dry skin. Use only whole-egg mayo. Apply it directly to your face and leave it on for 20 minutes. Then wipe off the excess with a tissue, and rinse with cool water.

Corn pone toner

Need a facial but don't want to spend the money? Do it yourself with this recipe. Mix cornmeal with enough water to make a thick paste. You can also use oatmeal. Gently apply it to your face with your fingertips. It will tighten your skin as it dries. Then gently massage your skin to let it remove dry skin and blackheads. Rinse well.

Help from Mr. Potato Head

Help clear up facial breakouts and blackheads with a peeled slice of potato. Rub it gently over freshly washed skin.

To make your own face mask for oily skin, cook one large potato, peel, and mash. Mix it with one egg white, half teaspoon lemon juice, and two tablespoons of milk to form a smooth paste. Spread it over the face avoiding the eye area. Leave on for 15 to 20 minutes, then remove with warm water.

Oh no, not a pimple!

Try a small dab of toothpaste on a pimple before going to bed. It will help dry the pimple out overnight and make it less noticeable the next day. Or try dabbing a lemon on the blemish after washing your face. Citric acid also helps dry and heal pimples fast.

Dress up the rough spots

Rough elbows and feet are simple to treat with this common kitchen item – salad dressing (the kind that looks like mayonnaise). Just before bathing, apply it to your problem dry skin areas and massage well. Keep working it in – the dry skin will roll right off. Then wash the area as usual.

Soft skin secrets

Try Cleopatra's beauty secret for soft skin – add four cups of milk to your warm bath water and luxuriate for 15 minutes. Or try adding a cup or two of powdered milk. You'll feel like a queen!

***

For a simple, natural way to soften your skin, add about one-half cup of baking soda to your bath water and enjoy.

When your face is dragging

If you wake up with puffy bags under your eyes, just brew yourself a pot of tea. If you make it chamomile, and wear it instead of drink it, you'll be on your way to smoother skin. How? Chamomile is a naturally soothing herb that temporarily decreases puffiness. Just ice the tea, soak a couple of gauze pads, and place them over your eyes. Bye-bye bags!

Hair and nails

Hair today, clean tomorrow

Try this next time you run out of shampoo, and you'll save yourself some money. Wash your hair with a dime-size spot of ordinary dishwashing liquid.

As shiny as an apple

If the shine has worked its way right out of your hair, try treating your tresses with an apple cider rinse after every shampoo. Mix one-half cup of apple cider vinegar with two cups of warm water, and pour over your freshly washed hair.

To get soapy residue out after shampooing, make a hair rinse with regular vinegar. Simply combine one cup of water and four teaspoons of vinegar. It also will leave your hair fresh and shiny.

On one condition

You'll never believe this dry hair conditioner till you've tried it. Before washing or even wetting your hair, apply about a half cup of mayonnaise to your hair, and work it in well. Put a shower cap or plastic bag over your head to hold in your body heat. Leave it on about 15 minutes, then rinse it out, and wash your hair thoroughly. This treatment will also straighten out a permanent, so if you're ready to lose those curls, comb the mayo through well and then shampoo.

Time for a (hot) oil change

To give yourself soft, healthy hair, try a homemade hot oil treatment using plain vegetable oil. Warm up one-quarter cup of oil in the microwave in a non-metallic container (or by placing it in a baggie in another cup of hot water for a few minutes). Massage into scalp and all through your hair. Wrap your head in plastic, leave the oil on for about 30 minutes, then shampoo as usual. Do this every few weeks to maintain softer, smoother hair.

The California conditioner

For a quick and nutritious hair pack/oil treatment, use one very ripe avocado. Mash it up well, and apply it to dry hair from scalp to ends. Leave it on for up to 30 minutes. Then rinse out and wash as usual.

The 'green' way to douse dandruff

A sure cure for dandruff is in the aloe vera plant on your windowsill. Break a branch off your plant and slit it open, scraping out the pulpy gel. Apply this soothing ointment to your scalp, and leave it on for five minutes, then wash with your regular shampoo. Aloe vera gel is also available in health food stores. Just be sure it's the real thing.

For blondes only

Here's how to remove that greenish tint you sometimes get from the chlorine in swimming pools. Dissolve an aspirin in a cup of water and pour it over your hair, from roots to ends. Massage well into hair, then rinse.

Low-cost hair gel works in a pinch

Dissolve a teaspoon of gelatin in a cup of warm water, and you have an instant setting lotion for your hair.

A 'hand'y use for vinegar

Rub some vinegar on your nails before applying nail polish. This will clean them and help the new polish last longer.

They may turn blue, but they'll be dry!

If you're tired of smearing your freshly painted nails, here's a trick to make them dry faster. When nails are partly dry, place your hands in a bowl of cold water. Or even better, stick them in the freezer! The cold will speed-set the polish, and you'll be ready to go in no time.

Bothering with bottles

Do you have trouble opening your bottles of nail polish? The next time you buy a new polish, rub petroleum jelly inside the cover and on the grooves of the bottle. You'll never have sticky problems again.

A smooth move

If your nail polish is "gummed up," simply put it in a pan of boiling water to make it smooth again. To avoid that problem, store your polish in the refrigerator. It will stay smooth and ready to apply.

Budget cutters

A little tea with your bath?

You've heard of aromatherapy, and you might have even shopped for some of those expensive essential oils to add to your bath. Here's a recipe for an aromatherapy bath that will only cost you pennies. Hold a couple of herbal tea bags under the hot water, and add a couple of orange slices. You'll feel like you're at a health spa without spending all that money!

Bubbling over

For inexpensive bubble bath, try a small amount of your dishwashing liquid. For more fragrance, add a bit of essential oil or even a baking extract such as vanilla or almond.

Baking soda surprises

Toothpaste is getting so expensive, and it really does not have to be. You can clean your teeth effectively with nothing more than baking soda and salt. Put about one tablespoon of salt and one tablespoon of baking soda together in a small container and shake well. Sprinkle some on your wet toothbrush, and brush as usual.

Getting tired of paying a ridiculous amount for deodorant? Try these recipes applied to clean, dry armpits. Add enough water to about two tablespoons of baking soda to make a paste. Many fancy deodorants use a similar recipe. If you like cream deoderant, mix two teaspoons each of baking soda, petroleum jelly and talcum powder. Heat in a double boiler over low heat, stirring until it forms a smooth cream. Put it in a small container with a tight-fitting top.

Lip service

You can get chapped lips any time of year. It's a good thing the solution is nothing more complicated than good old petroleum jelly! Apply a thin layer, and then add a couple of drops of water. The petroleum jelly will help the moisture penetrate and soothe your lips. You can do this same treatment to a wind-burned or sunburned face.

It keeps going and going ...

Lipsticks are expensive. Make yours last longer by buying a lipstick brush and getting the last bits of lipstick out of the tube. To clean the brush when you're ready to move on to another color, add a little Vaseline or mineral oil to the brush, then wipe it clean on a tissue.

Smooth as a baby's bottom

If you're looking for cheap makeup removers, you'll find them right next to the diapers. How about baby wipes? They're loaded with soothing ingredients that will take off your makeup in a flash.

The razor's edge

To prolong the life of razor blades, keep a cup of mineral oil in the bathroom, and store the razor in it after every use. The oil prevents oxidation, which helps keep the blade from getting imperfections that can cause nicks when you shave the next time.

New life for your brushes

Hairbrushes need a good cleaning now and then to get rid of dust and dirt, not to mention excess hair. Make your brushes sweet-smelling and clean by washing them with a solution of baking soda and warm water.

Would you like a clean, fresh toothbrush without buying a new one? How about throwing your old one in the dishwasher? It might sound strange, but the high heat and detergent that kills bacteria on your dishes can do wonders for personal hygiene items. So while you're at it, throw in your nail brushes, loofahs, or other sponges, and give them all a new lease on life.

Cut to the chase

Add up the yearly cost of haircuts for your family; you may be surprised at how much it is. For the price of a pair of good haircutting scissors, available at most discount or department stores, you can save that money by cutting your family's hair. A video or book from your local library will give you detailed instructions on cutting hair. Even if you only use your scissors for trims in between professional haircuts, you can cut your number of haircuts in half, and you'll still save a bundle.

HEALTH AND FIRST AID

Healthy living

Some fruitful ideas

Oranges aren't just for getting your quota of vitamin C. They can also relieve mood swings and revive your energy. Place grated orange rind or twists of orange rind in small squares of cheesecloth. Fold and tie with a ribbon or twist tie. Take a sniff of the refreshing scent whenever your energy drops.

Golden oldie

Apples are useful in nervous dyspepsia; they are nutritious, medicinal and vitalizing. They aid digestion, clear the voice, correct the acidity of the stomach, are valuable in rheumatism, insomnia, and liver trouble. An apple contains as much nutriment as a potato, in a pleasanter, more wholesome form.

Household Hand Book, 1860

When you're out of mints

If you need to cover up bad breath quickly, eat something sweet. Sugars and complex carbohydrates, such as a piece of bread, work well.

It will also help to drink buttermilk or eat yogurt with active cultures. The lactobacilli in these products make it hard for odor-causing bacteria to grow.

Have a ball with your workout

Wondering what to do with worn-out tennis balls that have lost their bounce? Dr. James D. Walter of Philadelphia recommends you turn them into exercise equipment for increasing hand and forearm strength.

Iron out the cause of fatigue

If you've been feeling tired and worn down lately, check the color of your tongue. A pale tongue may mean you have anemia and need more iron.

If you have three balls, you can make different cuts in each to create varying levels of resistance. In the first ball, make a small cut (about 1 inch). This will be your most resistant ball. In the second ball, make a slightly larger cut (about 2 1/4 inches). Finally, cut the third ball in half. This offers the least resistance of all. To improve your hand and forearm strength, begin doing 10 repetitions with each hand using the least resistant ball. Increase to the next level when it feels comfortable.

It beats yelling and pounding your fists

Caught in the middle of rush hour and feeling stressed out? Try a quick breathing exercise. Put one hand on your stomach, then inhale slowly and deeply while counting from one to four. Exhale as you count backward from four to one. According to Dr. Alice Domar of the Mind/Body Center at Beth Israel Deaconess Hospital in Boston, this mini meditation reduces stress, blood pressure, and heart rate.

Ring around the finger?

There are a lot of different remedies for stuck rings. Charles E. Powell, an EMT in Moscow, Idaho, favors the following technique. Take a relatively wide rubber band and snip it so it forms one long band of rubber. Take the rubber band, and beginning at the tip of the finger, wrap the finger all the way down to the ring. Apply some type of lubricant to the rubber band, such as liquid soap or lotion, and gently work the ring off over the rubber band.

Here's another way to remove a stuck ring. Take a piece of string, and lubricate it well with liquid soap. Thread the string under the ring, then wrap the remaining string tightly around the finger. Gently rotate and pull the ring until it slides off.

Cuts and bruises

Split skin savvy

If you suffer with split skin at the end of your fingertips that moisturizers just won't mend, soothe your skin with the superglue solution. Put a small amount of glue over the split to ease pain and prevent the split from growing larger. However, don't use superglue for very deep or bleeding splits. Once you apply the glue, be careful not to touch your finger to your eyes until the glue has dried thoroughly.

Another remedy for split skin is zinc oxide ointment, according to Dr. David Finlay of Falls Church, Virginia. You can buy the ointment over the counter at most pharmacies. Put the cream on your areas of split skin and cover with an adhesive bandage. As a mild antibiotic, zinc oxide will promote healing while it relieves discomfort.

The big squeeze

Hitting your finger with a hammer or crushing it in a door is one of life's miseries. However, you can minimize bruising and keep from losing your nail if you immediately squeeze the fingertip firmly and maintain the pressure for five full minutes. This gives the blood time to clot and seal off broken vessels. The squeezing prevents blood from oozing into the fingertip area and causing the possible loss of a nail.

Say bye-bye to bruises

Once the swelling from a bruise has gone down, you can discourage discoloration of the skin by using a hot salt pack. Heat two cups of sea salt in a dry skillet for a couple of minutes. Take care not to scorch the salt. Pour the warm salt into a thick sock and hold against the bruised area.

Burns

Cool comfort from the kitchen

How you treat a burn depends on how severe it is. For minor burns (a small reddened area with no blisters), place the affected area under cool, running water or cover with a cold wet compress until pain diminishes. Cover with a clean bandage. Never apply butter to a burn and never break blisters caused by a burn.

You can also take care of a minor burn with a little help from your kitchen cupboard. Vanilla extract will not only soothe the area, it will keep blisters from forming.

Sunburn solutions in your cupboard

A good soak is the best remedy for sunburn unless your skin blisters or you develop signs of shock and confusion. In that case, see a doctor right away. For

---

A cool glass of iced tea — for your face?

Did you know that tea can take the sting out of sunburn? It's the tannins that do the trick. If you've ever noticed after drinking tea that your mouth feels rather dry, those are the tannins at work. In this case, however, you don't drink the tea, you apply it directly to the sunburned area. After brewing up a batch of black or green tea, be sure to let it cool completely before you soak a soft cloth in the tea and place it directly on your skin.

milder cases of sunburn, dissolve a pound of baking soda into lukewarm water. Soak for 20 to 30 minutes to relieve pain. Later, soften and moisturize your sunburn-damaged skin by adding one to two cups of milk to another lukewarm tub of water. Soak for 20 to 30 minutes more.

For a very bad sunburn, turn to the trusty potato. Applying grated potato directly to the burn site will relieve pain and actually help prevent blistering. Wrap the area with gauze or cotton cloth to keep the potato gratings in place.

Although it will undoubtedly put you in a sticky situation, spreading raw honey over sunburned areas is also very soothing.

Golden oldie

Advice from a women's health editor: "If you will faithfully practice an exercise for reducing the hips, you will see results in a month." The exercise? "Running about the room."

Ladies Home Journal circa 1920

Strains and sprains

RICE is good advice

Remember the RICE technique for safe, effective relief of sprains and strains. Rest the injured limb.

Ice the affected area for 10 to 20 minutes every couple of hours. Compress the area with a loosely applied compression bandage wrapped around and slightly above and below the injury. Elevate the affected part. Keep it higher than heart level if possible.

Remember your ABCs

To strengthen an ankle that's undergone the stress of a sprain, Dr. James Garrick of San Francisco suggests the following exercise. With the ankle submerged in warm water, use your big toe to trace out the letters of the alphabet in large capital letters (4 to 5 inches high). Do this four minutes. Repeat this exercise with the ankle submerged in cold water. Repeat the entire sequence, switching from hot to cold water, four times.

Fire and ice

A good rule of thumb to remember: Use ice to treat an injury for the first 48 hours. After that, if the swelling has gone down, you can use heat to relax the muscles and ease pain.

Cure it with cold

When icing injuries, follow these tips from Dean R. Dryburgh, DC, of Ontario, Canada, for maximum safety and effectiveness:

▶ Never apply an ice pack directly to the skin. Wrap it in a dampened paper towel. Using a thicker towel will make the ice pack ineffective.

▶ Remember that using an ice pack will make the area feel cold at first. Then, the cold sensation will be replaced by pain and burning before the area becomes numb. Numbness will occur within 7 to 10 minutes of applying the ice pack.

▶ Don't use the ice pack for longer than 20 minutes. Wait 10 minutes before you reapply the pack. However, it's best to wait two hours between cold treatments.

Here's another handy way to ice an injury. According to John P. Kelley of Tucker, Georgia, this technique is especially useful for weekend warriors and others who may suffer injuries after a game or other athletic event. Freeze water in a Styrofoam cup. Transport frozen cups in a cooler to the event. If needed, simply pull out a prefrozen cup, peel off the top section of foam, and use the base as a holder while you use the ice cup to massage painful areas.

And when you're done, you can eat it

Need an ice pack now? Check your freezer. Chances are you already have one ready made in the form of frozen packages of beans, peas, or corn. These frozen food packs work well for sprains and strains because they mold so easily to the affected area. Once defrosted, either refreeze and reuse, or enjoy some veggies with dinner.

Rock and roll for relief

For cheap and effective relief of heel spurs, place your bare foot on an empty glass soft drink bottle, and roll your foot back and forth. Before you begin, make sure the bottle doesn't have any chips or cracks that could cut you. Some people find a frozen can of fruit juice works even better because it offers the doubly helpful combination of cold therapy and stretching.

Animal pops for sprain pain

For a kid with a sprain, the idea of holding an ice pack to the sore spot is not such a cool idea. Dr. John Canalizo of Ormond Beach, Florida offers some suggestions on how to make ice packs more appealing.

▶ Cut colorful cellulose sponges into fun animals or other shapes. Next, wet the sponges and freeze them. Kids find these "ice animals" fun, and the frozen sponges are more comfortable than regular ice packs. Plus, they still significantly reduce pain and swelling.

▶ Place cubed or crushed ice into a freezer bag and add a little rubbing alcohol. Have the child add a few drops of his or her favorite food coloring to the bag. The alcohol ensures that the ice pack stays a little slushy (and not quite as cold), and the kids find the colored ice packs fun.

Bites, stings, and scratches

Poultices from your pantry

Feeling the sting of an angry bee? For instant relief, mash some fresh papaya and apply it to the site of the sting. If you don't have any papaya handy, a paste of meat tenderizer and water will offer similar relief. If you don't have any meat tenderizer either, it's probably a good bet you do have baking soda. A paste of baking soda and water will also soothe stings. All of the above will also reduce swelling and relieve pain and itching.

Spiders don't sting; they bite. However, their method of self-protection can be at least as painful and sometimes more so than a sting from an ant, bee, hornet, yellow jacket, or wasp. To ease the ache, mash half of a white onion, and spread it around the site of the bite. Wrap a clean cloth around the injury to hold the onion in place.

The medicine cabinet might be the place to go to ease the ache of a bug bite or sting. But skip the creams and ointments, and reach for the aspirin instead. Wet the sore spot, then rub with an aspirin tablet, and you should find fairly quick relief.

Stings from the sea

A jellyfish sting is no joking matter. Reactions can range from itching and pain to nausea and vomiting. If you have nausea, fever, muscle aches, or pain that doesn't go away after a few hours, see a doctor as soon as possible. Otherwise, remembering these rules can help you handle a jellyfish sting.

▶ Don't wash the area with fresh water. This will only prolong the stinging sensation.

▶ Soak the sore spot with vinegar. This will help neutralize the jellyfish toxins (poisons).

▶ Combine four parts flour with one part salt, and mix with enough water to make a paste. Apply this after you've soaked the affected area with vinegar. Wrap the area with a clean cloth to hold the paste in place. This should give you relief in about an hour.

▶ Since the paste sticks so well, you'll probably have to soak the area with water before you can rinse the rest of the paste off. But it's a small price to pay for relief from this painful attack.

Don't turn into a mosquito cocktail

You may enjoy having a drink or two with your outdoor picnic supper. But you're better off avoiding alcohol if you want to ward off mosquitoes. Drinking alcohol dilates your blood vessels, making you a more desirable dinner choice for hungry mosquitoes.

Scrape up some homemade solutions

If you get a cut or scrape, but have no antibiotic ointments available, just look in your cupboard for a handy solution. You can prevent infection by applying raw honey to the wound.

―――――――――

Your fruit and vegetable bin can also save the day. Try peeling a banana and pressing the inner skin against a minor scrape for almost immediate relief. Or cut a thin slice of raw potato and press it against the abrasion, holding it in place with gauze or tape.

―――――――――

Another way to soothe your minor cuts, scrapes, and burns is with an aloe vera plant. A bit of juicy aloe vera can replace many expensive ointments and creams. Just split open a leaf and rub the gel on the affected area. You can even use aloe gel as an insect repellent.

Stop that itch in its tracks

If you know you've been exposed to poison oak or ivy, you can often prevent an itchy rash if you wash the exposed areas immediately with soap and cold water. Don't use warm water. It will just encourage the toxic oils from the plant to seep into your skin.

Leaves of three — let them be

Commit that simple phrase to memory. When it comes to poison ivy, oak, and sumac, prevention is the best cure. To identify these plants, just remember that their leaves always grow in threes. They commonly grow on the ground as shrubs or as climbing vines in trees.

Stop a poison oak or ivy rash from spreading with a baking-soda paste. Simply add enough water to some baking soda to make it spread easily. Apply to the affected area. Let the paste harden then wash it off with cold water. Apply honey to the exposed areas to soothe your skin and prevent infection.

Can anything else stop the terrible itching of a poison oak or ivy rash? A soothing oat bath may be just the answer. Grind a cup of whole oats into a fine flour. Add to lukewarm bath water, and soak for 20 to 30 minutes. Don't try to rinse off the film left by the oat bath; just gently pat yourself dry.

Medicine made easy

Pull in the reins on a racing heart

To slow a racing heart, soak a towel in ice water, and hold the towel to your face. If you suffer from occasional heart palpitations or tachycardia, applying an ice-cold towel to your face can slow down your racing heart, according to emergency room doctors. However, you should check with your doctor before using this technique if you have a history of chest pain or if your angina typically becomes worse in cold weather.

When its OK to swallow toothpaste

An attack of heartburn can be scary when there are no antacids around. Never fear if you find yourself in this situation. Drinking a cold glass of water will provide relief for some people. If that doesn't work, this practically foolproof remedy from Dr. Basil Rodansky of Lincoln Park, Michigan probably will. Take one or two teaspoons of mentholated toothpaste and wash it down with water or tea. But avoid toothpastes that contain baking soda or hydrogen peroxide. These may actually make heartburn worse.

Medication meltdown

To make your medicines last longer and preserve their potency, don't store them in the bathroom cabinet. High humidity and wide temperature variations can age medicines early. Try keeping your medicines in an area where they will stay at a constantly moderate temperature. As always, be sure to keep all medicines well out of the reach of children.

A salty solution

If you need a heat pack for your headache, try this effective remedy. Place salt in a dry pan and heat until it's very warm but not hot. Wrap the salt in a thin dishtowel. If the headache is in front, press the pack to the back of your head and rub. The dry heat will draw the pain away from where it's hurting.

When heat cramps your style

Head off heat cramps by drinking 18 to 24 ounces of water one to two hours before exercise. If you exercise for an extended period of time, remember to drink fluids during exercise, too.

Cheap cough cure

If you need some relief from coughing, try this simple remedy: a cup of warm milk with two teaspoons of honey. This relaxing beverage will soothe the throat, stop the cough, and help you sleep.

If massage or stretching isn't working to relieve a heat cramp in progress, try using your thumb and index finger to firmly squeeze the cramping area.

You might smell bad, but you won't cough

The next time you're suffering with a case of chest congestion, try this chest clearing ointment. Peel and mince seven garlic cloves. Put them in a pint-sized jar; add enough shortening to cover the minced cloves. Place the open jar into a pan of boiling water and let it boil for three hours. For extra effectiveness, add 1/8 teaspoon of eucalyptus oil to the melted shortening. Let cool, then rub ointment on the chest, stomach, and back. Cover with a heavy bath towel.

Be nice to your nose

Unstuff your stuffy nose without spending big bucks on nasal decongestants at the drugstore. Make your own saline nasal spray by mixing 1/2 teaspoon of table salt with 8 ounces of warm water. Store in an empty nasal spray bottle. Spraying this solution in the nose will remove irritants, allergens, and excess mucus that can make it difficult to breathe.

Is a stuffed-up nose keeping you from sleeping soundly at night? Before you turn to decongestant drugs, try what's sometimes called a mechanical decongestant – better known as a nose spring or nose "Band-Aid." This adhesive strip includes a little expander that gently widens the passages of your nose and makes breathing easier without the expense or side effects of drugs.

A little squirt may help

A foreign object stuck up the nose is nothing to sniff at. Instead of trying to dig the object out and possibly doing serious damage to your nose, let a decongestant do the dirty work. Squirt a couple of streams of liquid decongestant up your nose. This will sometimes constrict the blood vessels in the nose and relieve swelling enough that you can blow the foreign body right out. If this doesn't unstick whatever's stuck in your nose, see a doctor immediately.

Popsicle nose

For a neat way to control a nosebleed, try the technique recommended by Dr. John Ellis of Oakland, California. Take two popsicle sticks and wrap the ends on one side with 1-inch cloth tape. This provides padding for your nose. Next, tape the other ends together. This will form a clamp. To change the pressure the clamp provides, simply move the tape closer or further from the padded end of the sticks. Now, use the clamp to pinch the end of your nose shut. Leave it on for at least 10 minutes. You can stop your nosebleed and still go about your business with your hands unhampered!

Swallowing trick

If you have trouble swallowing capsules, try this trick recommended by Dr. Deborah L. Morris of Cary, North Carolina. Place the capsule in your mouth, take a big mouthful of water, tilt your head down, then swallow. Because the capsule usually floats to the back of your mouth when you tilt your head down, swallowing is much simpler.

Snore-free slumber

If you or your spouse has a snoring problem, the solution may be as simple as not sleeping on your back. To break yourself of this habit, sew a tennis ball into the back of your pajama top. You'll definitely feel more comfortable in another position, and it may be all you need to get a good night's sleep.

Frozen hiccups

A doctor in Bellingham, Washington has discovered that he can block the nerve signals that cause hiccups with a couple of ice cubes. He says to put an ice cube on either side of your Adam's apple. If that doesn't do the trick, move the ice cubes farther out to the sides of your neck, still at the level of your Adam's apple. You should be able to freeze those hiccups right in their tracks.

Little folks

Poison preventing 'sundae'

If your child has ingested poison and the Poison Control Center tells you to use activated charcoal to counteract the toxin's effect, you'll need a trick or two up your sleeve just to get the kid to swallow the stuff. Dr. Britt Durham of Los Angeles suggests combining the activated charcoal with vanilla ice cream. That combo creates what looks like a syrupy sundae that kids are quick to eat.

Ready, set ... burp

For the easiest way to burp a calm baby, try the technique Dr. Ron Reynolds uses with his own children. Sit the baby up with head supported and legs extended. Now, lean the baby 30 to 45 degrees to the left. Most babies burp immediately. However, if the baby does not burp, keep leaning the baby to the left while also leaning the child backward or forward about 30 degrees. Whatever position you find to be effective should work every time.

Smooth move for calming baby

If you have a colicky baby, try the maneuver Dr. Glen C. Griffin of Mapleton, Utah uses to soothe a tummy troubled with too much swallowed air. Lay the baby on his or her back on your lap, and tilt the child's head slightly to the left. Slip your left hand under the baby's head and neck. Place your right index and middle fingers on the left side of the stomach, just under the ribs. Lift the baby to a sitting position and apply gentle pressure to the stomach with the right hand. This helps push excess air out of the baby's stomach. Repeat before and after feeding as well as during if needed. You can also do it each time the baby is picked up as a simple colic preventative.

Ouchless splinters

When your child gets a splinter, reach for the scotch tape before resorting to tweezers or a needle. Simply put the scotch tape over the splinter, then pull it off. Scotch tape removes most splinters painlessly and easily.

Easy ways with eyedrops

A simple way to administer eyedrops to a child or an adult with a bad case of the blinks: Have the person lie down and close his or her eyes. Place one or two drops in the corner of the affected eye. When the eye opens, the drops flow right in.

According to Donald L. Turner, DO, of Huber Heights, Ohio, the easiest way to administer eyedrops to babies and small children is to put them in while the child is sleeping on his or her back. You'll avoid both tantrums and tears.

Get 'snippy' with your straw

For both younger children and older adults, sucking liquid through a straw can require more strength than they can muster. Dr. Louis C. Barricelli suggests a simple solution – simply snip the straw in half. Then it won't require quite so much effort.

INDEX

Fingernail polish *(continued)*
  stains 177
Fingernails 362
Fire safety 255
Fireplaces 112-113, 268
First aid kits 284
Fish 176
Flashlights 76
Flatware 210
Fleas 98, 328
Flies 52, 93
Floors 34, 103-105, 120, 132
Flour 37, 53, 368
Flowerpots 60, 78, 311.
  See also Planters
Flowers 58, 81, 88-90
Fly paper 52
Fly swatters 34
Frames, picture 208
Freezers 48, 224
Fruit 10-12, 25, 178
Furniture
  antique 125
  care of 59-60, 71, 128, 132-134
  cedar 130
  outdoor 134
  refinishing 129-132
  repairs 125-128
  shopping for 123-124
  unfinished 124
  upholstered 62, 72, 128-129
Furniture polish 126, 132, 199, 278

G

Garage sales 124
Garages 260, 277-278, 286
Garbage cans 47, 52, 71, 325
Garbage disposals 39, 47
Garden hoses 98, 113, 263, 299, 309

Gardening 301-315
  companion planting 298-299
  composting 303-305
  fertilizer 308
  mulching 303, 309, 315-316, 319
  seeds and seedlings 305-308, 310-311, 319
Garlic 16, 299, 372
Gelatin 25-26
Gift tags 80
Gifts, gift wrap 58, 78-81, 92, 96
Ginger 16
Gingersnaps 26
Glassware 45, 91, 214-216
Gloves
  leather 170
  white 205
Glue 127, 257, 362
Gnats 93
Golf shoes 319
Graham crackers 26
Grass. *See* Lawn
Grease 72
  clogs in drains 138
  fires 54
  for lubrication 246
  on hardwood floors 104
  on walls 110, 117
  stains 72, 101, 180, 195, 199, 251-252
Greeting cards 80
Grocery lists 3, 4
Grocery shopping 3-6, 54
Gutters 243-246

H

Hair 351-353, 357
Hair dryers 189, 196, 214

Hairbrushes 356
Haircuts 357
Hairspray 200
Hammers 258-259, 266, 268
Handkerchiefs 187
Hats, straw 202
Headaches 371
Headlights 279, 281
Heart rate, lowering 361, 370
Heartburn 371
Heat packs 371
Heating and air conditioning 132, 142-147
Hedges. *See* Trees and shrubs
Hems 189
Herbicides 293-296
Herbs 16, 20
Hiccups 374
Hinges 112
Home accessories 57-60
Honey 26, 364, 369-370
Hoses, vacuum cleaner 98
Hotels 336-337, 339
Household organization 72-75
Houseplants 60, 83-87, 308
Hubcaps 286
Humidifiers 132, 146

I

Ice 19, 47, 85, 184, 287, 329, 365-367,
Ice cream 25, 375
Ice trays 201
Index cards 73
Injuries
  burns 363
  cuts and scrapes 369
  smashed fingers 362